Mary Shelley MONSTERHUNTER ™

VOLUME 1

ABOMINATION

ADAM GLASS

OLIVIA CUARTERO-BRIGGS

HAYDEN SHERMAN

SAL CIPRIANO

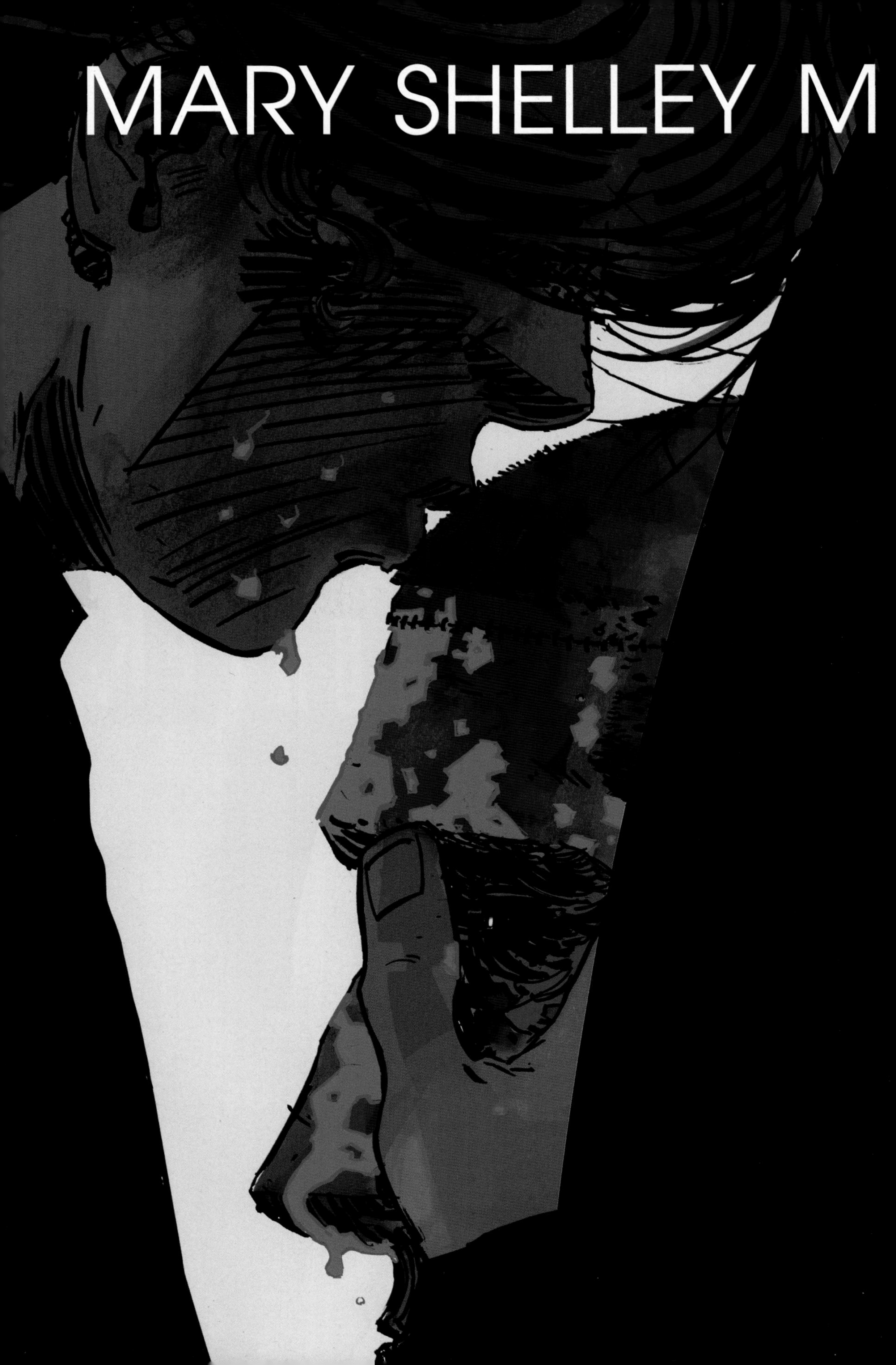
MARY SHELLEY M

ONSTER HUNTER™

VOLUME 1
ABOMINATION

ADAM GLASS co-creator & writer

OLIVIA CUARTERO-BRIGGS co-creator & writer

HAYDEN SHERMAN artist

SAL CIPRIANO letterer

HAYDEN SHERMAN front & original covers

JAVIER AVILA, BERNARD CHANG, GREG KIRKPATRICK, BRANDON PATERSON, STEVE WILCOX w/ DEE CUNNIFFE and **ANNA ZHOU** variant covers

SAL CIPRIANO logo designer

COREY BREEN book designer

MIKE MARTS editor

AFTERSHOCK™

MIKE MARTS - Editor-in-Chief   •   JOE PRUETT - Publisher/CCO   •   LEE KRAMER - President   •   JON KRAMER - Chief Executive Officer
STEVE ROTTERDAM - SVP, Sales & Marketing   •   DAN SHIRES - VP, Film & Television UK   •   CHRISTINA HARRINGTON - Managing Editor
MARC HAMMOND - Sr. Retail Sales Development Manager   •   RUTHANN THOMPSON - Sr. Retailer Relations Manager   •   BLAKE STOCKER - Director of Finance
AARON MARION - Publicist   •   LISA MOODY - Finance   •   RYAN CARROLL - Development Coordinator   •   STEPHAN NILSON - Publishing Operations
JAWAD QURESHI - Technology Advisor/Strategist   •   CHARLES PRITCHETT - Comics Production   •   COREY BREEN - Collections Production
TEDDY LEO - Editorial Assistant   •   STEPHANIE CASEBIER & SARAH PRUETT - Publishing Assistants

AfterShock Logo Design by COMICRAFT
Publicity: contact AARON MARION (aaron@publichausagency.com) & RYAN CROY (ryan@publichausagency.com) at PUBLICHAUS
Special thanks to: IRA KURGAN, MARINE KSADZHIKYAN & ANTONIA LIANOS

AFTERSHOCKCOMICS.COM Follow us on social media 🐦 📷 f

INTRODUCTION

Today, the name Mary Shelley is synonymous with *Frankenstein*, a harrowing story of revenge that still inspires books, movies and television shows two hundred years after its publication. Not bad for a nineteen-year-old, pre-Victorian writer.

But there is much more to Mary Shelley than the creation of the genre we now know as horror. She was an ideological philosopher, a traveler, and a well-known rebel in a time when women didn't even have the rights to their own children, let alone own property, vote, or so much as request a divorce.

Carrying on her late mother's legacy, Mary Wollstonecraft, now considered the grandmother of modern feminism, Mary Shelley (or Mary Godwin, as we will come to know her) enjoyed an open relationship with the eccentric poet Percy Shelley, and traipsed around Europe, accompanied by her lover, her fiery stepsister, and the notorious ladies' man, Lord Byron. Branded "the league of incest and atheism" by the British press, this sometimes admired, sometimes exiled group and their adventures serve as the foundation of our frightening tale.

Mary Shelley was a woman ahead of her time. A feminist warrior who suffered the loss of nearly everyone she ever loved, and yet soldiered on—producing four novels, hundreds of articles and preserving the legacy of both her deceased husband and mother for generations to come. Her mark on our current culture is profound, and while MARY SHELLEY MONSTER HUNTER is indeed a work of fiction, it is inspired by the true events of the writer's life, to both entertain and enlighten its audiences to one of the true pioneers of women's equality.

They say 2019 is the year of the woman. I say that's just the beginning.

MARY SHELLEY MONSTER HUNTER is a story for this generation of readers, a reminder of the greatness of women, as well as a harrowing, historical thrill ride through Georgian-era counterculture. It is an honor to breathe life into the character of Mary Shelley, and a privilege to share this, the "real" story behind the creation of *Frankenstein*, kept secret, until now...

OLIVIA CUARTERO-BRIGGS
October 2019

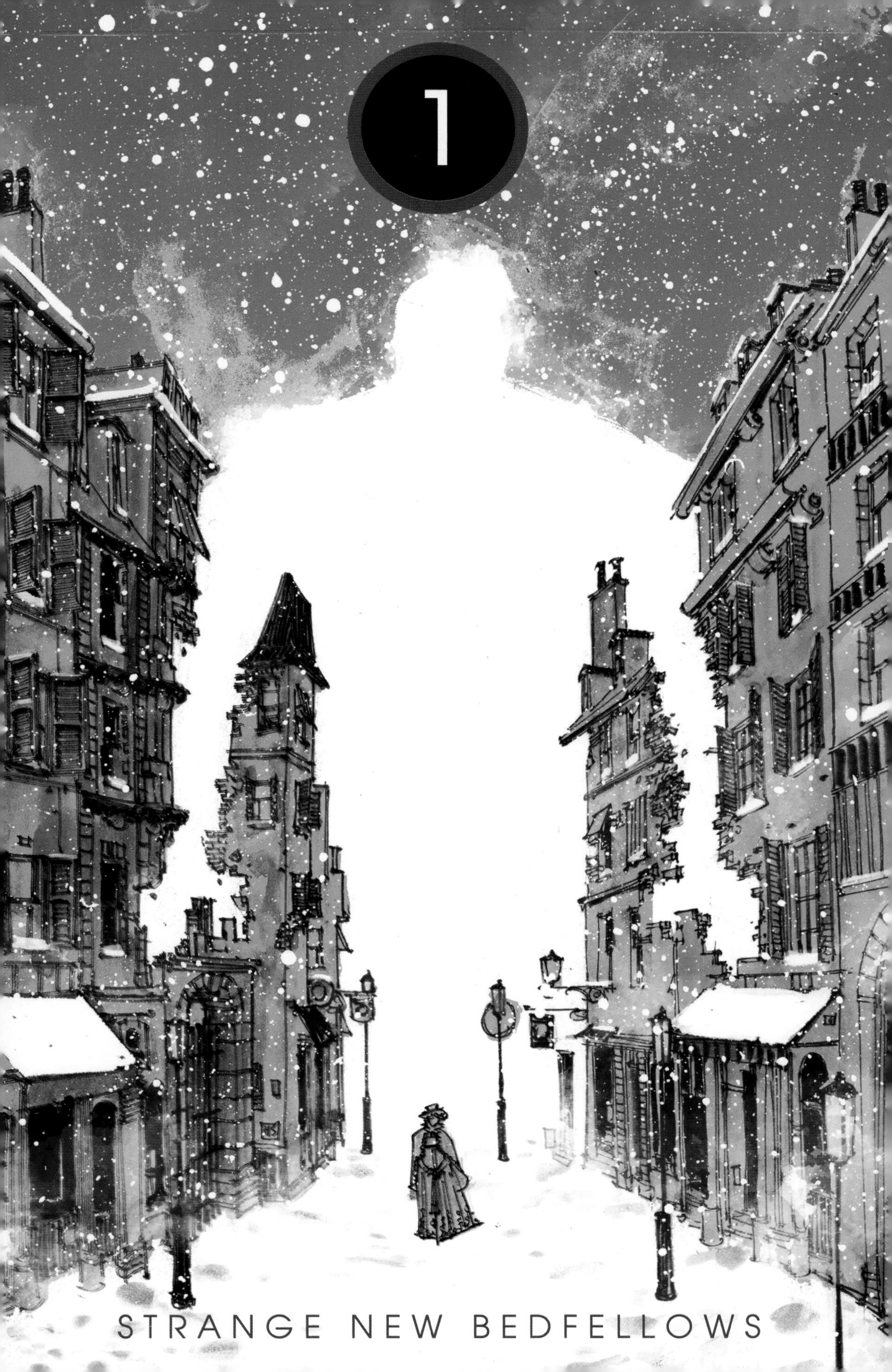

1

STRANGE NEW BEDFELLOWS

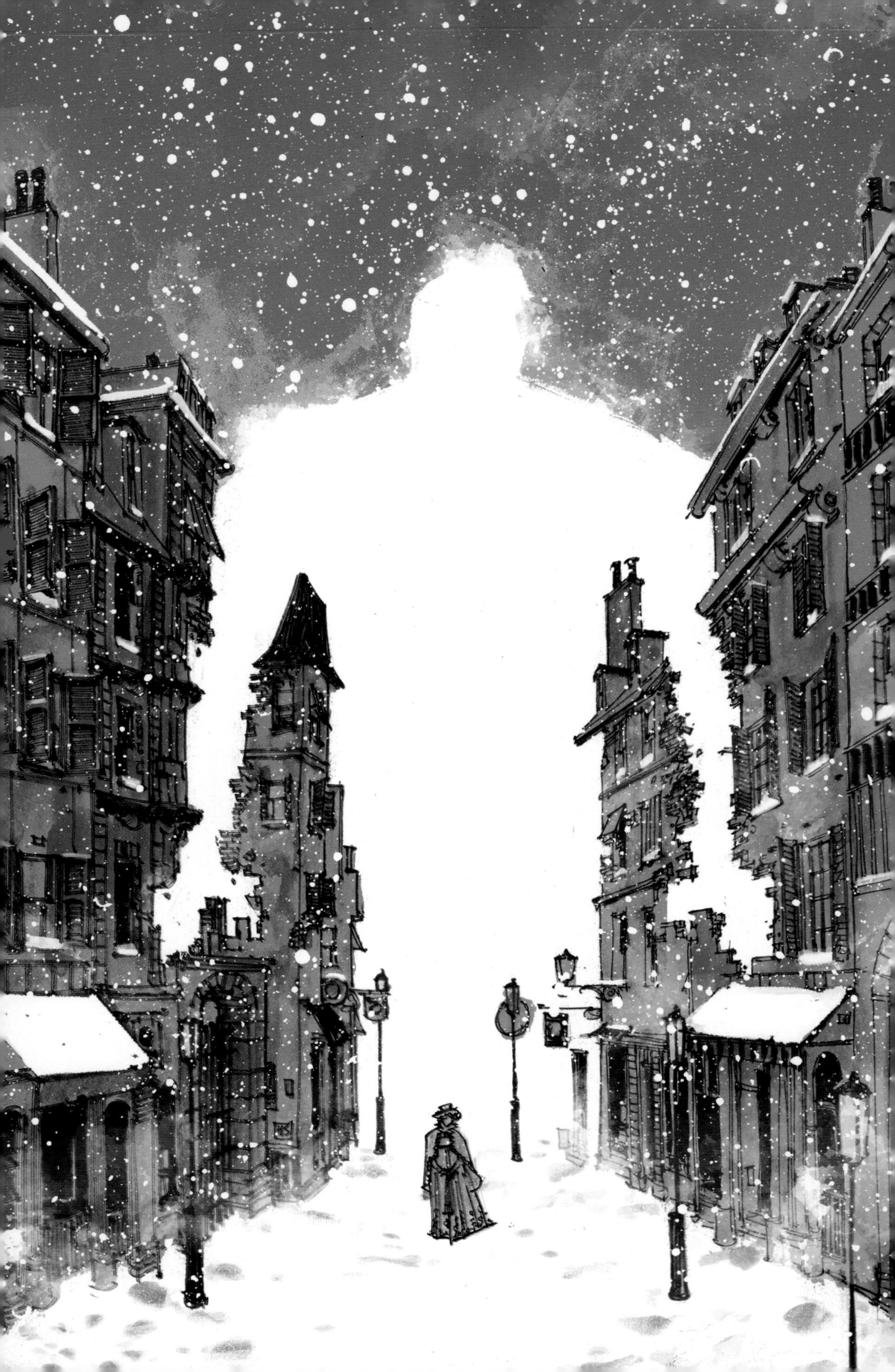

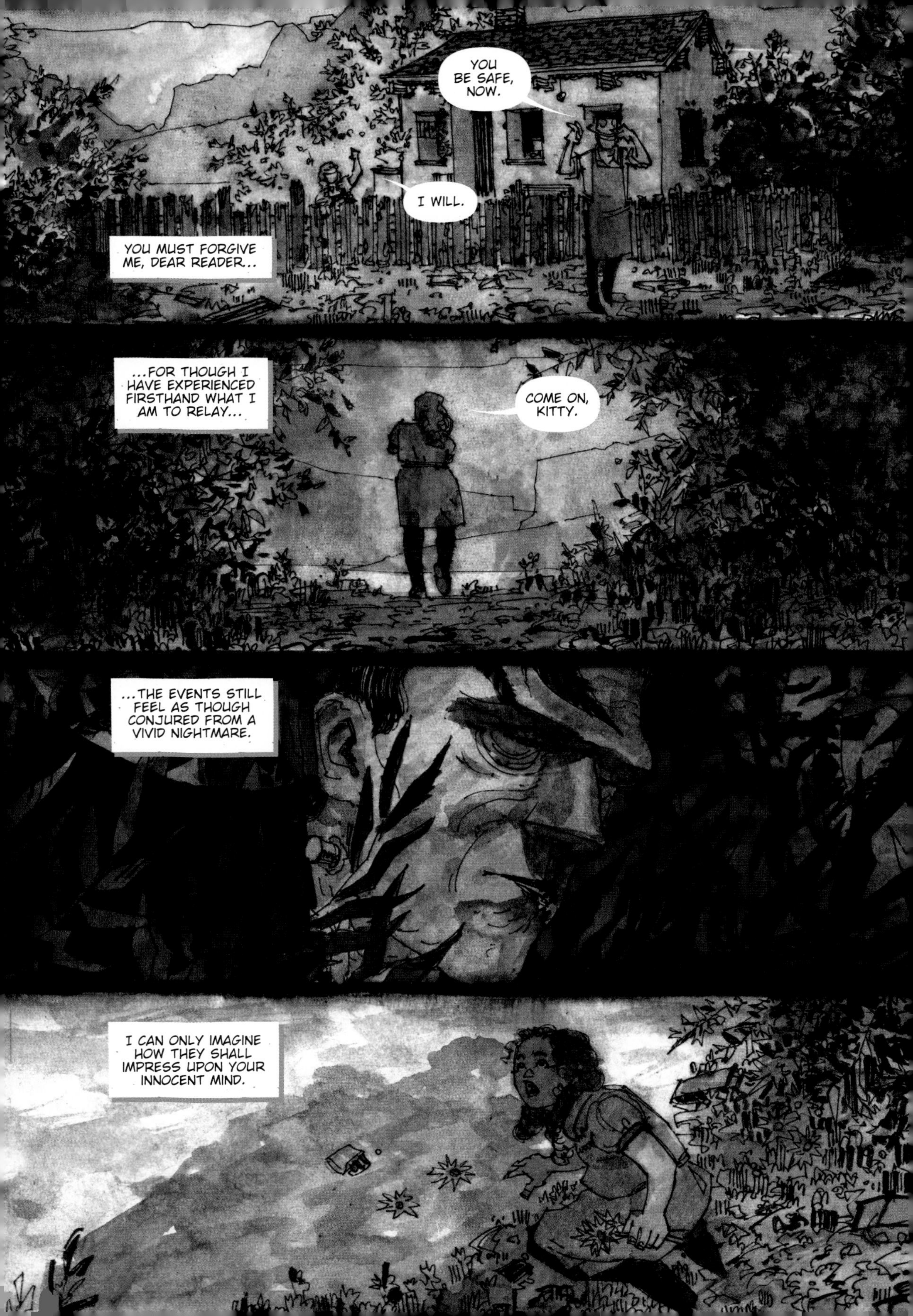
YOU BE SAFE, NOW.
I WILL.
YOU MUST FORGIVE ME, DEAR READER...
...FOR THOUGH I HAVE EXPERIENCED FIRSTHAND WHAT I AM TO RELAY...
COME ON, KITTY.
...THE EVENTS STILL FEEL AS THOUGH CONJURED FROM A VIVID NIGHTMARE.
I CAN ONLY IMAGINE HOW THEY SHALL IMPRESS UPON YOUR INNOCENT MIND.

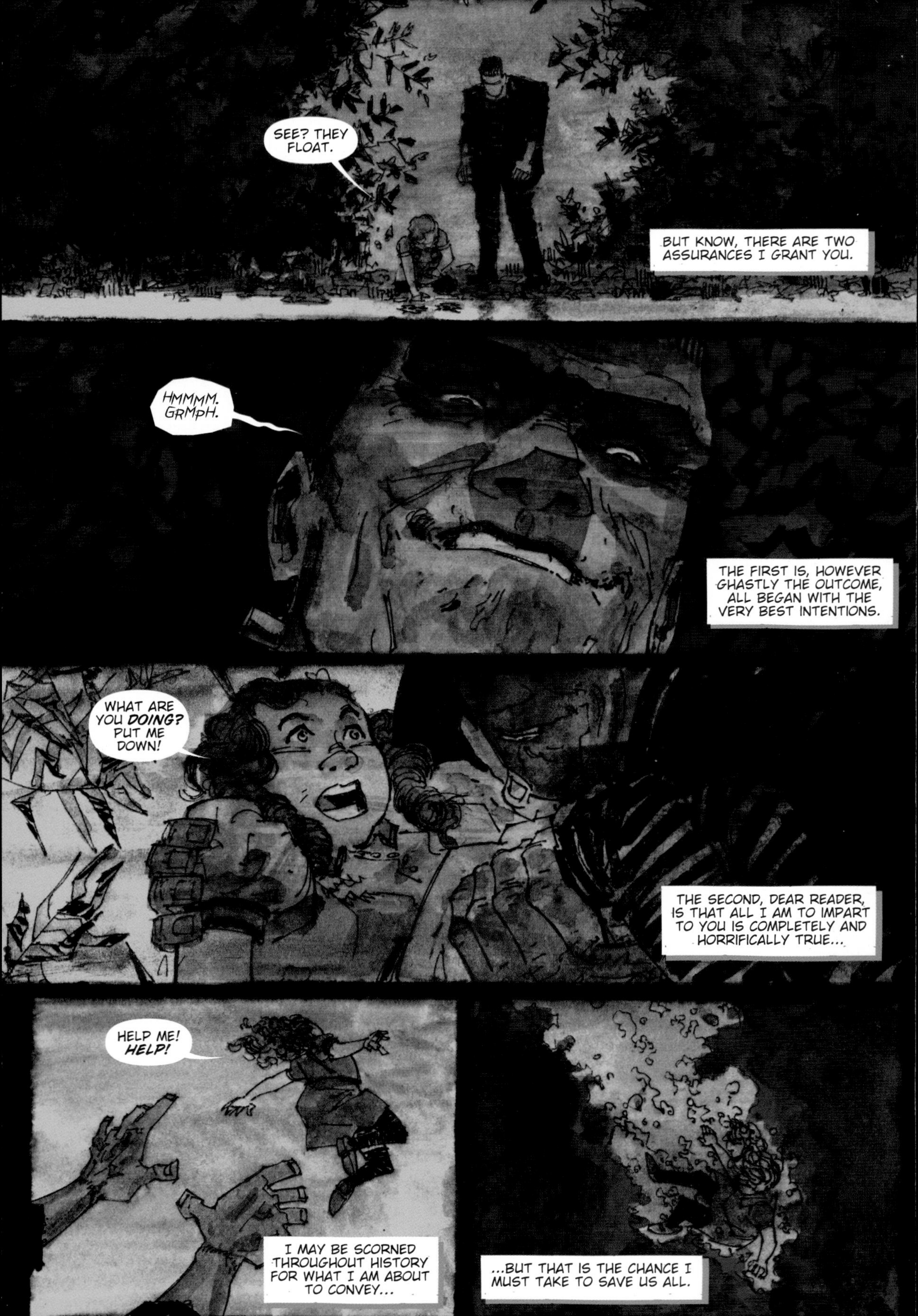
SEE? THEY FLOAT.
BUT KNOW, THERE ARE TWO ASSURANCES I GRANT YOU.
HMMMM. GRMPH.
THE FIRST IS, HOWEVER GHASTLY THE OUTCOME, ALL BEGAN WITH THE VERY BEST INTENTIONS.
WHAT ARE YOU DOING? PUT ME DOWN!
THE SECOND, DEAR READER, IS THAT ALL I AM TO IMPART TO YOU IS COMPLETELY AND HORRIFICALLY TRUE...
HELP ME! HELP!
I MAY BE SCORNED THROUGHOUT HISTORY FOR WHAT I AM ABOUT TO CONVEY...
...BUT THAT IS THE CHANCE I MUST TAKE TO SAVE US ALL.

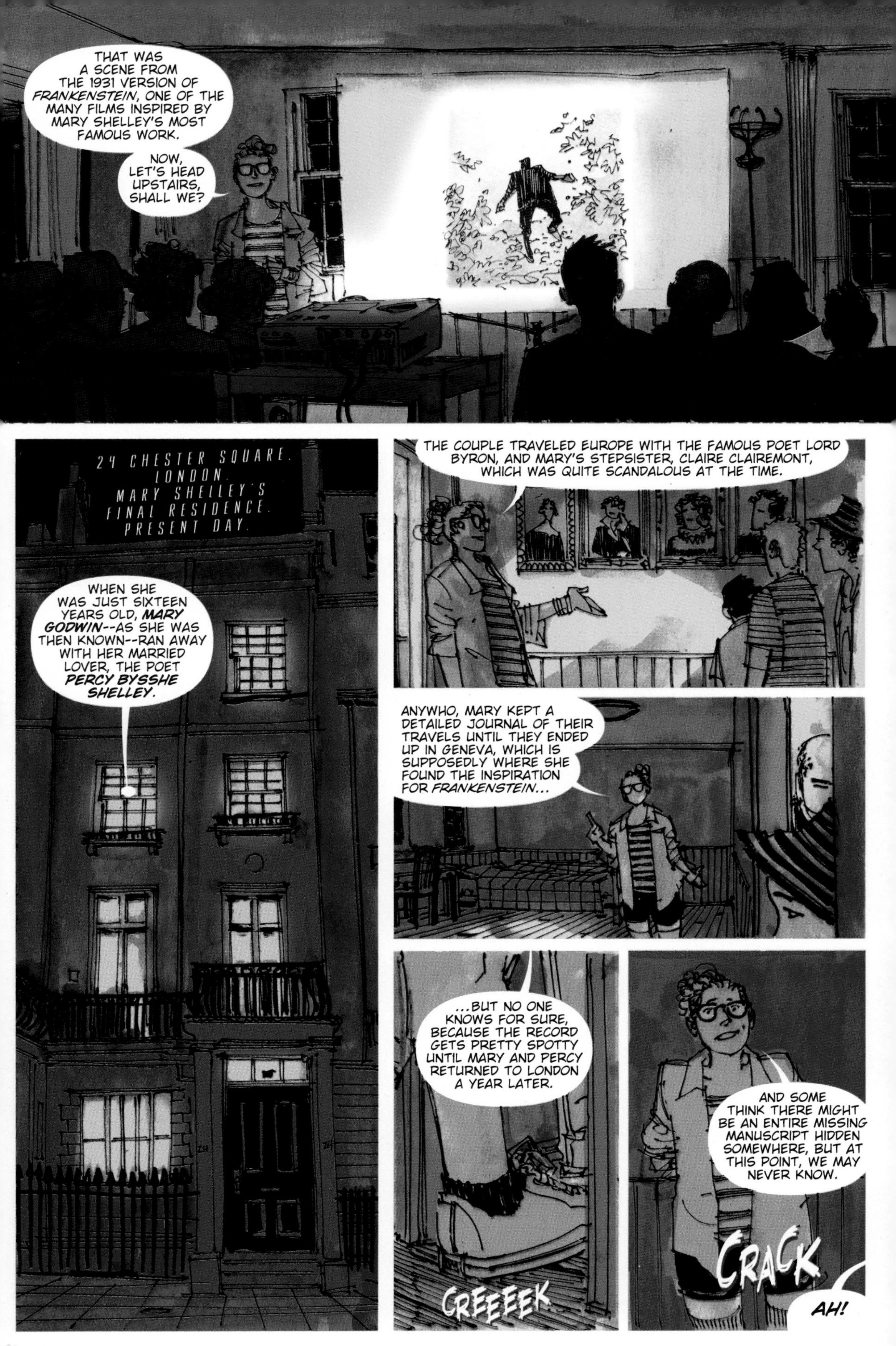
THAT WAS A SCENE FROM THE 1931 VERSION OF *FRANKENSTEIN*, ONE OF THE MANY FILMS INSPIRED BY MARY SHELLEY'S MOST FAMOUS WORK.
NOW, LET'S HEAD UPSTAIRS, SHALL WE?
24 CHESTER SQUARE. LONDON. MARY SHELLEY'S FINAL RESIDENCE. PRESENT DAY.
WHEN SHE WAS JUST SIXTEEN YEARS OLD, **MARY GODWIN**--AS SHE WAS THEN KNOWN--RAN AWAY WITH HER MARRIED LOVER, THE POET **PERCY BYSSHE SHELLEY**.
THE COUPLE TRAVELED EUROPE WITH THE FAMOUS POET LORD BYRON, AND MARY'S STEPSISTER, CLAIRE CLAIREMONT, WHICH WAS QUITE SCANDALOUS AT THE TIME.
ANYWHO, MARY KEPT A DETAILED JOURNAL OF THEIR TRAVELS UNTIL THEY ENDED UP IN GENEVA, WHICH IS SUPPOSEDLY WHERE SHE FOUND THE INSPIRATION FOR *FRANKENSTEIN*...
...BUT NO ONE KNOWS FOR SURE, BECAUSE THE RECORD GETS PRETTY SPOTTY UNTIL MARY AND PERCY RETURNED TO LONDON A YEAR LATER.
CREEEEK
AND SOME THINK THERE MIGHT BE AN ENTIRE MISSING MANUSCRIPT HIDDEN SOMEWHERE, BUT AT THIS POINT, WE MAY NEVER KNOW.
CRACK
AH!

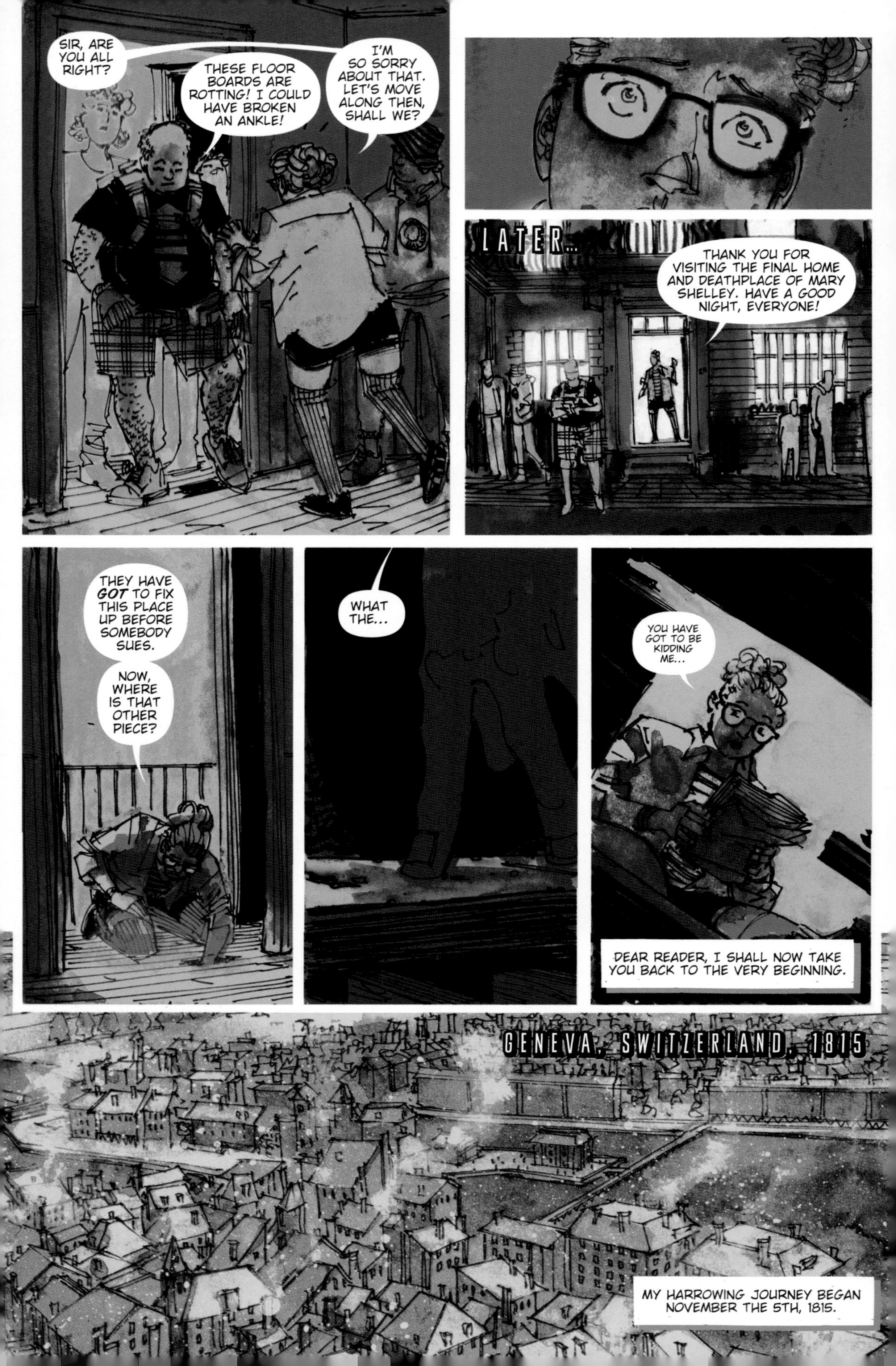
SIR, ARE YOU ALL RIGHT?
THESE FLOOR BOARDS ARE ROTTING! I COULD HAVE BROKEN AN ANKLE!
I'M SO SORRY ABOUT THAT. LET'S MOVE ALONG THEN, SHALL WE?
LATER...
THANK YOU FOR VISITING THE FINAL HOME AND DEATHPLACE OF MARY SHELLEY. HAVE A GOOD NIGHT, EVERYONE!
THEY HAVE GOT TO FIX THIS PLACE UP BEFORE SOMEBODY SUES.
NOW, WHERE IS THAT OTHER PIECE?
WHAT THE...
YOU HAVE GOT TO BE KIDDING ME...
DEAR READER, I SHALL NOW TAKE YOU BACK TO THE VERY BEGINNING.
GENEVA, SWITZERLAND, 1815
MY HARROWING JOURNEY BEGAN NOVEMBER THE 5TH, 1815.

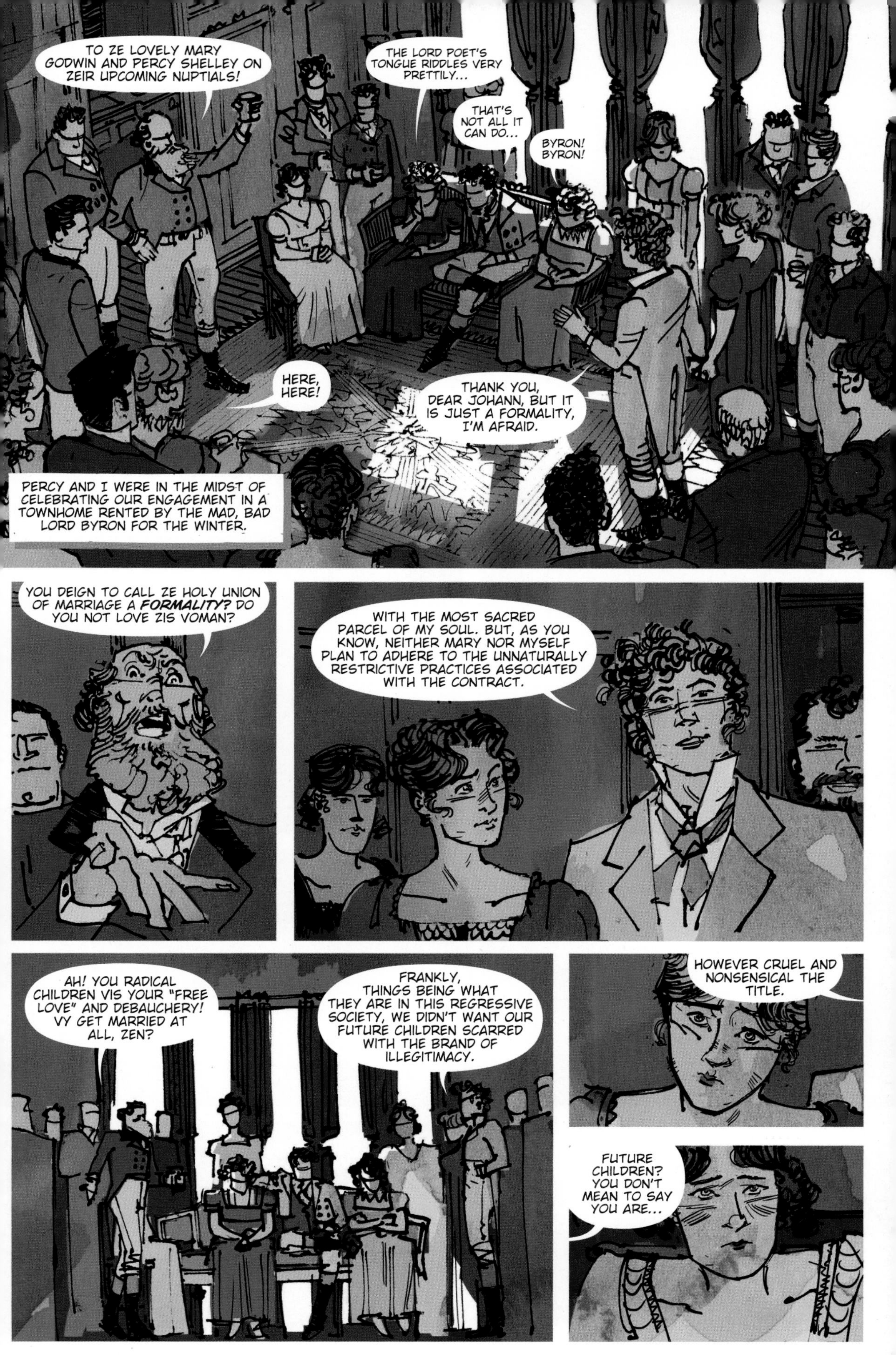
TO ZE LOVELY MARY GODWIN AND PERCY SHELLEY ON ZEIR UPCOMING NUPTIALS!
THE LORD POET'S TONGUE RIDDLES VERY PRETTILY...
THAT'S NOT ALL IT CAN DO...
BYRON! BYRON!
HERE, HERE!
THANK YOU, DEAR JOHANN, BUT IT IS JUST A FORMALITY, I'M AFRAID.
PERCY AND I WERE IN THE MIDST OF CELEBRATING OUR ENGAGEMENT IN A TOWNHOME RENTED BY THE MAD, BAD LORD BYRON FOR THE WINTER.
YOU DEIGN TO CALL ZE HOLY UNION OF MARRIAGE A ***FORMALITY?*** DO YOU NOT LOVE ZIS VOMAN?
WITH THE MOST SACRED PARCEL OF MY SOUL. BUT, AS YOU KNOW, NEITHER MARY NOR MYSELF PLAN TO ADHERE TO THE UNNATURALLY RESTRICTIVE PRACTICES ASSOCIATED WITH THE CONTRACT.
AH! YOU RADICAL CHILDREN VIS YOUR "FREE LOVE" AND DEBAUCHERY! VY GET MARRIED AT ALL, ZEN?
FRANKLY, THINGS BEING WHAT THEY ARE IN THIS REGRESSIVE SOCIETY, WE DIDN'T WANT OUR FUTURE CHILDREN SCARRED WITH THE BRAND OF ILLEGITIMACY.
HOWEVER CRUEL AND NONSENSICAL THE TITLE.
FUTURE CHILDREN? YOU DON'T MEAN TO SAY YOU ARE...

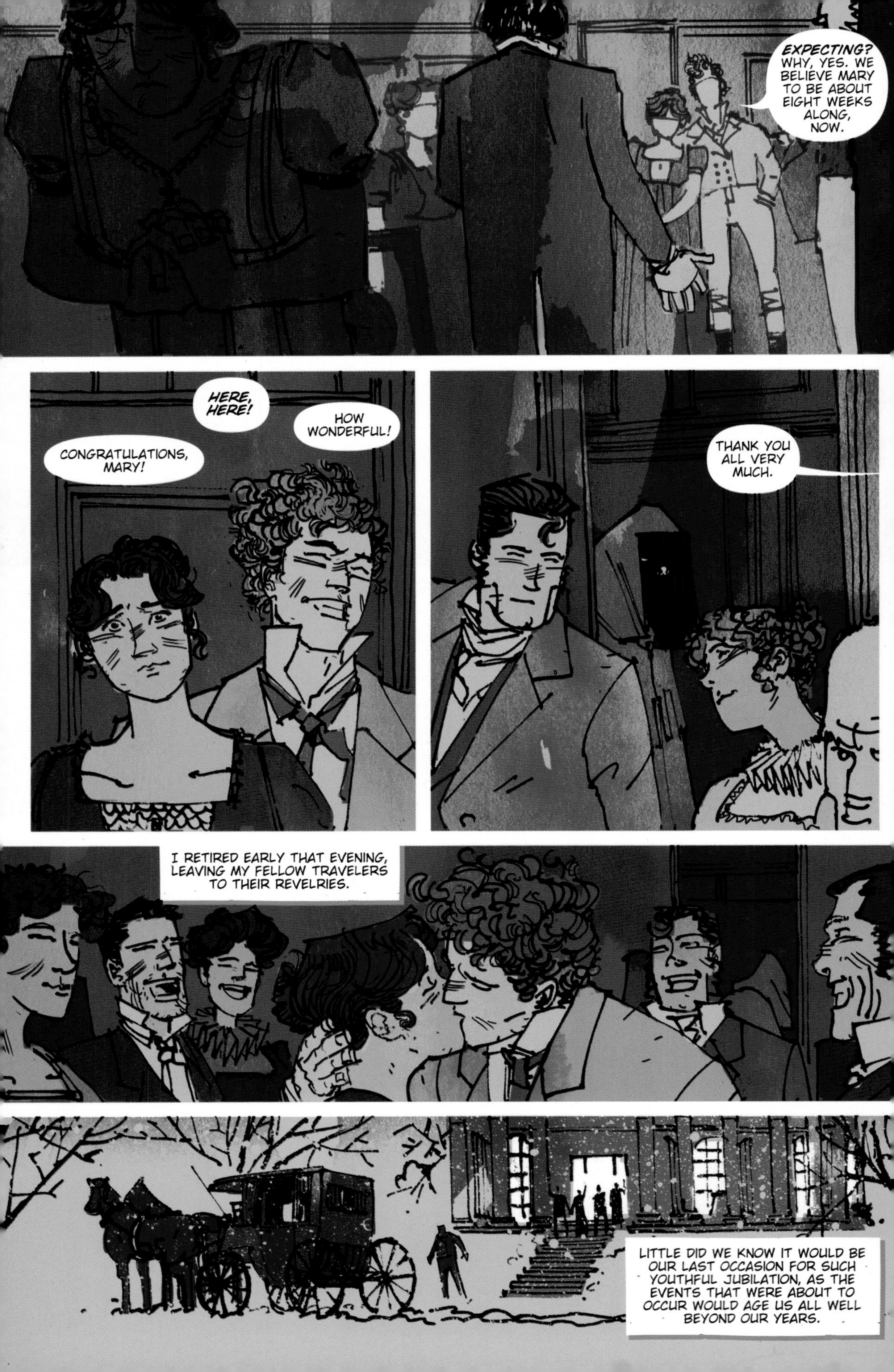
EXPECTING? WHY, YES. WE BELIEVE MARY TO BE ABOUT EIGHT WEEKS ALONG, NOW.
CONGRATULATIONS, MARY!
HERE, HERE!
HOW WONDERFUL!
THANK YOU ALL VERY MUCH.
I RETIRED EARLY THAT EVENING, LEAVING MY FELLOW TRAVELERS TO THEIR REVELRIES.
LITTLE DID WE KNOW IT WOULD BE OUR LAST OCCASION FOR SUCH YOUTHFUL JUBILATION, AS THE EVENTS THAT WERE ABOUT TO OCCUR WOULD AGE US ALL WELL BEYOND OUR YEARS.

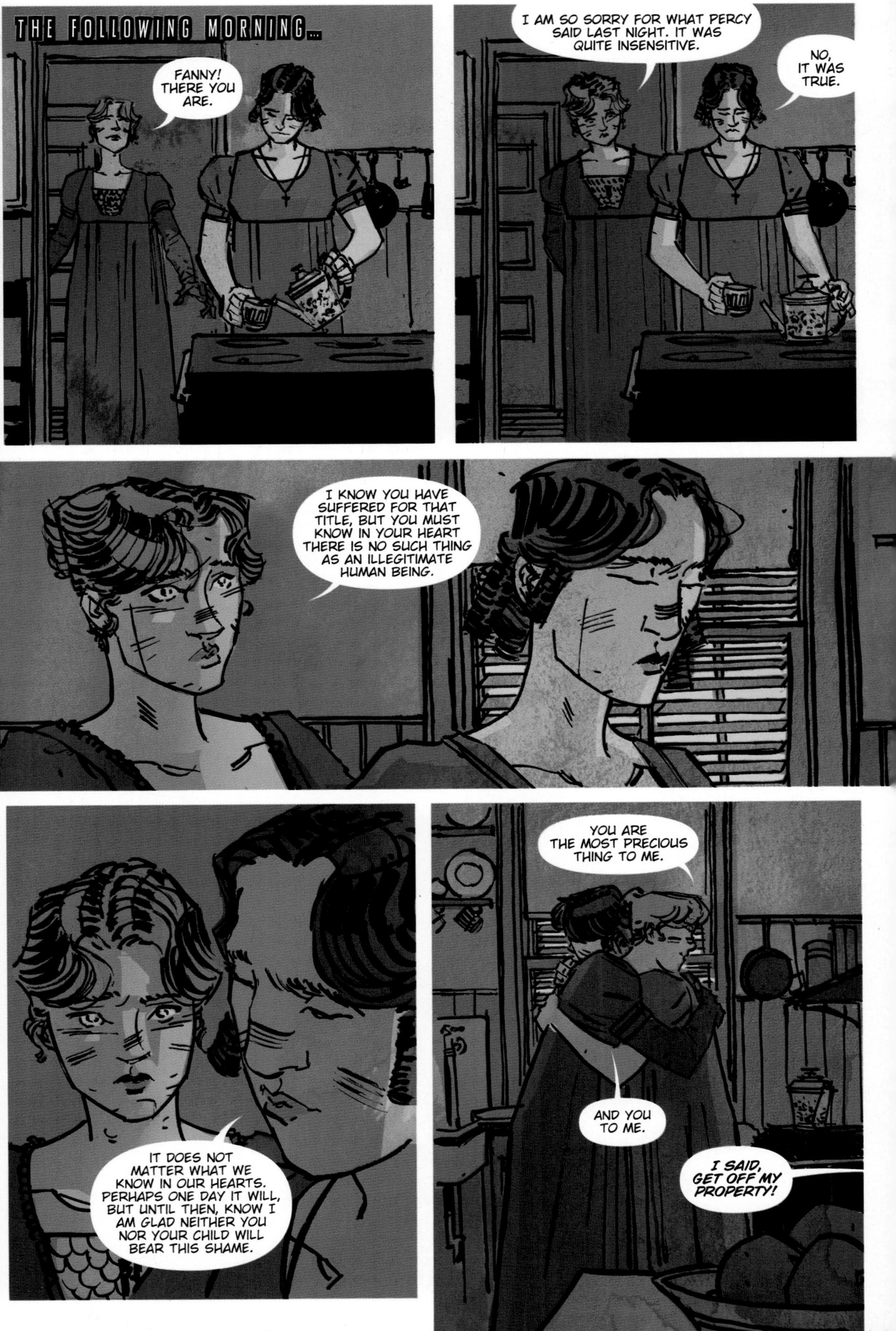
THE FOLLOWING MORNING...
FANNY! THERE YOU ARE.
I AM SO SORRY FOR WHAT PERCY SAID LAST NIGHT. IT WAS QUITE INSENSITIVE.
NO, IT WAS TRUE.
I KNOW YOU HAVE SUFFERED FOR THAT TITLE, BUT YOU MUST KNOW IN YOUR HEART THERE IS NO SUCH THING AS AN ILLEGITIMATE HUMAN BEING.
IT DOES NOT MATTER WHAT WE KNOW IN OUR HEARTS. PERHAPS ONE DAY IT WILL, BUT UNTIL THEN, KNOW I AM GLAD NEITHER YOU NOR YOUR CHILD WILL BEAR THIS SHAME.
YOU ARE THE MOST PRECIOUS THING TO ME.
AND YOU TO ME.
I SAID, GET OFF MY PROPERTY!

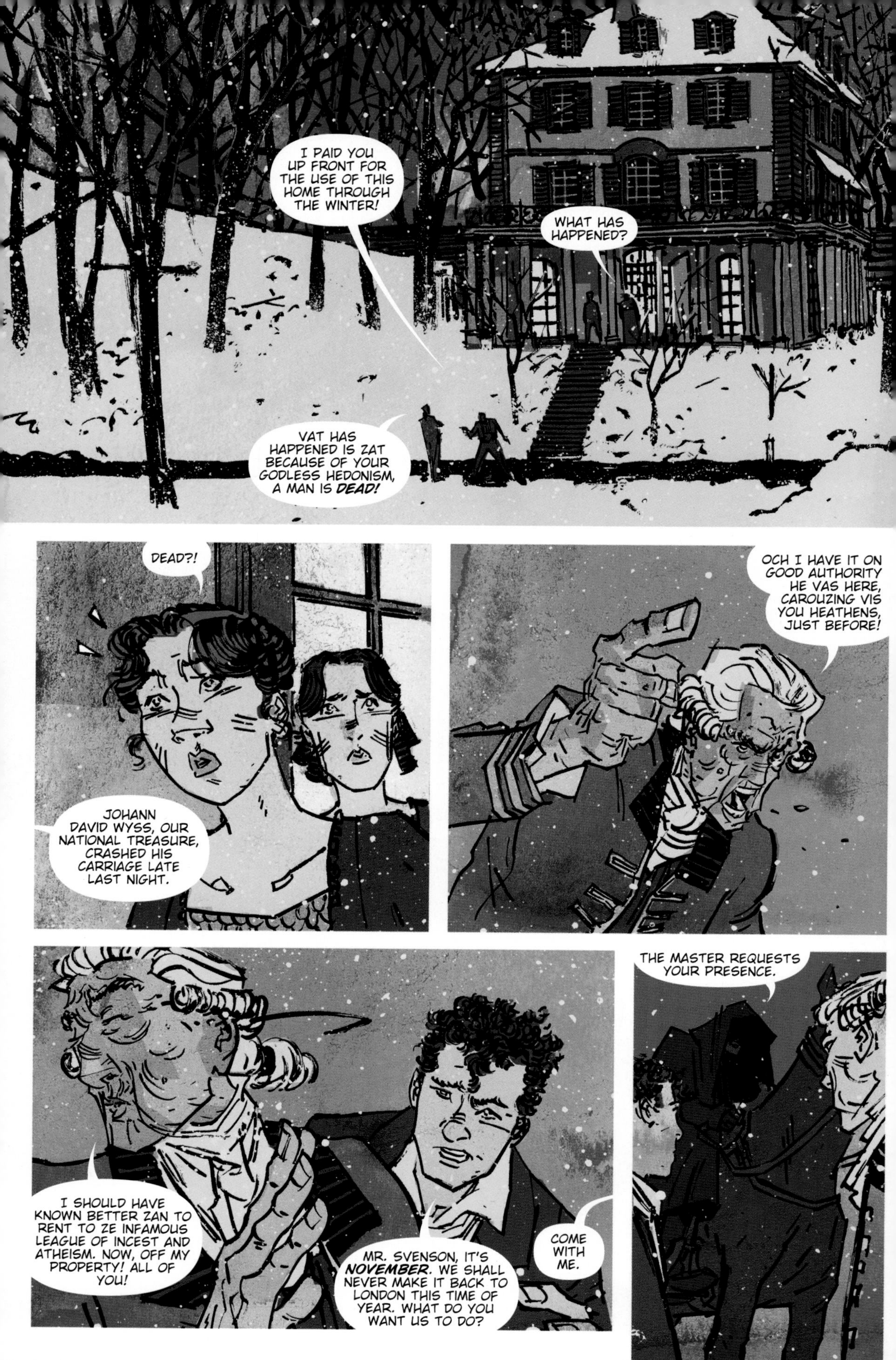
I PAID YOU UP FRONT FOR THE USE OF THIS HOME THROUGH THE WINTER!
WHAT HAS HAPPENED?
VAT HAS HAPPENED IS ZAT BECAUSE OF YOUR GODLESS HEDONISM, A MAN IS ***DEAD!***
DEAD?!
JOHANN DAVID WYSS, OUR NATIONAL TREASURE, CRASHED HIS CARRIAGE LATE LAST NIGHT.
OCH I HAVE IT ON GOOD AUTHORITY HE VAS HERE, CAROUZING VIS YOU HEATHENS, JUST BEFORE!
I SHOULD HAVE KNOWN BETTER ZAN TO RENT TO ZE INFAMOUS LEAGUE OF INCEST AND ATHEISM. NOW, OFF MY PROPERTY! ALL OF YOU!
MR. SVENSON, IT'S ***NOVEMBER***. WE SHALL NEVER MAKE IT BACK TO LONDON THIS TIME OF YEAR. WHAT DO YOU WANT US TO DO?
COME WITH ME.
THE MASTER REQUESTS YOUR PRESENCE.

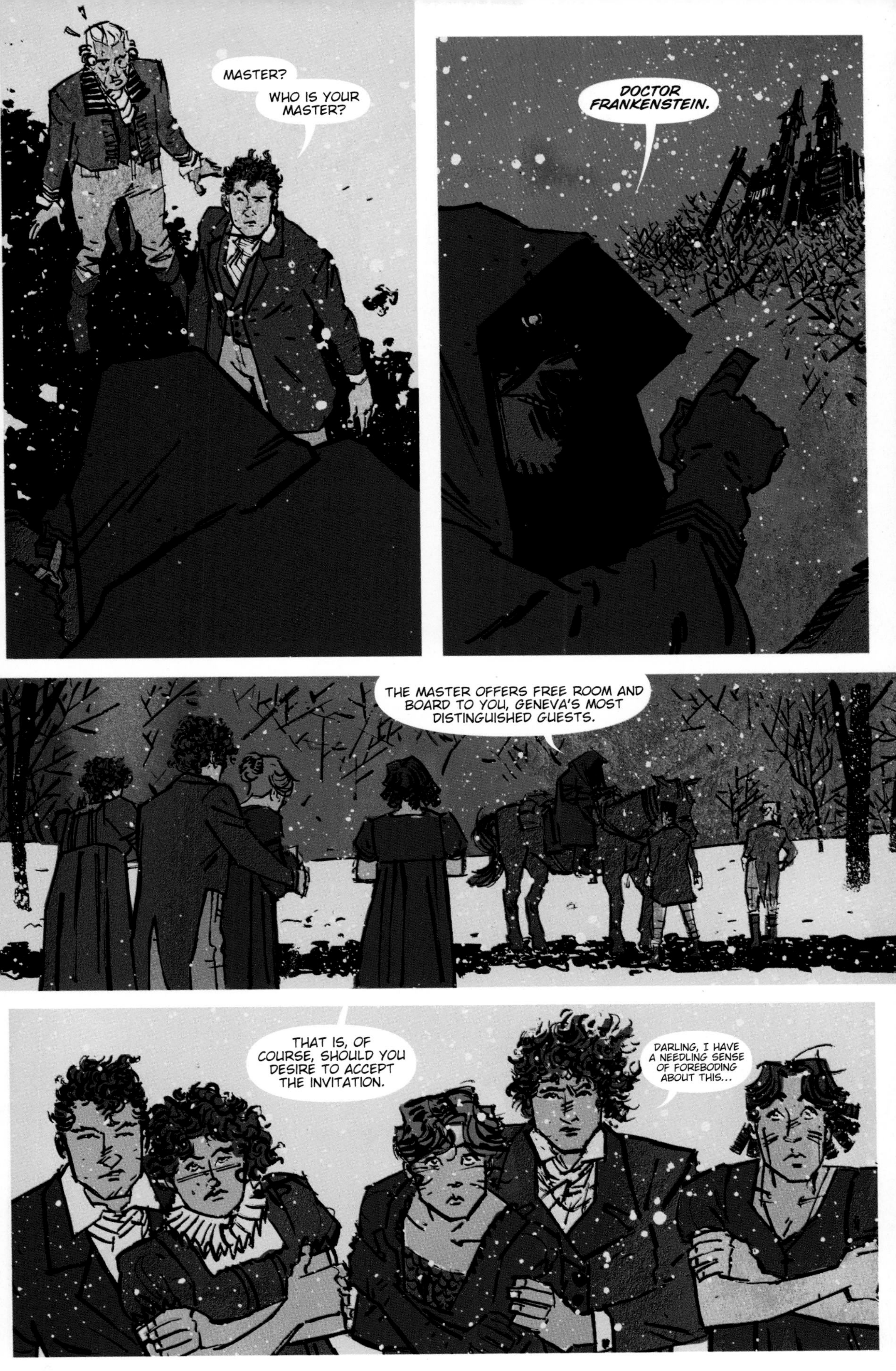
MASTER?
WHO IS YOUR MASTER?
DOCTOR FRANKENSTEIN.
THE MASTER OFFERS FREE ROOM AND BOARD TO YOU, GENEVA'S MOST DISTINGUISHED GUESTS.
THAT IS, OF COURSE, SHOULD YOU DESIRE TO ACCEPT THE INVITATION.
DARLING, I HAVE A NEEDLING SENSE OF FOREBODING ABOUT THIS...

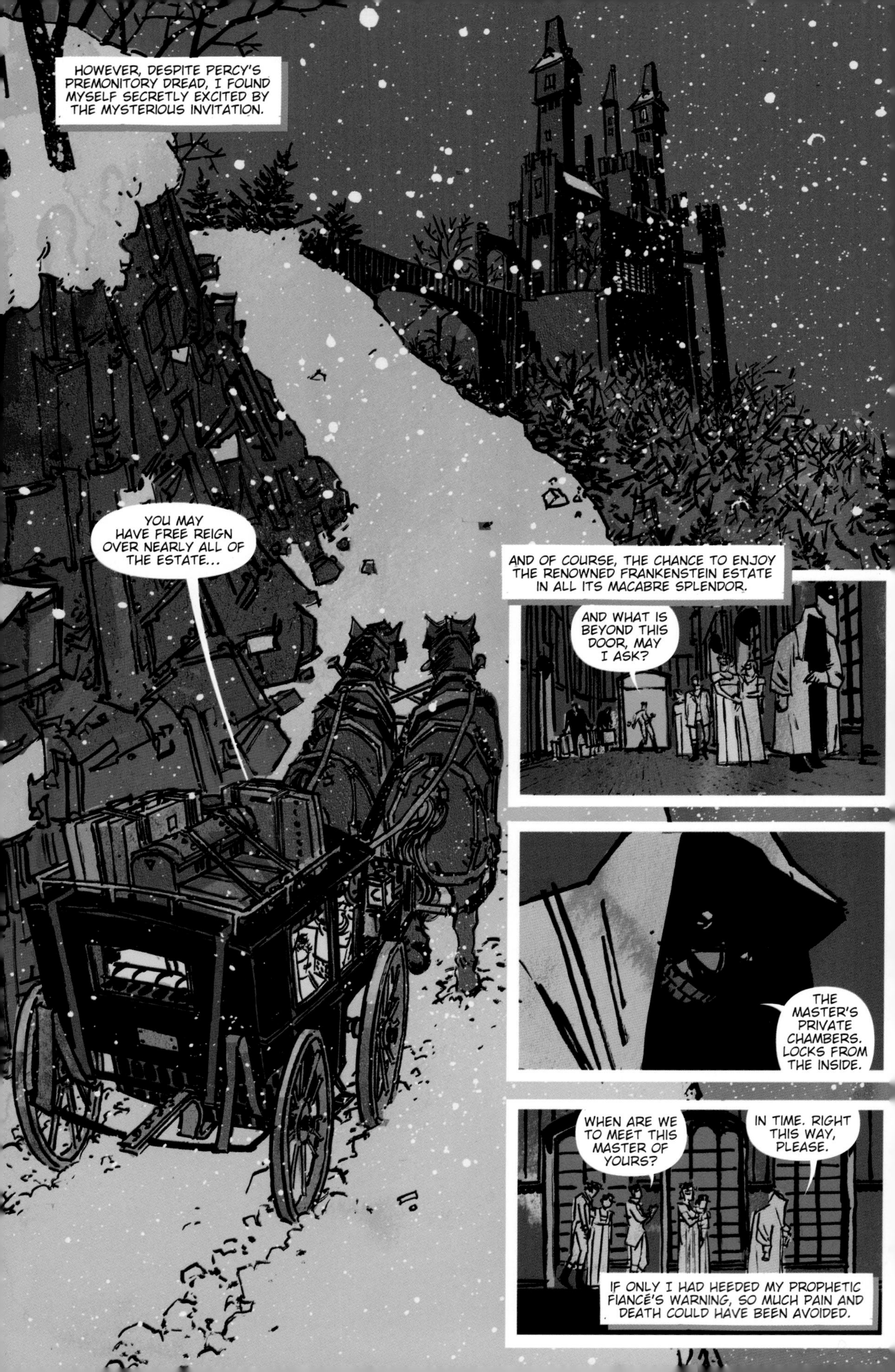
HOWEVER, DESPITE PERCY'S PREMONITORY DREAD, I FOUND MYSELF SECRETLY EXCITED BY THE MYSTERIOUS INVITATION.
YOU MAY HAVE FREE REIGN OVER NEARLY ALL OF THE ESTATE...
AND OF COURSE, THE CHANCE TO ENJOY THE RENOWNED FRANKENSTEIN ESTATE IN ALL ITS MACABRE SPLENDOR.
AND WHAT IS BEYOND THIS DOOR, MAY I ASK?
THE MASTER'S PRIVATE CHAMBERS. LOCKS FROM THE INSIDE.
WHEN ARE WE TO MEET THIS MASTER OF YOURS?
IN TIME. RIGHT THIS WAY, PLEASE.
IF ONLY I HAD HEEDED MY PROPHETIC FIANCÉ'S WARNING, SO MUCH PAIN AND DEATH COULD HAVE BEEN AVOIDED.

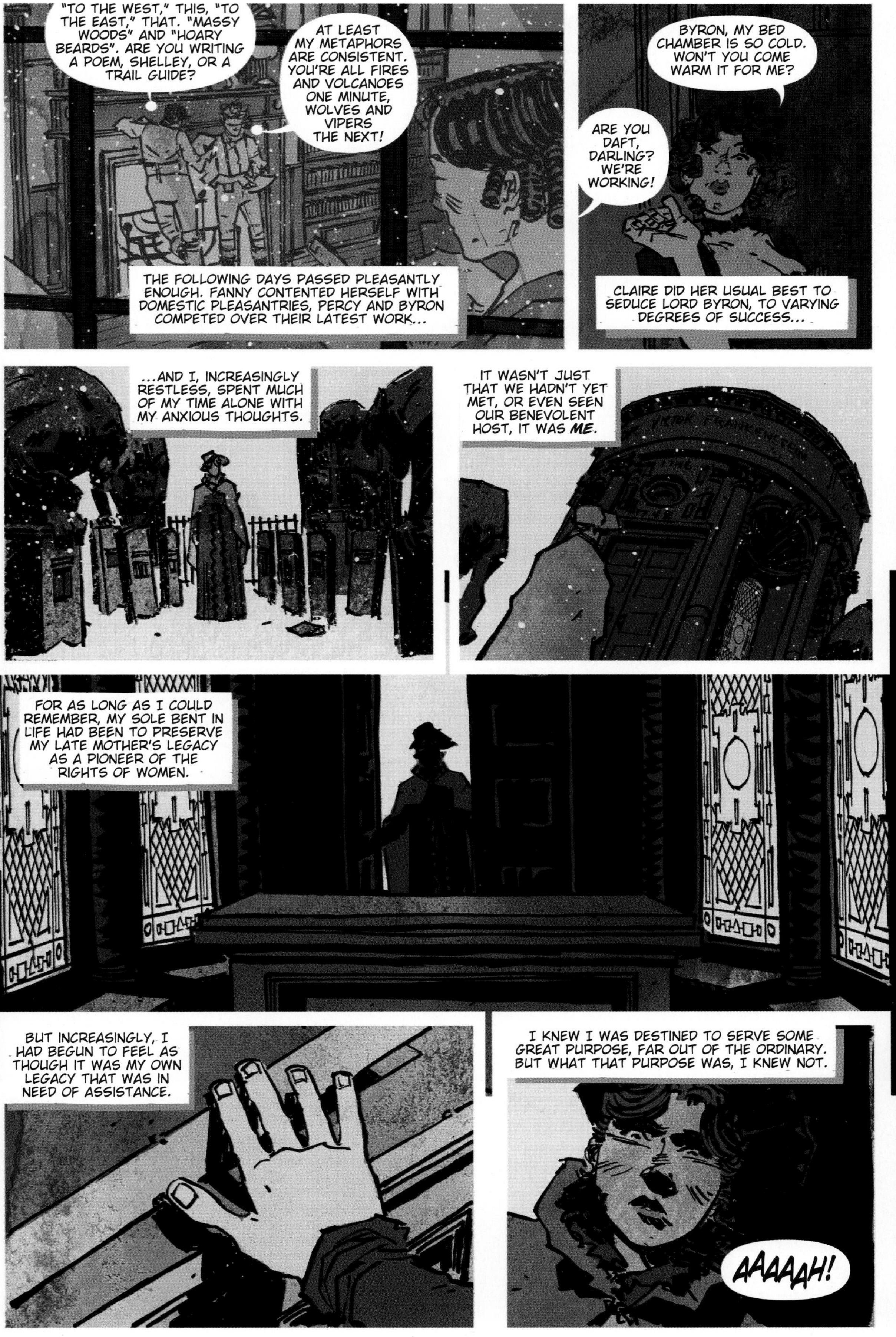
"TO THE WEST," THIS, "TO THE EAST," THAT. "MASSY WOODS" AND "HOARY BEARDS". ARE YOU WRITING A POEM, SHELLEY, OR A TRAIL GUIDE?
AT LEAST MY METAPHORS ARE CONSISTENT. YOU'RE ALL FIRES AND VOLCANOES ONE MINUTE, WOLVES AND VIPERS THE NEXT!
THE FOLLOWING DAYS PASSED PLEASANTLY ENOUGH. FANNY CONTENTED HERSELF WITH DOMESTIC PLEASANTRIES, PERCY AND BYRON COMPETED OVER THEIR LATEST WORK...
BYRON, MY BED CHAMBER IS SO COLD. WON'T YOU COME WARM IT FOR ME?
ARE YOU DAFT, DARLING? WE'RE WORKING!
CLAIRE DID HER USUAL BEST TO SEDUCE LORD BYRON, TO VARYING DEGREES OF SUCCESS...
...AND I, INCREASINGLY RESTLESS, SPENT MUCH OF MY TIME ALONE WITH MY ANXIOUS THOUGHTS.
IT WASN'T JUST THAT WE HADN'T YET MET, OR EVEN SEEN OUR BENEVOLENT HOST, IT WAS *ME*.
VICTOR FRANKENSTEIN
FOR AS LONG AS I COULD REMEMBER, MY SOLE BENT IN LIFE HAD BEEN TO PRESERVE MY LATE MOTHER'S LEGACY AS A PIONEER OF THE RIGHTS OF WOMEN.
BUT INCREASINGLY, I HAD BEGUN TO FEEL AS THOUGH IT WAS MY OWN LEGACY THAT WAS IN NEED OF ASSISTANCE.
I KNEW I WAS DESTINED TO SERVE SOME GREAT PURPOSE, FAR OUT OF THE ORDINARY. BUT WHAT THAT PURPOSE WAS, I KNEW NOT.
AAAAAH!

FANNY! ARE YOU ALL RIGHT?

IT WAS NOT LONG, HOWEVER, BEFORE MY GREATER PURPOSE WOULD REVEAL ITSELF.

GOOD LORD...

SANK YOU FOR LETTING US KNOW. ZERE HAVE BEEN SOME ROBBERIES AT OUR LOCAL MORGUE. PERHAPS ZE CULPRIT CAME ZIS VAY.

ROBBERIES? HOW WOULD THAT EXPLAIN A DISCARDED FOOT?

ZE ROBBERS DID NOT TAKE MONEY, MADAME. ONLY HUMAN REMAINS.

THE FOOT MARKED THE BEGINNING...

CLANG   CRASH

...THEN CAME THE HARROWING NOISES IN THE NIGHT, THE PUTRID SMELLS...

MRRRAAA...

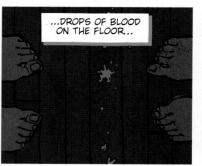

...DROPS OF BLOOD ON THE FLOOR...

...ALL EMANATING FROM THE MYSTERIOUS MASTER'S CHAMBERS.

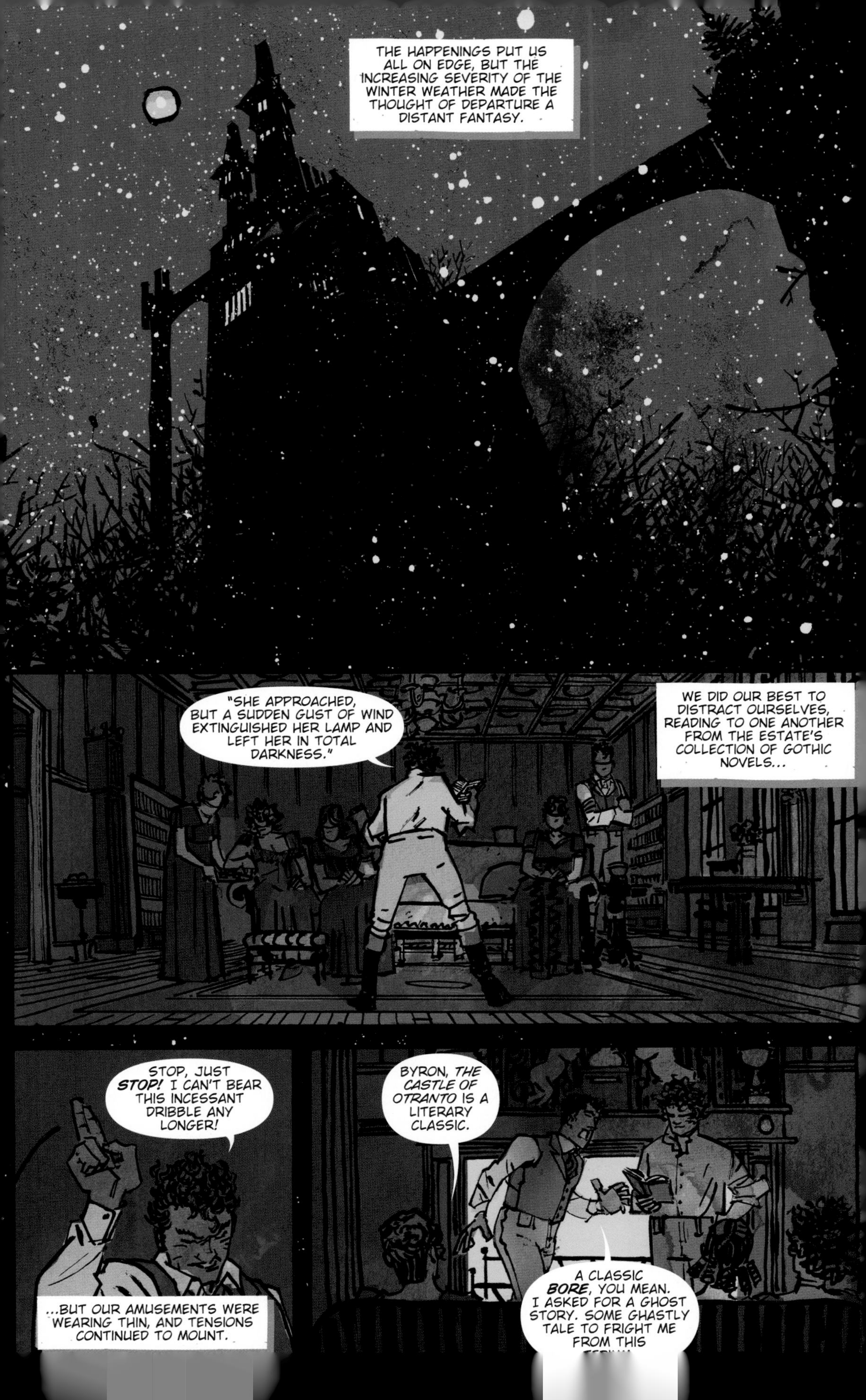
THE HAPPENINGS PUT US ALL ON EDGE, BUT THE INCREASING SEVERITY OF THE WINTER WEATHER MADE THE THOUGHT OF DEPARTURE A DISTANT FANTASY.
"SHE APPROACHED, BUT A SUDDEN GUST OF WIND EXTINGUISHED HER LAMP AND LEFT HER IN TOTAL DARKNESS."
WE DID OUR BEST TO DISTRACT OURSELVES, READING TO ONE ANOTHER FROM THE ESTATE'S COLLECTION OF GOTHIC NOVELS...
STOP, JUST ***STOP!*** I CAN'T BEAR THIS INCESSANT DRIBBLE ANY LONGER!
...BUT OUR AMUSEMENTS WERE WEARING THIN, AND TENSIONS CONTINUED TO MOUNT.
BYRON, *THE CASTLE OF OTRANTO* IS A LITERARY CLASSIC.
A CLASSIC ***BORE***, YOU MEAN. I ASKED FOR A GHOST STORY. SOME GHASTLY TALE TO FRIGHT ME FROM THIS

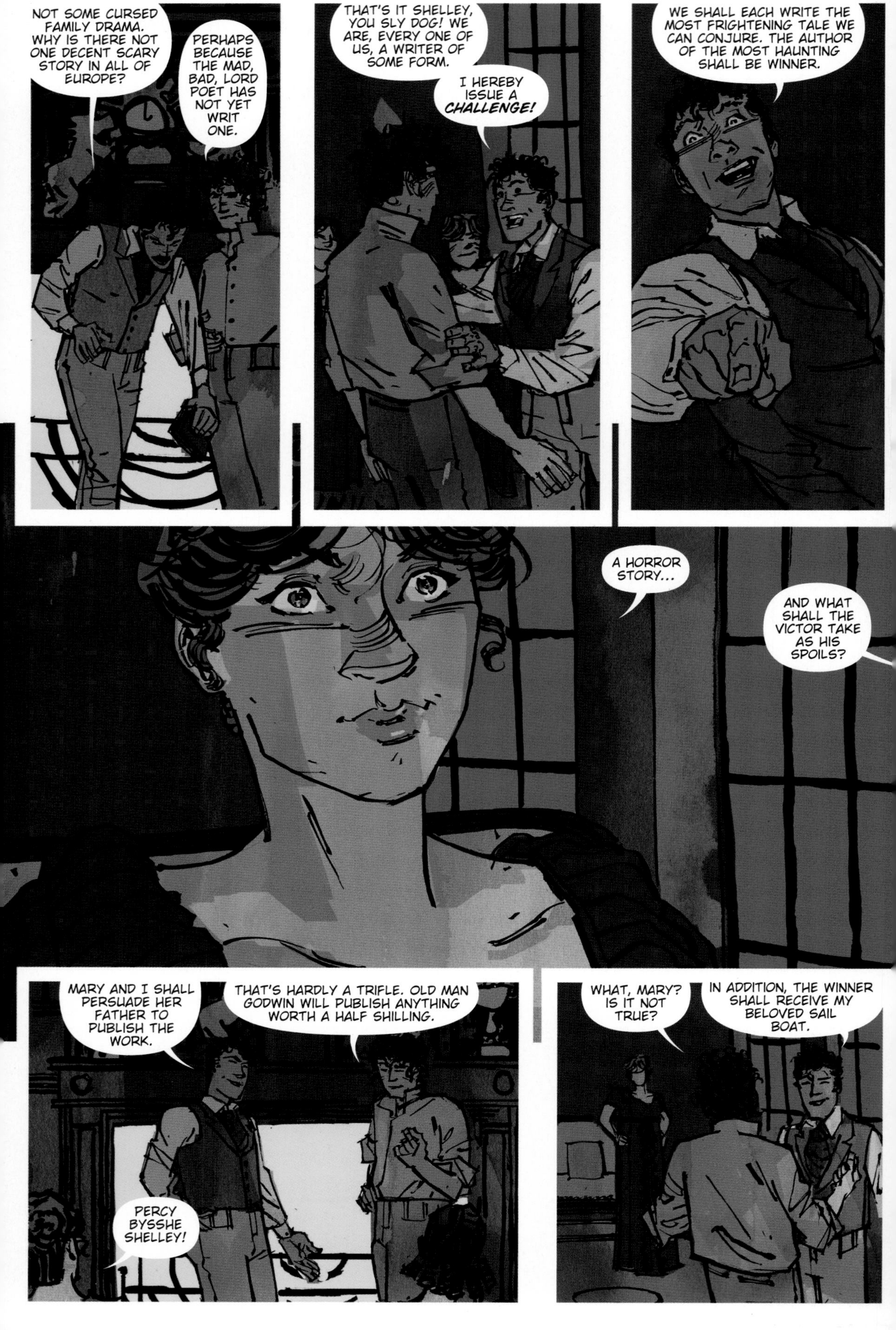
NOT SOME CURSED FAMILY DRAMA. WHY IS THERE NOT ONE DECENT SCARY STORY IN ALL OF EUROPE?
PERHAPS BECAUSE THE MAD, BAD, LORD POET HAS NOT YET WRIT ONE.
THAT'S IT SHELLEY, YOU SLY DOG! WE ARE, EVERY ONE OF US, A WRITER OF SOME FORM.
I HEREBY ISSUE A CHALLENGE!
WE SHALL EACH WRITE THE MOST FRIGHTENING TALE WE CAN CONJURE. THE AUTHOR OF THE MOST HAUNTING SHALL BE WINNER.
A HORROR STORY...
AND WHAT SHALL THE VICTOR TAKE AS HIS SPOILS?
MARY AND I SHALL PERSUADE HER FATHER TO PUBLISH THE WORK.
THAT'S HARDLY A TRIFLE. OLD MAN GODWIN WILL PUBLISH ANYTHING WORTH A HALF SHILLING.
PERCY BYSSHE SHELLEY!
WHAT, MARY? IS IT NOT TRUE?
IN ADDITION, THE WINNER SHALL RECEIVE MY BELOVED SAIL BOAT.

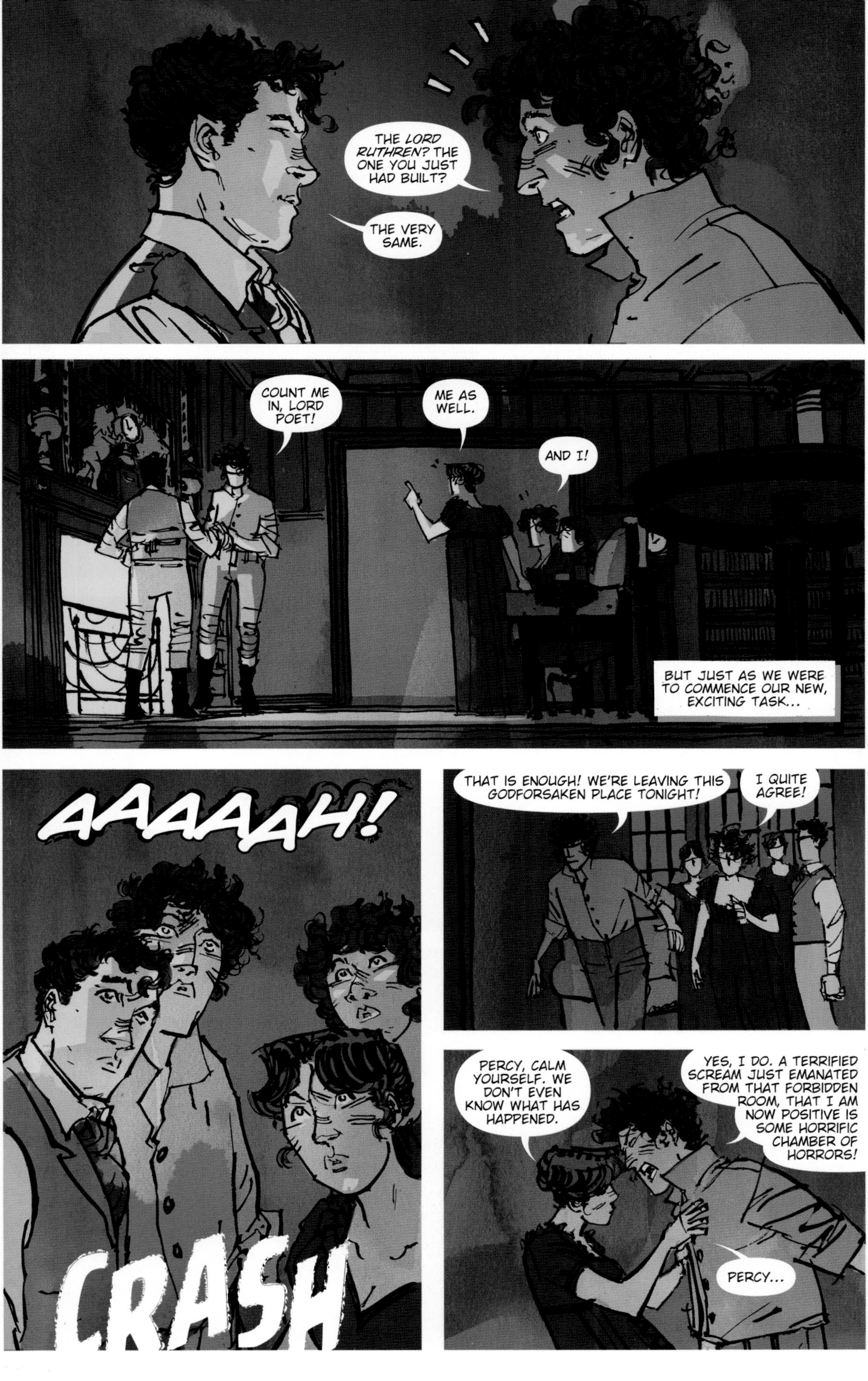
THE *LORD RUTHREN*? THE ONE YOU JUST HAD BUILT?
THE VERY SAME.
COUNT ME IN, LORD POET!
ME AS WELL.
AND I!
BUT JUST AS WE WERE TO COMMENCE OUR NEW, EXCITING TASK...
AAAAAH!
CRASH
THAT IS ENOUGH! WE'RE LEAVING THIS GODFORSAKEN PLACE TONIGHT!
I QUITE AGREE!
PERCY, CALM YOURSELF. WE DON'T EVEN KNOW WHAT HAS HAPPENED.
YES, I DO. A TERRIFIED SCREAM JUST EMANATED FROM THAT FORBIDDEN ROOM, THAT I AM NOW POSITIVE IS SOME HORRIFIC CHAMBER OF HORRORS!
PERCY...

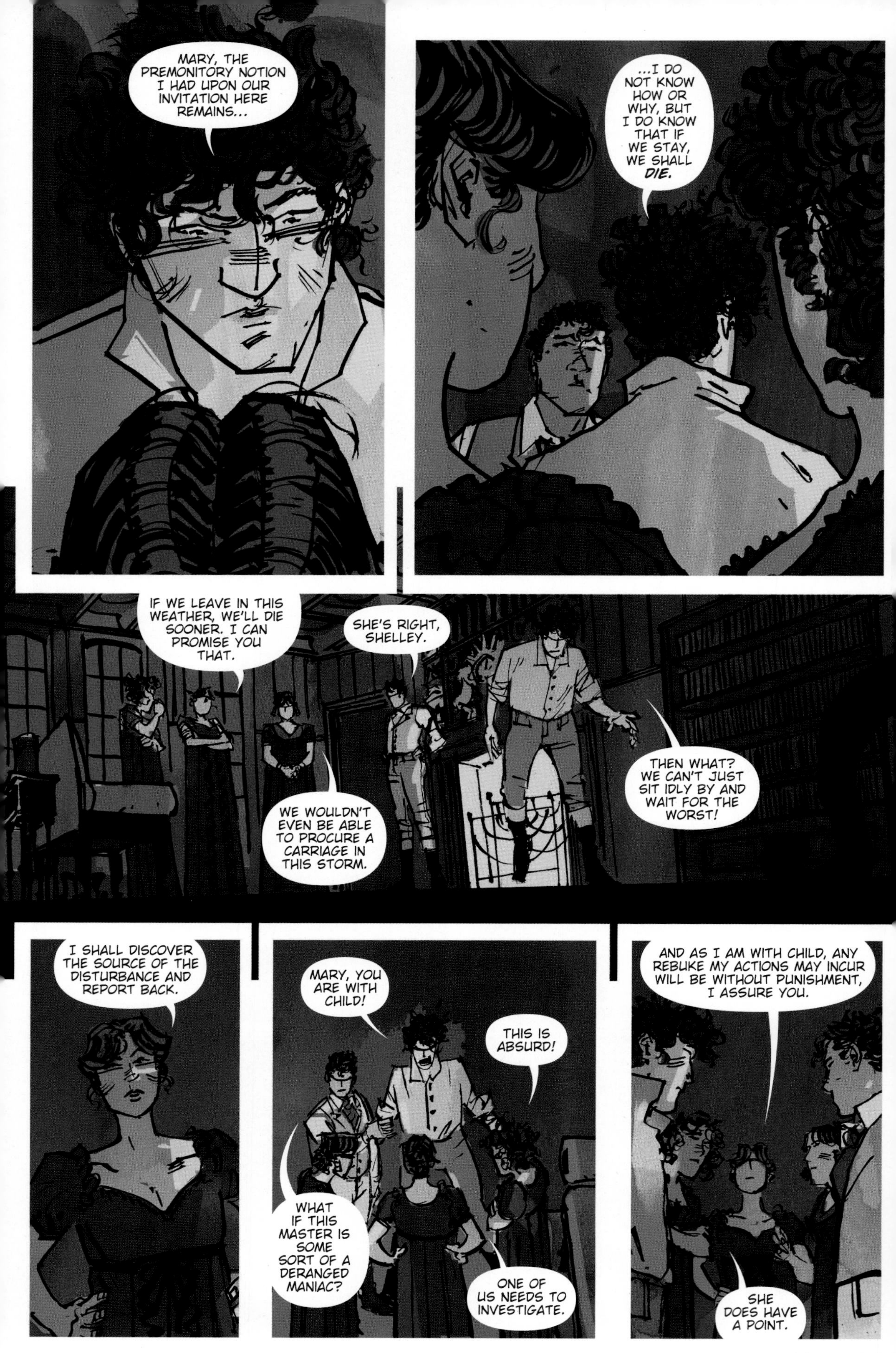
MARY, THE PREMONITORY NOTION I HAD UPON OUR INVITATION HERE REMAINS...
...I DO NOT KNOW HOW OR WHY, BUT I DO KNOW THAT IF WE STAY, WE SHALL *DIE.*
IF WE LEAVE IN THIS WEATHER, WE'LL DIE SOONER. I CAN PROMISE YOU THAT.
SHE'S RIGHT, SHELLEY.
WE WOULDN'T EVEN BE ABLE TO PROCURE A CARRIAGE IN THIS STORM.
THEN WHAT? WE CAN'T JUST SIT IDLY BY AND WAIT FOR THE WORST!
I SHALL DISCOVER THE SOURCE OF THE DISTURBANCE AND REPORT BACK.
MARY, YOU ARE WITH CHILD!
THIS IS ABSURD!
WHAT IF THIS MASTER IS SOME SORT OF A DERANGED MANIAC?
ONE OF US NEEDS TO INVESTIGATE.
AND AS I AM WITH CHILD, ANY REBUKE MY ACTIONS MAY INCUR WILL BE WITHOUT PUNISHMENT, I ASSURE YOU.
SHE DOES HAVE A POINT.

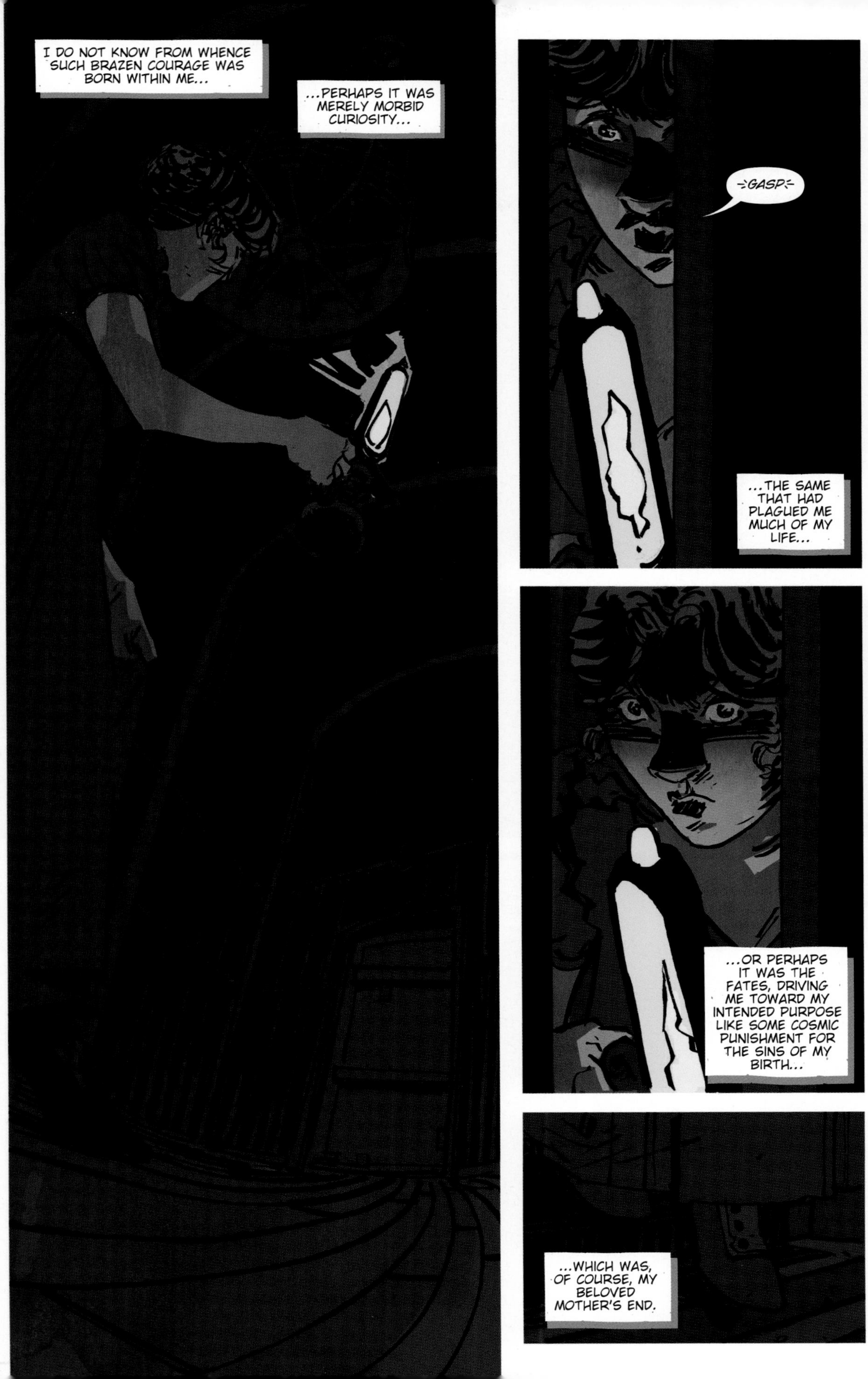
I DO NOT KNOW FROM WHENCE SUCH BRAZEN COURAGE WAS BORN WITHIN ME...
...PERHAPS IT WAS MERELY MORBID CURIOSITY...
GASP
...THE SAME THAT HAD PLAGUED ME MUCH OF MY LIFE...
...OR PERHAPS IT WAS THE FATES, DRIVING ME TOWARD MY INTENDED PURPOSE LIKE SOME COSMIC PUNISHMENT FOR THE SINS OF MY BIRTH...
...WHICH WAS, OF COURSE, MY BELOVED MOTHER'S END.

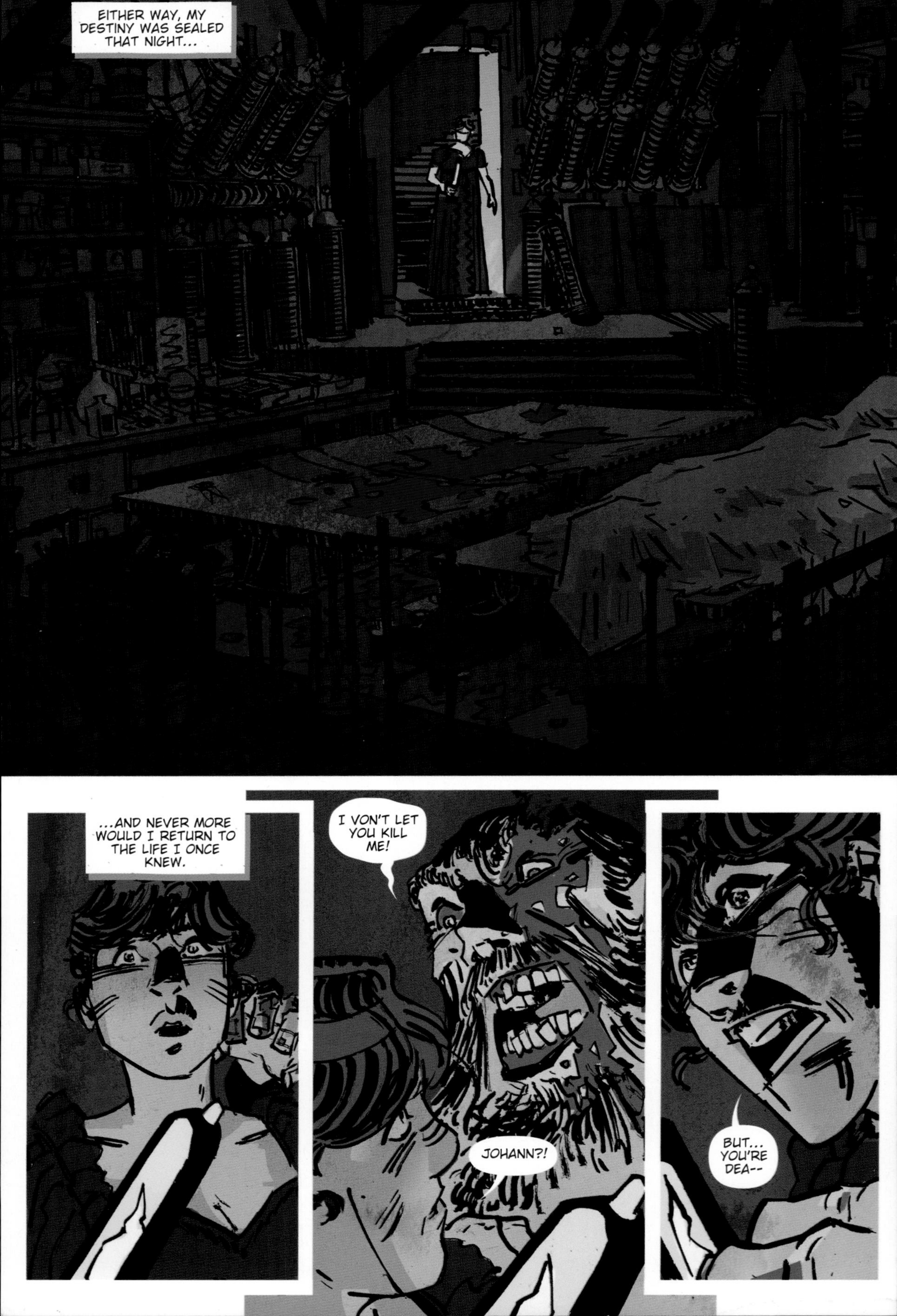

EITHER WAY, MY DESTINY WAS SEALED THAT NIGHT...
...AND NEVER MORE WOULD I RETURN TO THE LIFE I ONCE KNEW.
I VON'T LET YOU KILL ME!
JOHANN?!
BUT... YOU'RE DEA--

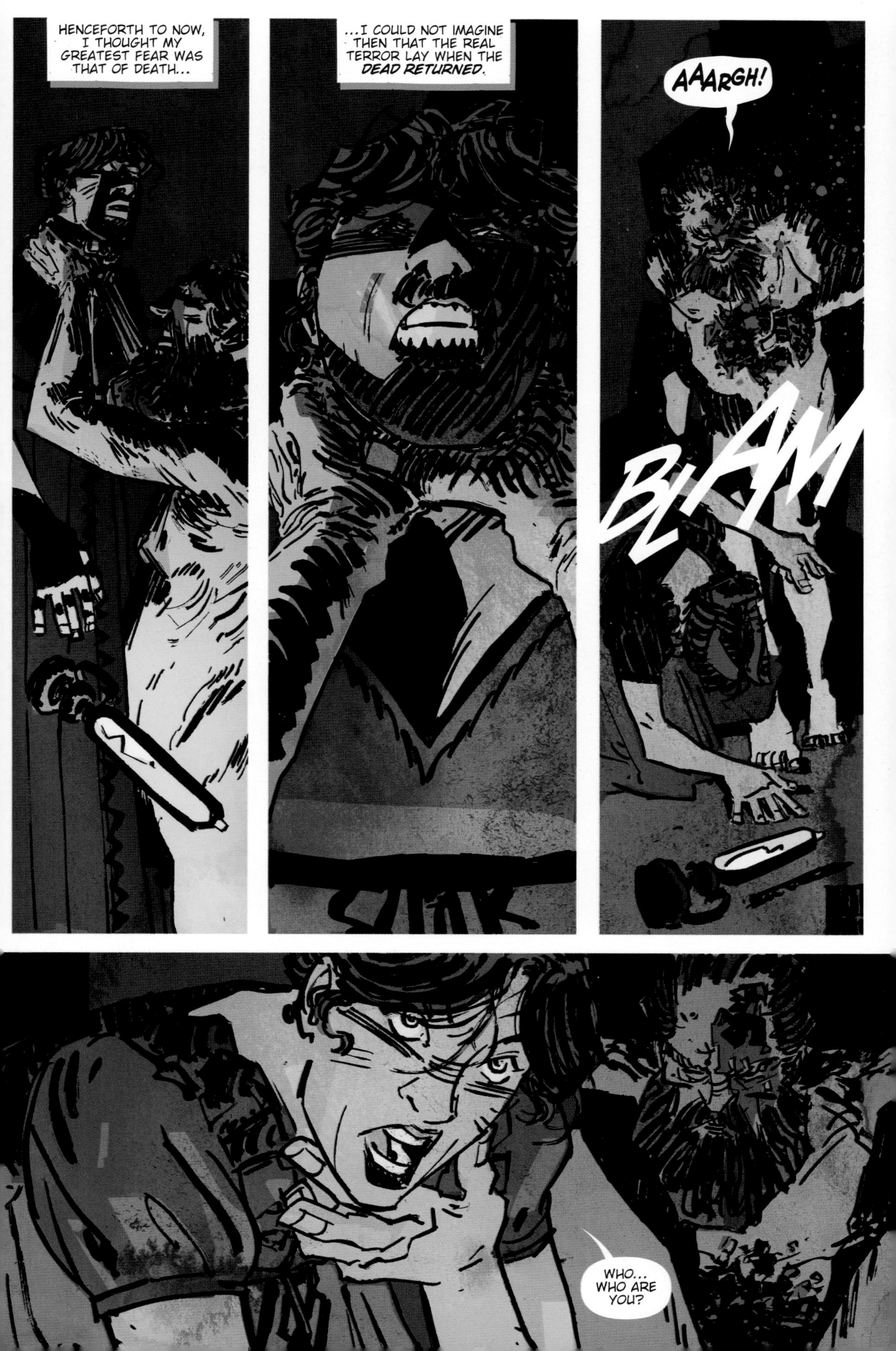
HENCEFORTH TO NOW, I THOUGHT MY GREATEST FEAR WAS THAT OF DEATH...
...I COULD NOT IMAGINE THEN THAT THE REAL TERROR LAY WHEN THE *DEAD RETURNED*.
AAARGH!
BLAM
WHO... WHO ARE YOU?

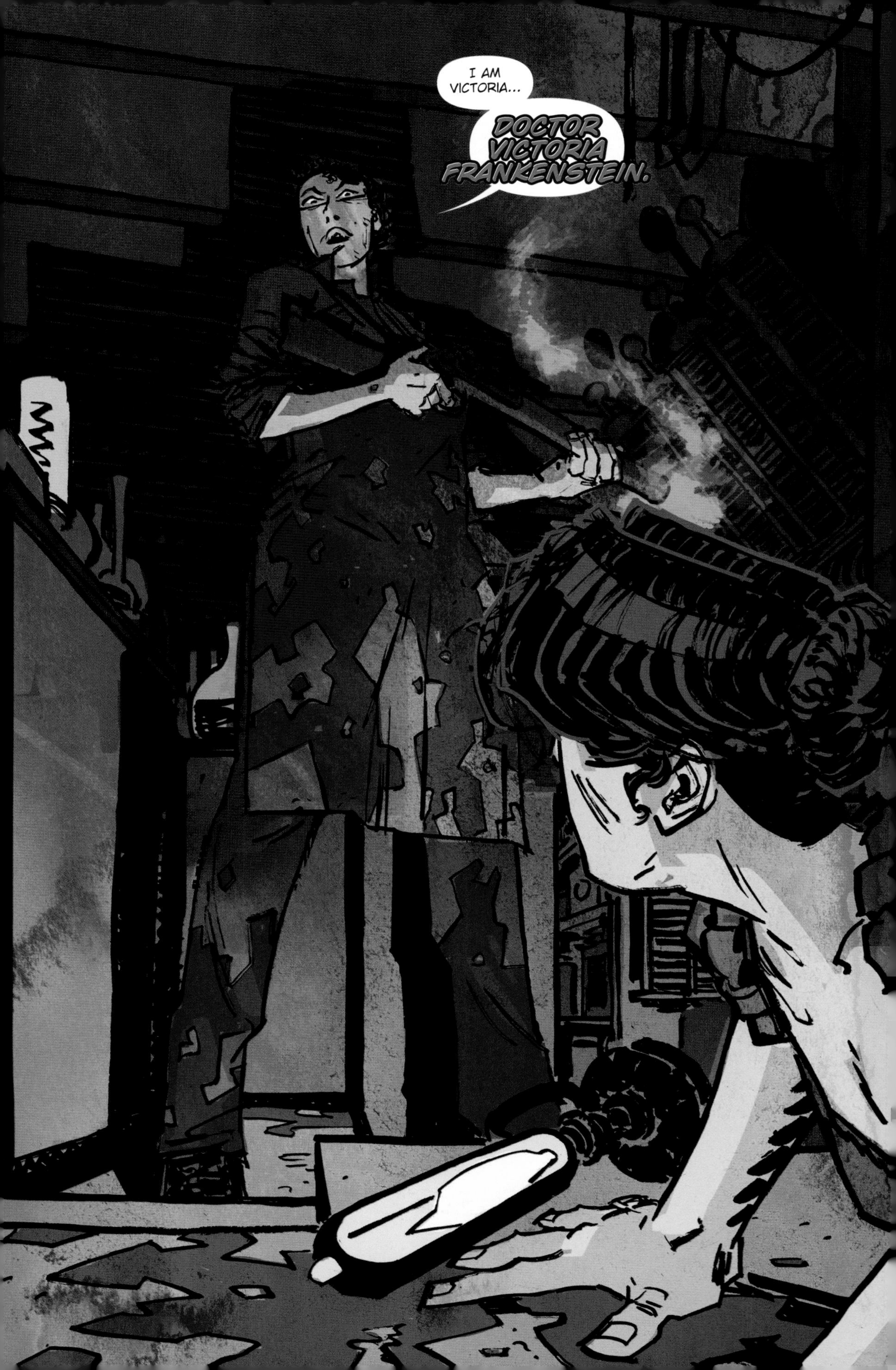
I AM VICTORIA...
DOCTOR VICTORIA FRANKENSTEIN.

2

AN UNLIKELY PARTNERSHIP

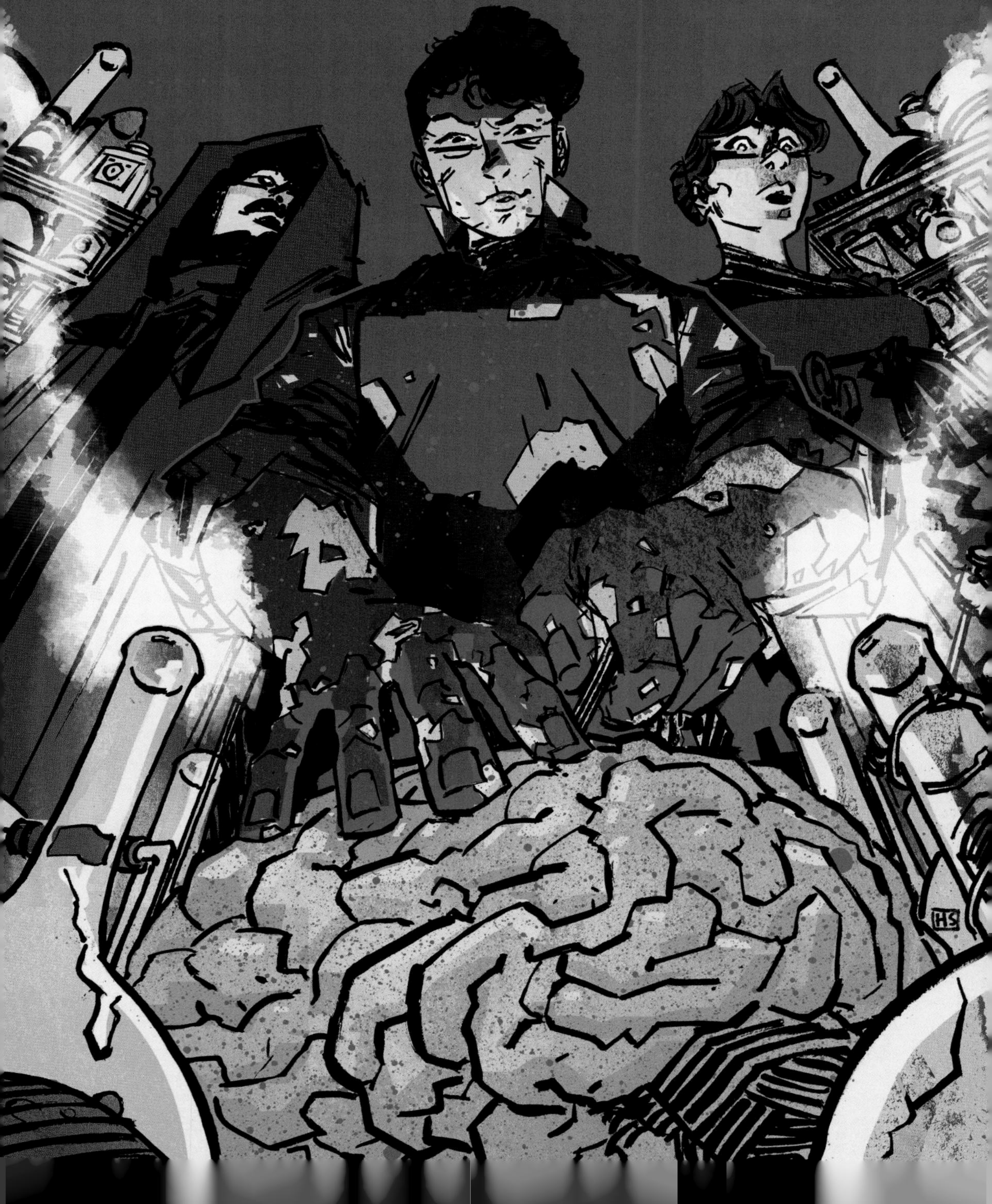
HS

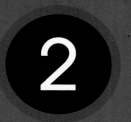

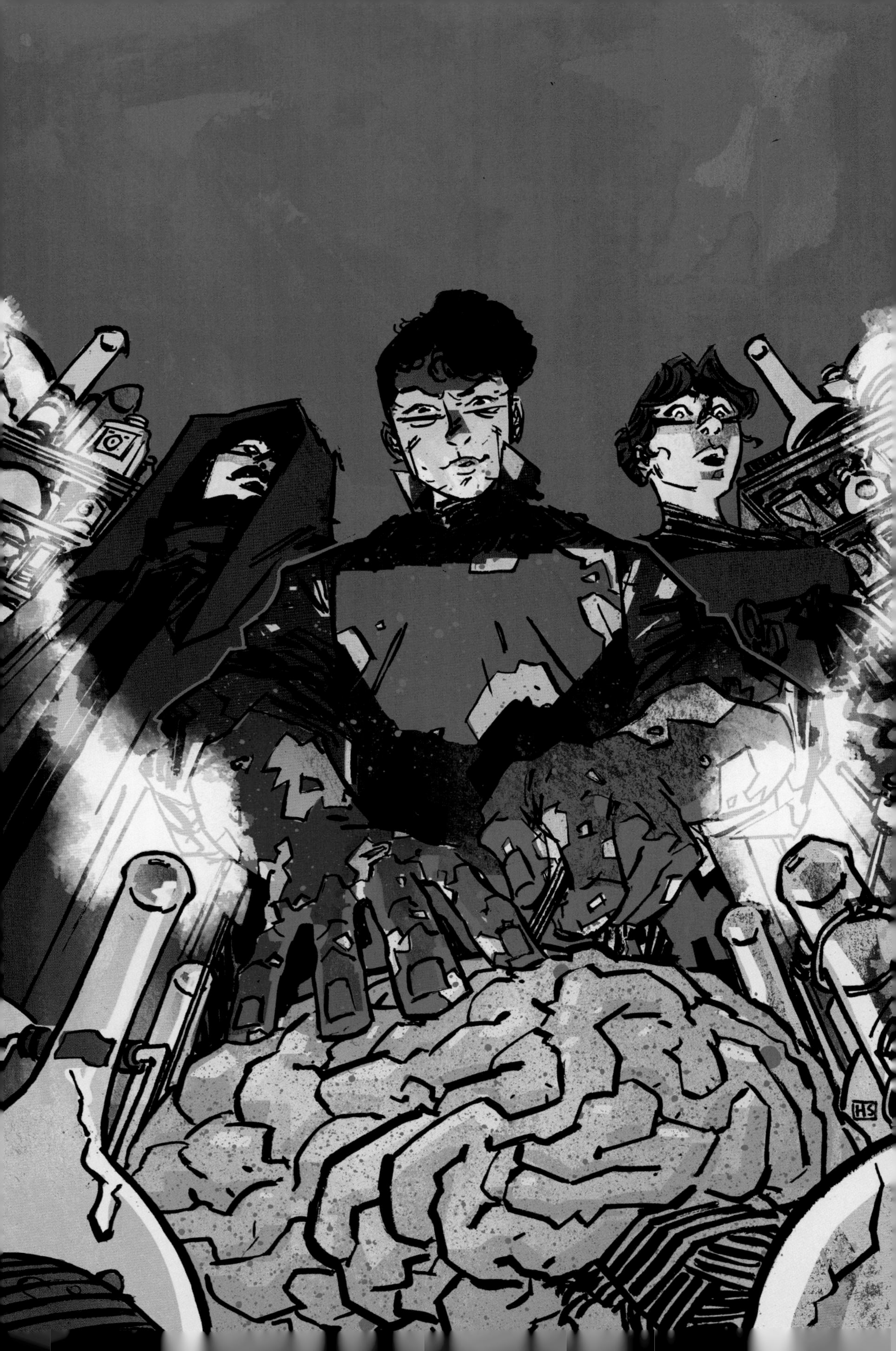
HS

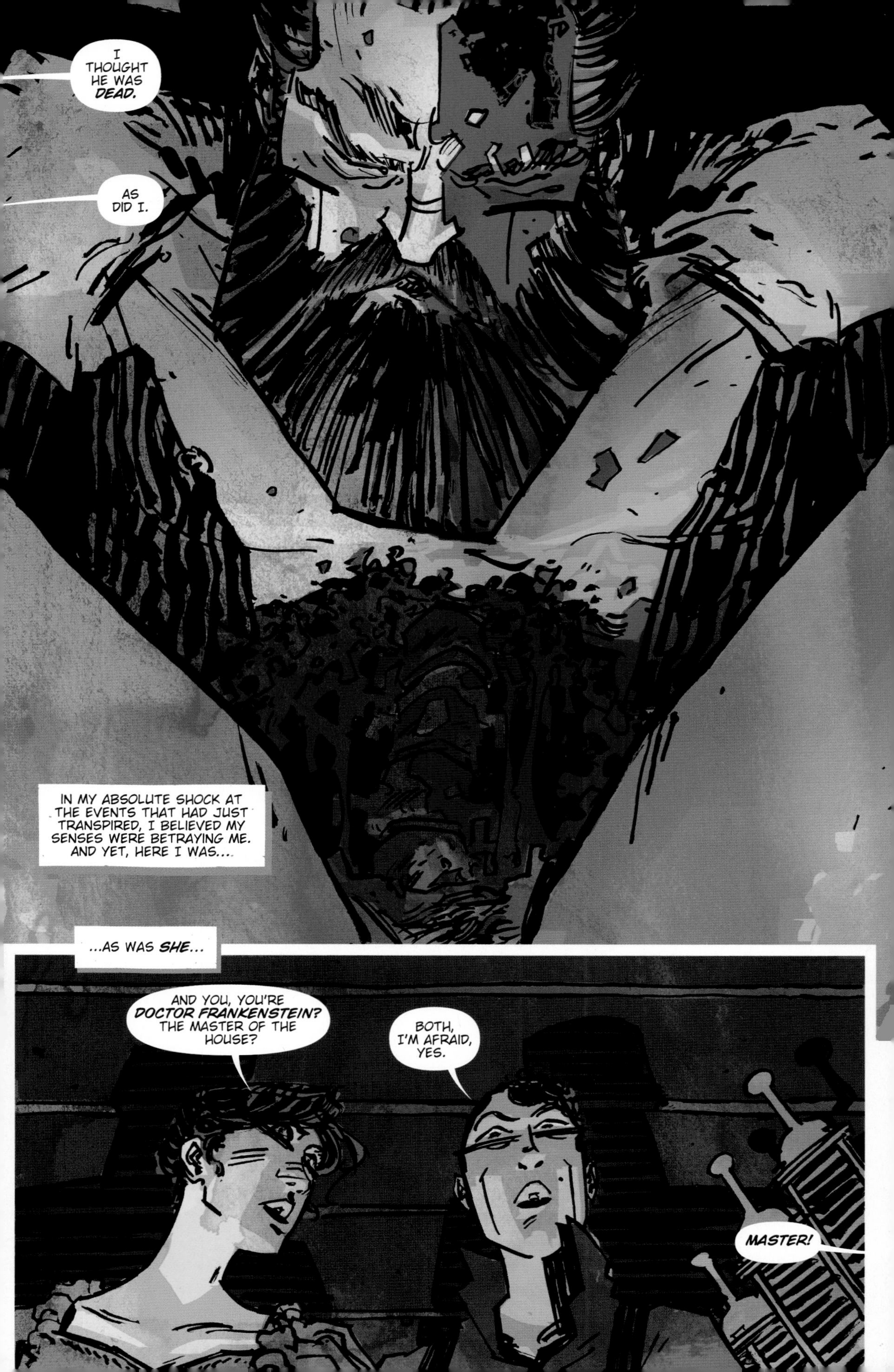
I THOUGHT HE WAS **DEAD.**
AS DID I.
IN MY ABSOLUTE SHOCK AT THE EVENTS THAT HAD JUST TRANSPIRED, I BELIEVED MY SENSES WERE BETRAYING ME. AND YET, HERE I WAS...
...AS WAS **SHE**...
AND YOU, YOU'RE **DOCTOR FRANKENSTEIN?** THE MASTER OF THE HOUSE?
BOTH, I'M AFRAID, YES.
MASTER!

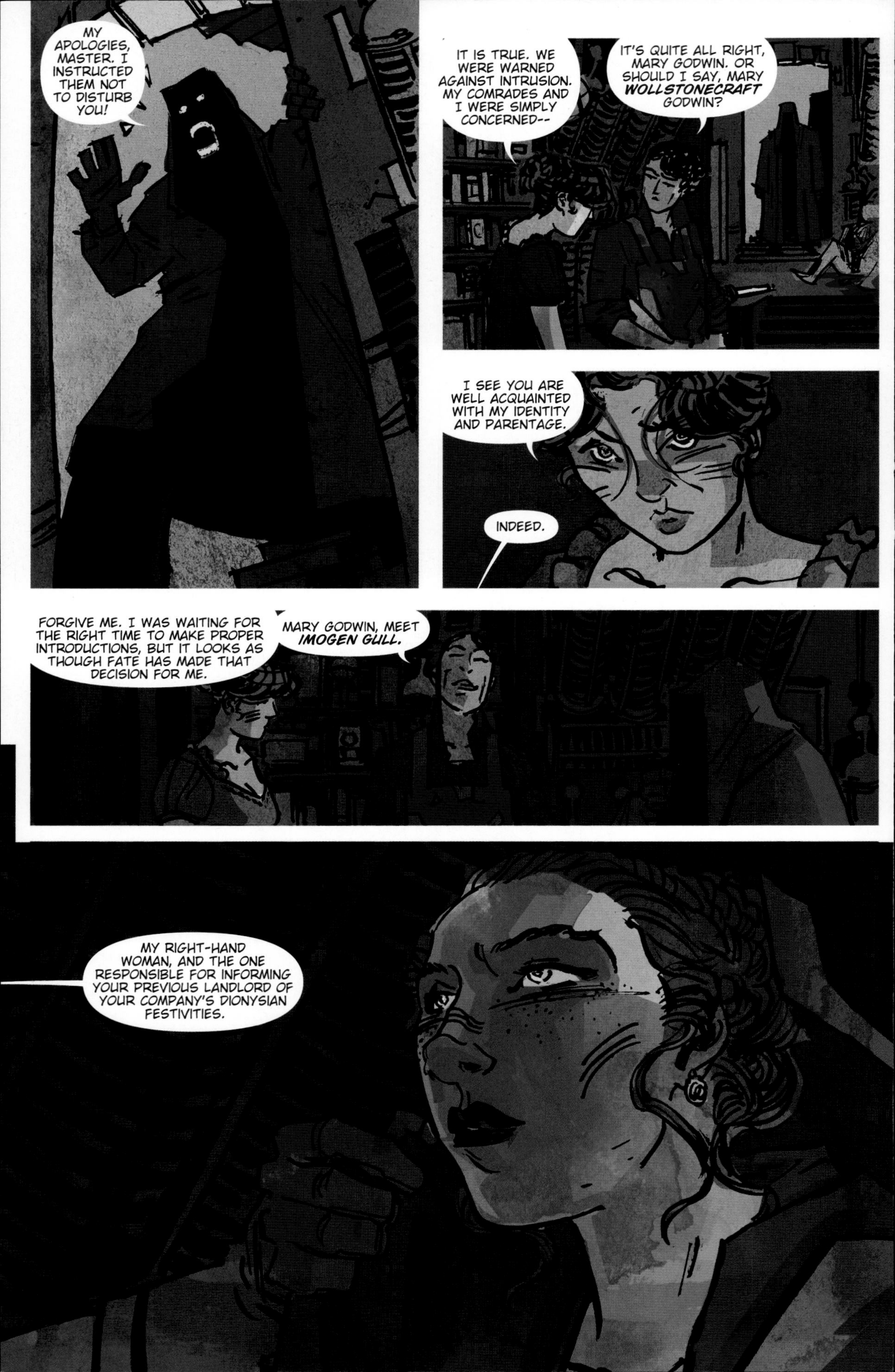
MY APOLOGIES, MASTER. I INSTRUCTED THEM NOT TO DISTURB YOU!
IT IS TRUE. WE WERE WARNED AGAINST INTRUSION. MY COMRADES AND I WERE SIMPLY CONCERNED--
IT'S QUITE ALL RIGHT, MARY GODWIN. OR SHOULD I SAY, MARY WOLLSTONECRAFT GODWIN?
I SEE YOU ARE WELL ACQUAINTED WITH MY IDENTITY AND PARENTAGE.
INDEED.
FORGIVE ME. I WAS WAITING FOR THE RIGHT TIME TO MAKE PROPER INTRODUCTIONS, BUT IT LOOKS AS THOUGH FATE HAS MADE THAT DECISION FOR ME.
MARY GODWIN, MEET IMOGEN GULL.
MY RIGHT-HAND WOMAN, AND THE ONE RESPONSIBLE FOR INFORMING YOUR PREVIOUS LANDLORD OF YOUR COMPANY'S DIONYSIAN FESTIVITIES.

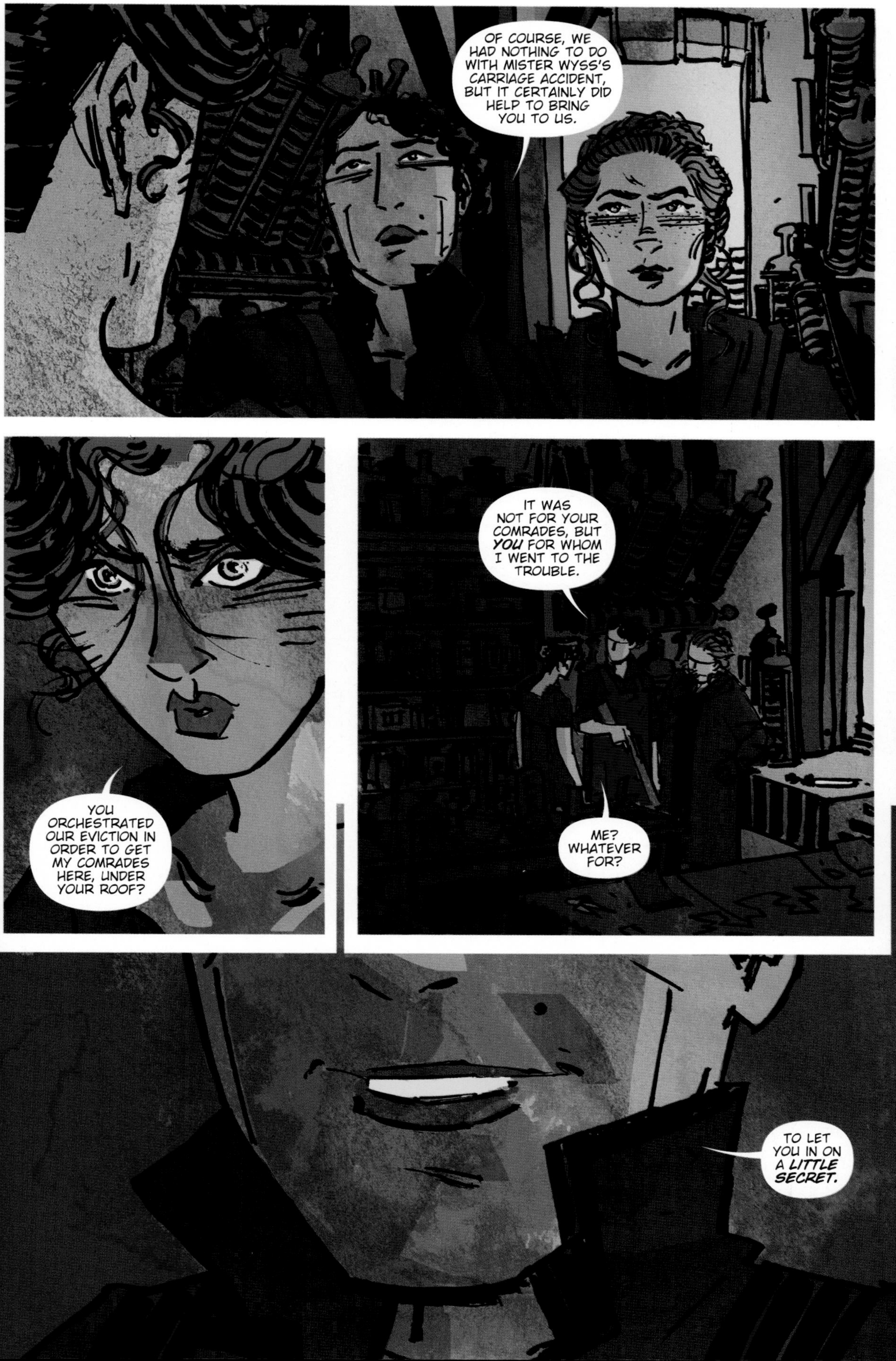
OF COURSE, WE HAD NOTHING TO DO WITH MISTER WYSS'S CARRIAGE ACCIDENT, BUT IT CERTAINLY DID HELP TO BRING YOU TO US.
YOU ORCHESTRATED OUR EVICTION IN ORDER TO GET MY COMRADES HERE, UNDER YOUR ROOF?
IT WAS NOT FOR YOUR COMRADES, BUT *YOU* FOR WHOM I WENT TO THE TROUBLE.
ME? WHATEVER FOR?
TO LET YOU IN ON A *LITTLE SECRET.*

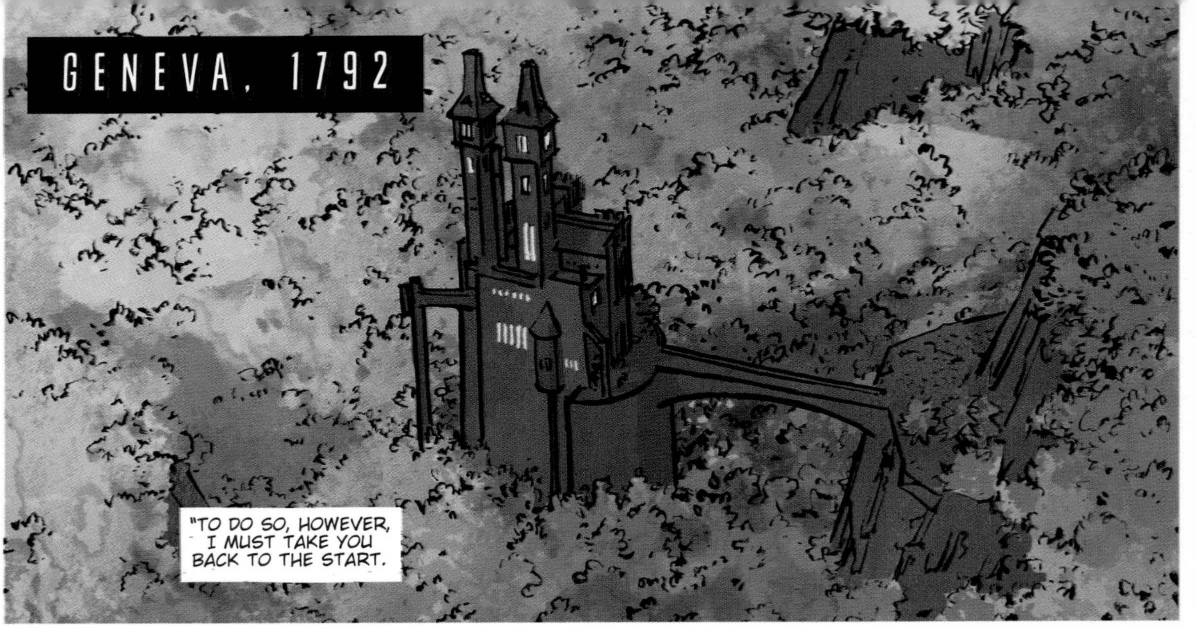
GENEVA, 1792
"TO DO SO, HOWEVER, I MUST TAKE YOU BACK TO THE START.

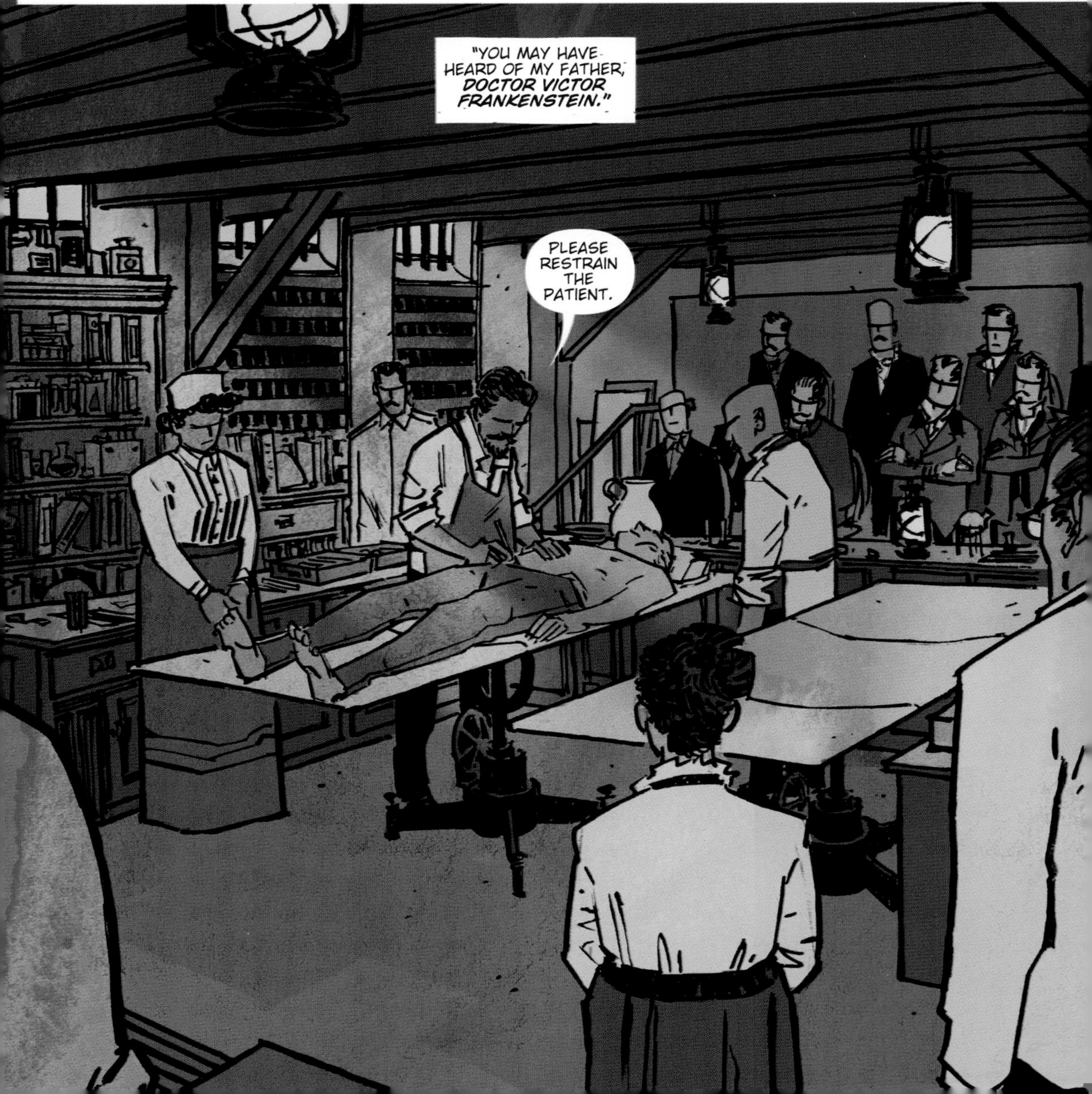
"YOU MAY HAVE HEARD OF MY FATHER, DOCTOR VICTOR FRANKENSTEIN."
PLEASE RESTRAIN THE PATIENT.

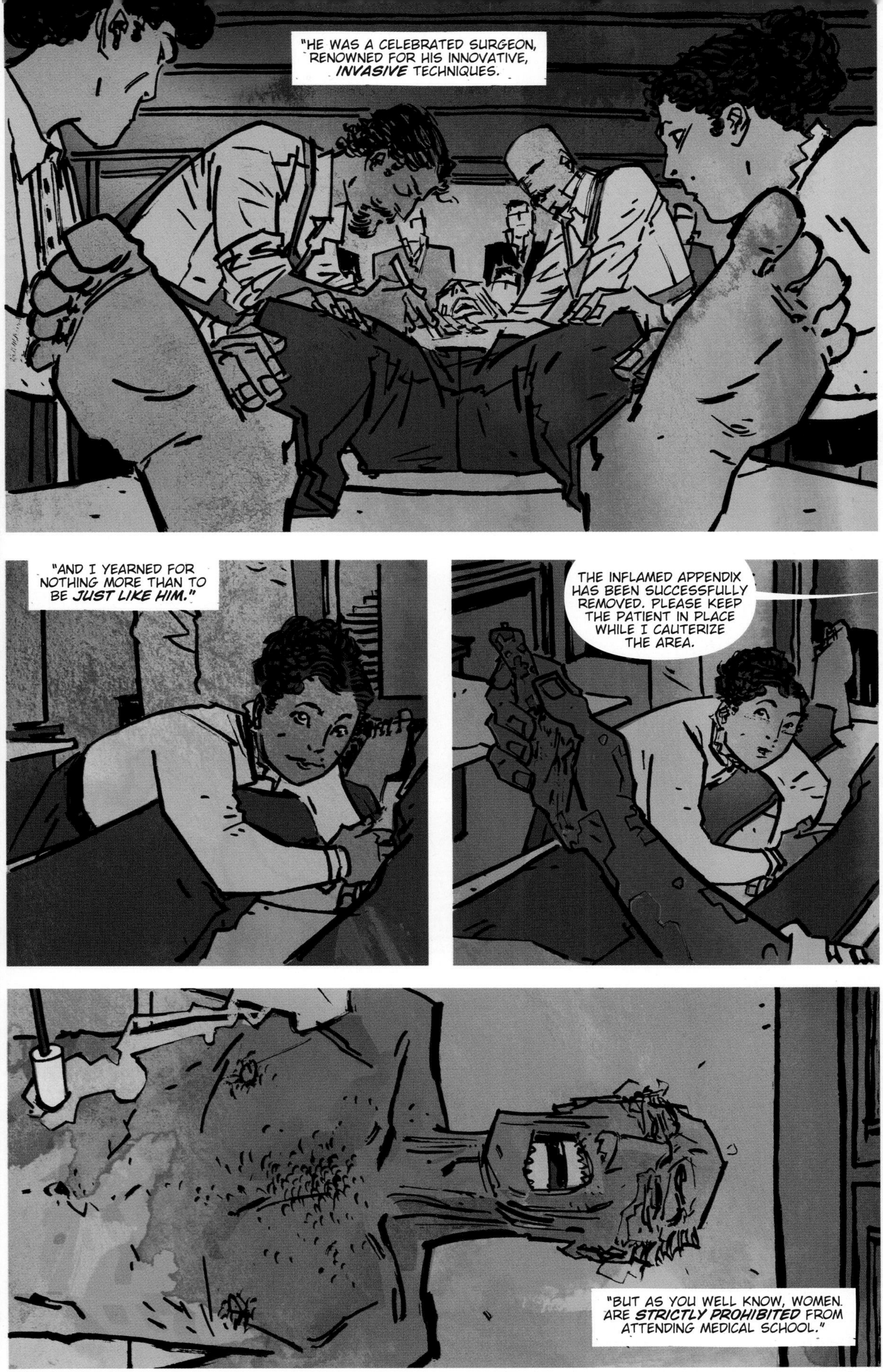
"HE WAS A CELEBRATED SURGEON, RENOWNED FOR HIS INNOVATIVE, *INVASIVE* TECHNIQUES.
"AND I YEARNED FOR NOTHING MORE THAN TO BE *JUST LIKE HIM.*"
THE INFLAMED APPENDIX HAS BEEN SUCCESSFULLY REMOVED. PLEASE KEEP THE PATIENT IN PLACE WHILE I CAUTERIZE THE AREA.
"BUT AS YOU WELL KNOW, WOMEN. ARE *STRICTLY PROHIBITED* FROM ATTENDING MEDICAL SCHOOL."

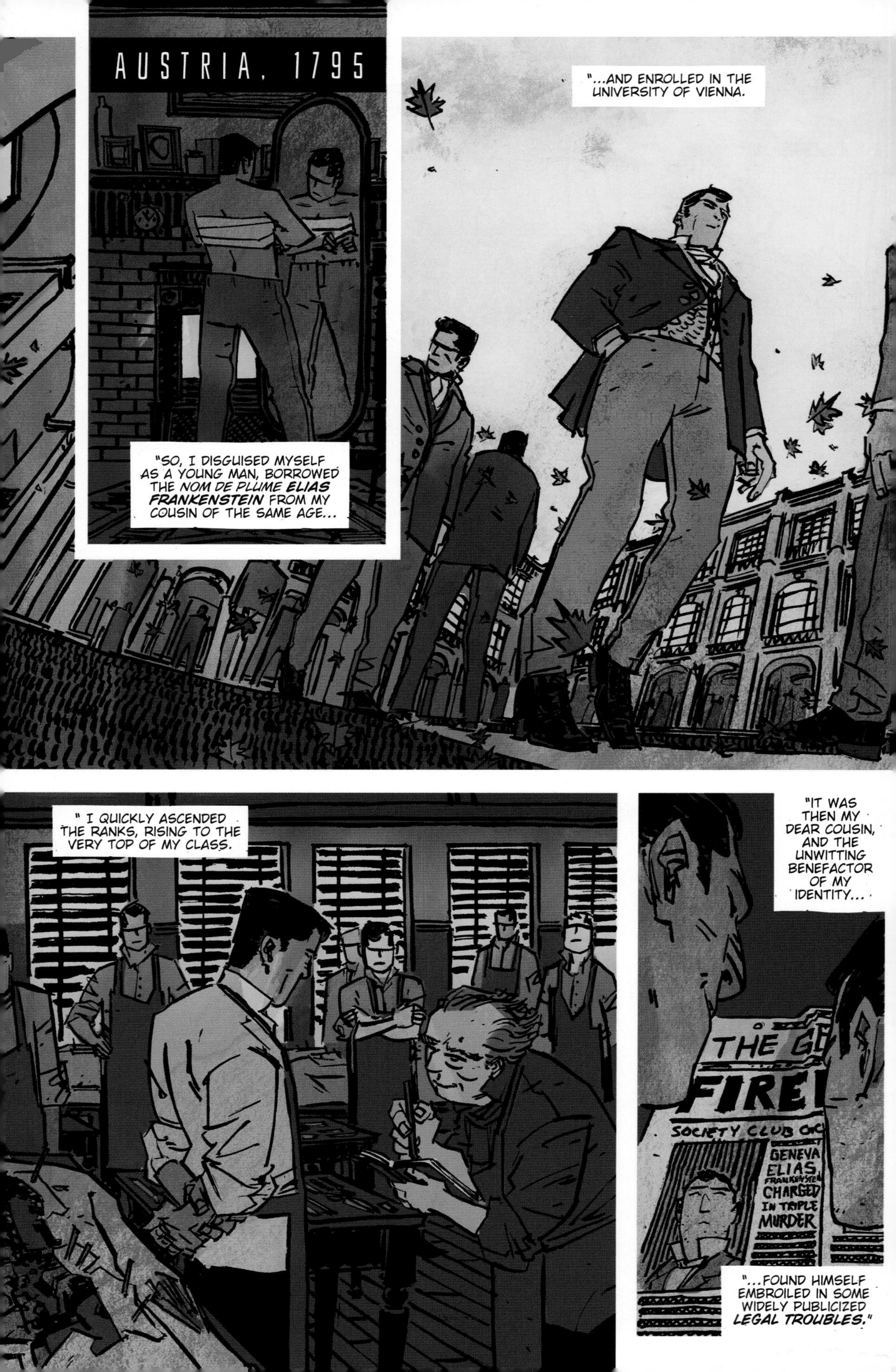
AUSTRIA, 1795
"SO, I DISGUISED MYSELF AS A YOUNG MAN, BORROWED THE *NOM DE PLUME* **ELIAS FRANKENSTEIN** FROM MY COUSIN OF THE SAME AGE...
"...AND ENROLLED IN THE UNIVERSITY OF VIENNA.
" I QUICKLY ASCENDED THE RANKS, RISING TO THE VERY TOP OF MY CLASS.
"IT WAS THEN MY DEAR COUSIN, AND THE UNWITTING BENEFACTOR OF MY IDENTITY...
THE G
FIRE
SOCIETY CLUB
GENEVA ELIAS FRANKENSTEIN CHARGED IN TRIPLE MURDER
"...FOUND HIMSELF EMBROILED IN SOME WIDELY PUBLICIZED **LEGAL TROUBLES.**"

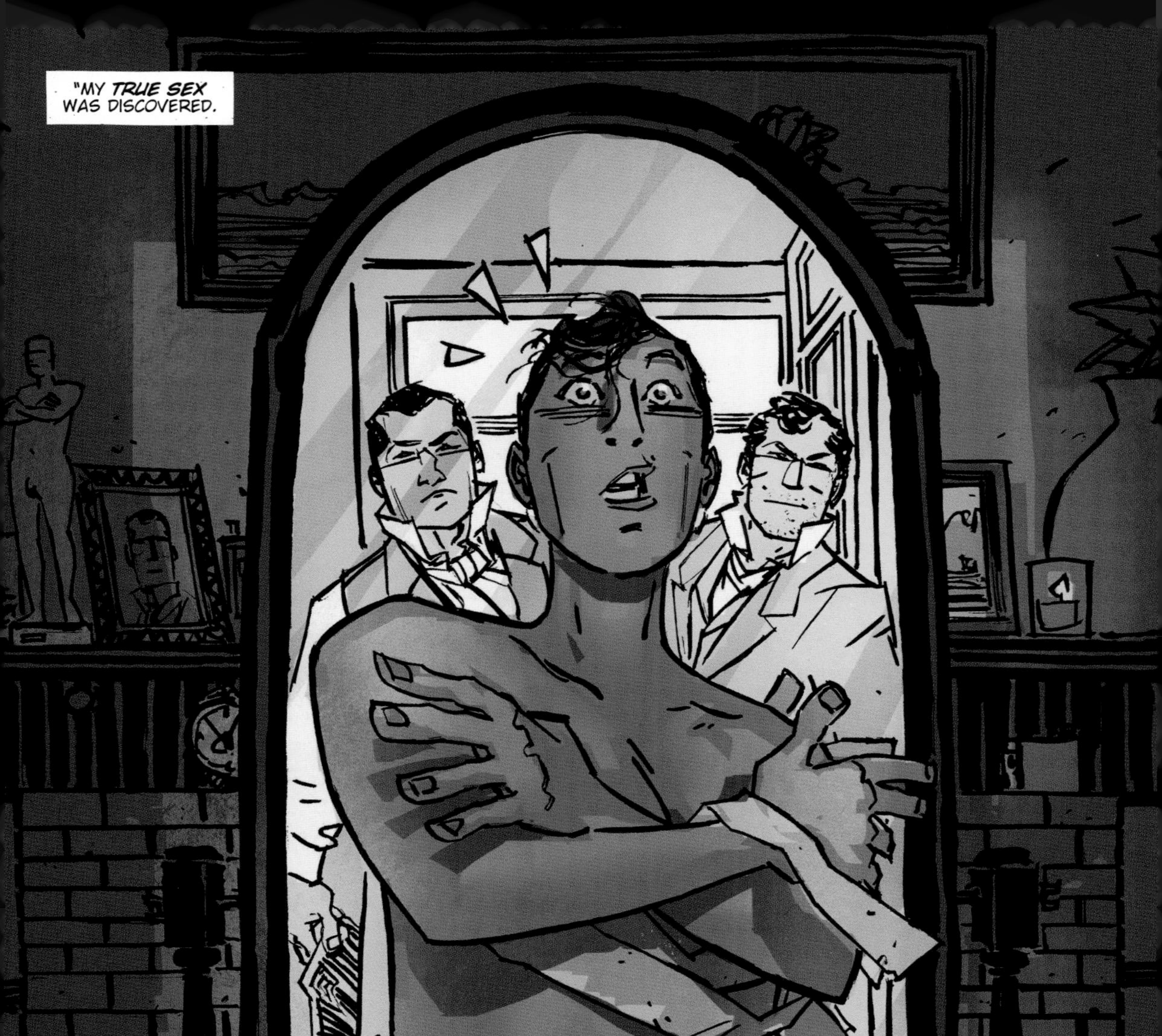
"MY TRUE SEX
WAS DISCOVERED.

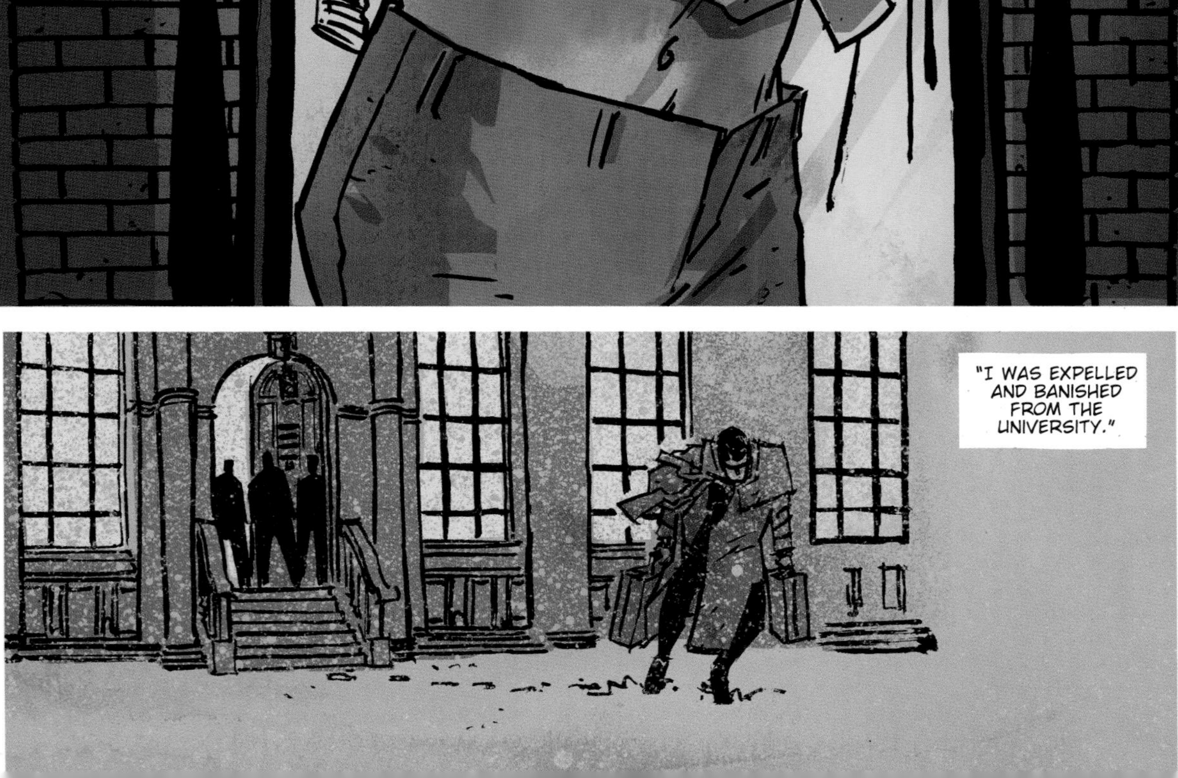
"I WAS EXPELLED
AND BANISHED
FROM THE
UNIVERSITY."

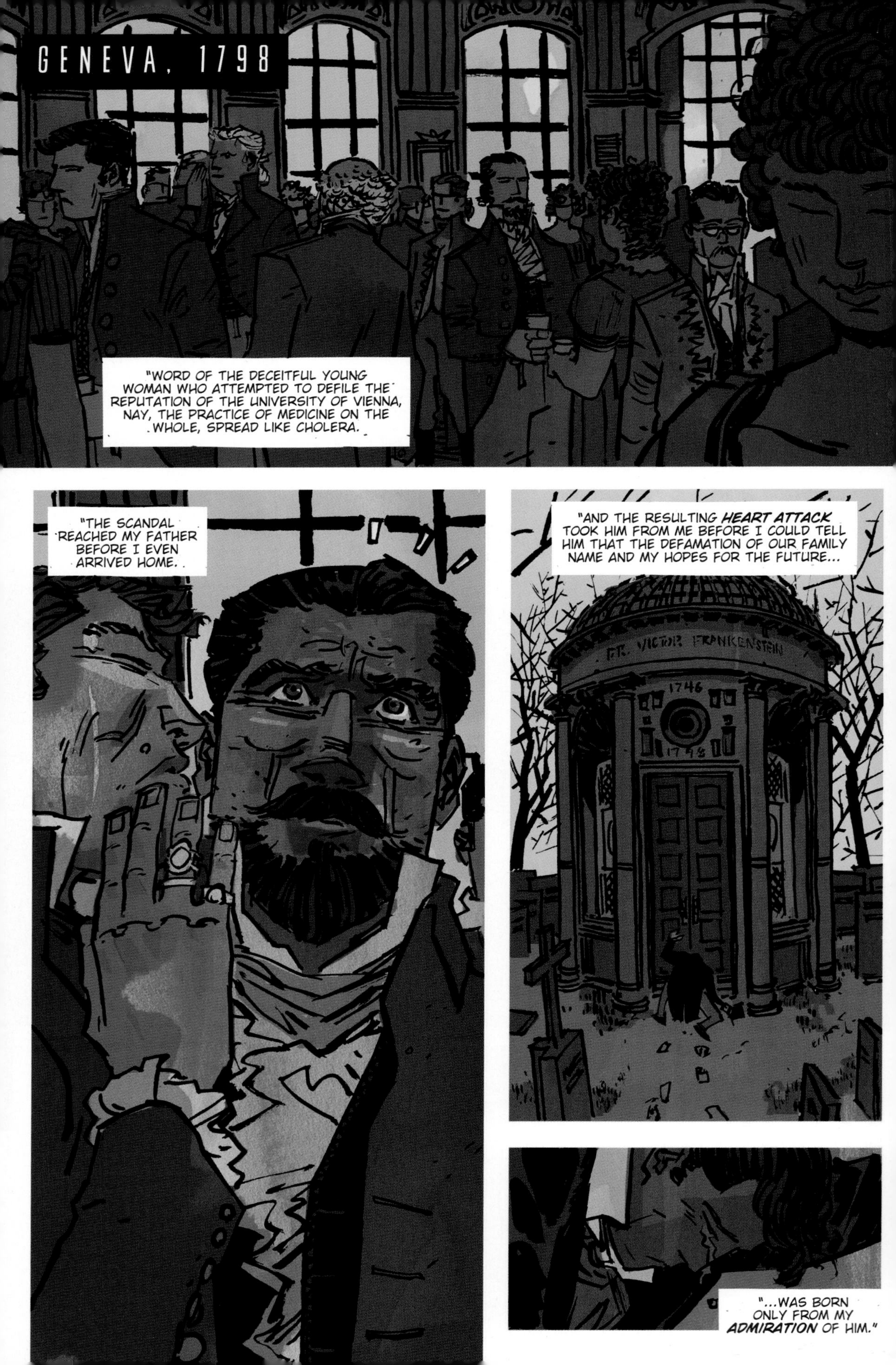
GENEVA, 1798
"WORD OF THE DECEITFUL YOUNG WOMAN WHO ATTEMPTED TO DEFILE THE REPUTATION OF THE UNIVERSITY OF VIENNA, NAY, THE PRACTICE OF MEDICINE ON THE WHOLE, SPREAD LIKE CHOLERA.
"THE SCANDAL REACHED MY FATHER BEFORE I EVEN ARRIVED HOME.
"AND THE RESULTING *HEART ATTACK* TOOK HIM FROM ME BEFORE I COULD TELL HIM THAT THE DEFAMATION OF OUR FAMILY NAME AND MY HOPES FOR THE FUTURE...
FR. VICTOR FRANKENSTEIN
1746
1798
"...WAS BORN ONLY FROM MY *ADMIRATION* OF HIM."

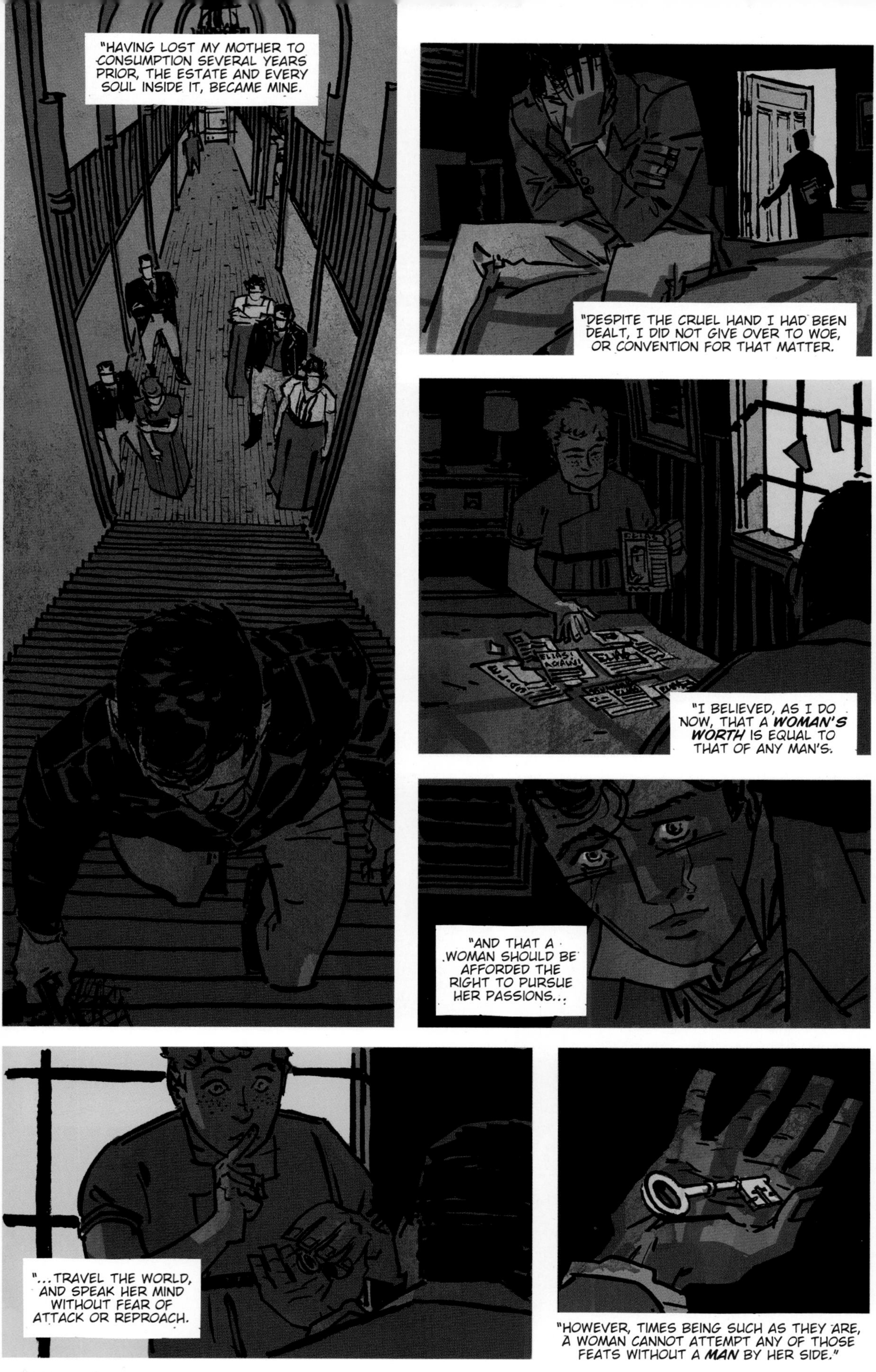
"HAVING LOST MY MOTHER TO CONSUMPTION SEVERAL YEARS PRIOR, THE ESTATE AND EVERY SOUL INSIDE IT, BECAME MINE.
"DESPITE THE CRUEL HAND I HAD BEEN DEALT, I DID NOT GIVE OVER TO WOE, OR CONVENTION FOR THAT MATTER.
"I BELIEVED, AS I DO NOW, THAT A WOMAN'S WORTH IS EQUAL TO THAT OF ANY MAN'S.
"AND THAT A WOMAN SHOULD BE AFFORDED THE RIGHT TO PURSUE HER PASSIONS...
"...TRAVEL THE WORLD, AND SPEAK HER MIND WITHOUT FEAR OF ATTACK OR REPROACH.
"HOWEVER, TIMES BEING SUCH AS THEY ARE, A WOMAN CANNOT ATTEMPT ANY OF THOSE FEATS WITHOUT A MAN BY HER SIDE."

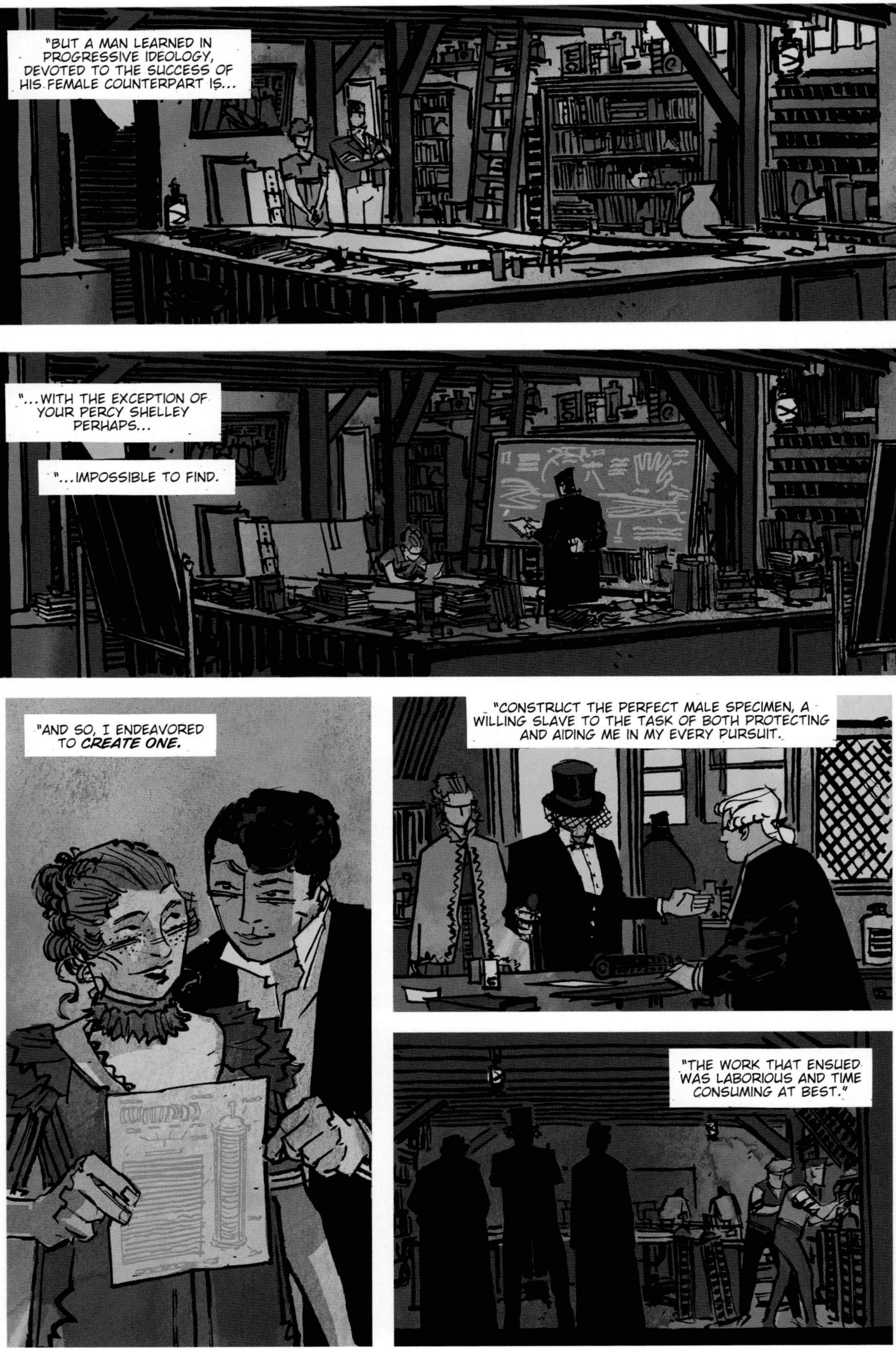
"BUT A MAN LEARNED IN PROGRESSIVE IDEOLOGY, DEVOTED TO THE SUCCESS OF HIS FEMALE COUNTERPART IS...
"...WITH THE EXCEPTION OF YOUR PERCY SHELLEY PERHAPS...
"...IMPOSSIBLE TO FIND.
"AND SO, I ENDEAVORED TO CREATE ONE.
"CONSTRUCT THE PERFECT MALE SPECIMEN, A WILLING SLAVE TO THE TASK OF BOTH PROTECTING AND AIDING ME IN MY EVERY PURSUIT.
"THE WORK THAT ENSUED WAS LABORIOUS AND TIME CONSUMING AT BEST."

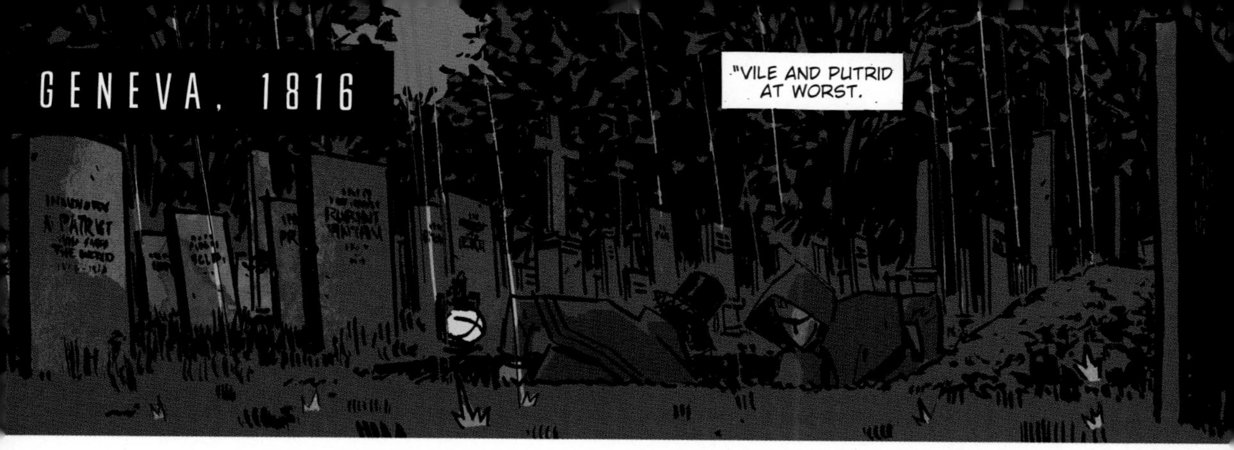
GENEVA, 1816
"VILE AND PUTRID AT WORST.

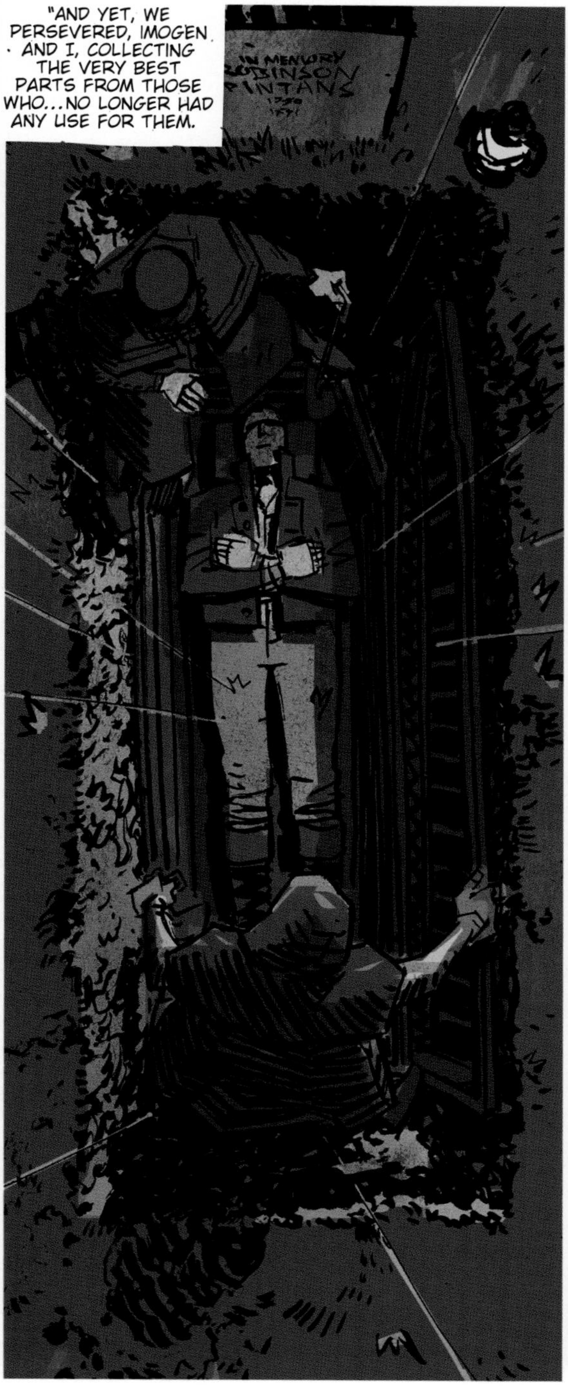
"AND YET, WE PERSEVERED, IMOGEN AND I, COLLECTING THE VERY BEST PARTS FROM THOSE WHO...NO LONGER HAD ANY USE FOR THEM.

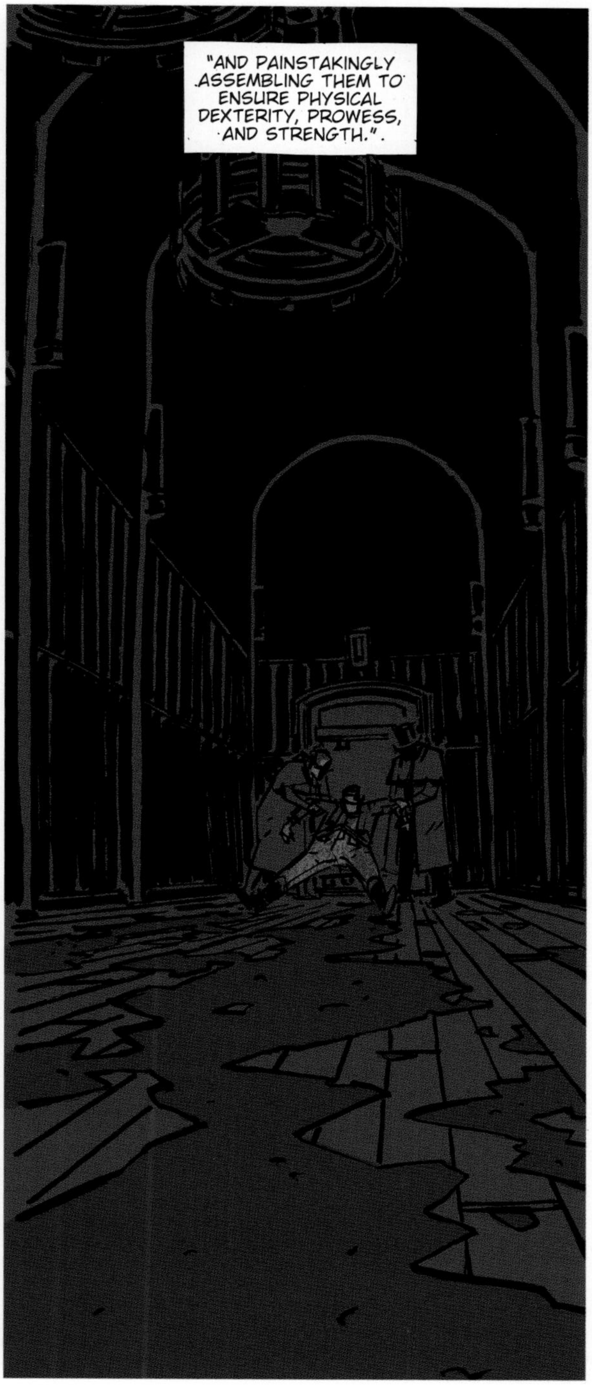
"AND PAINSTAKINGLY ASSEMBLING THEM TO ENSURE PHYSICAL DEXTERITY, PROWESS, AND STRENGTH."

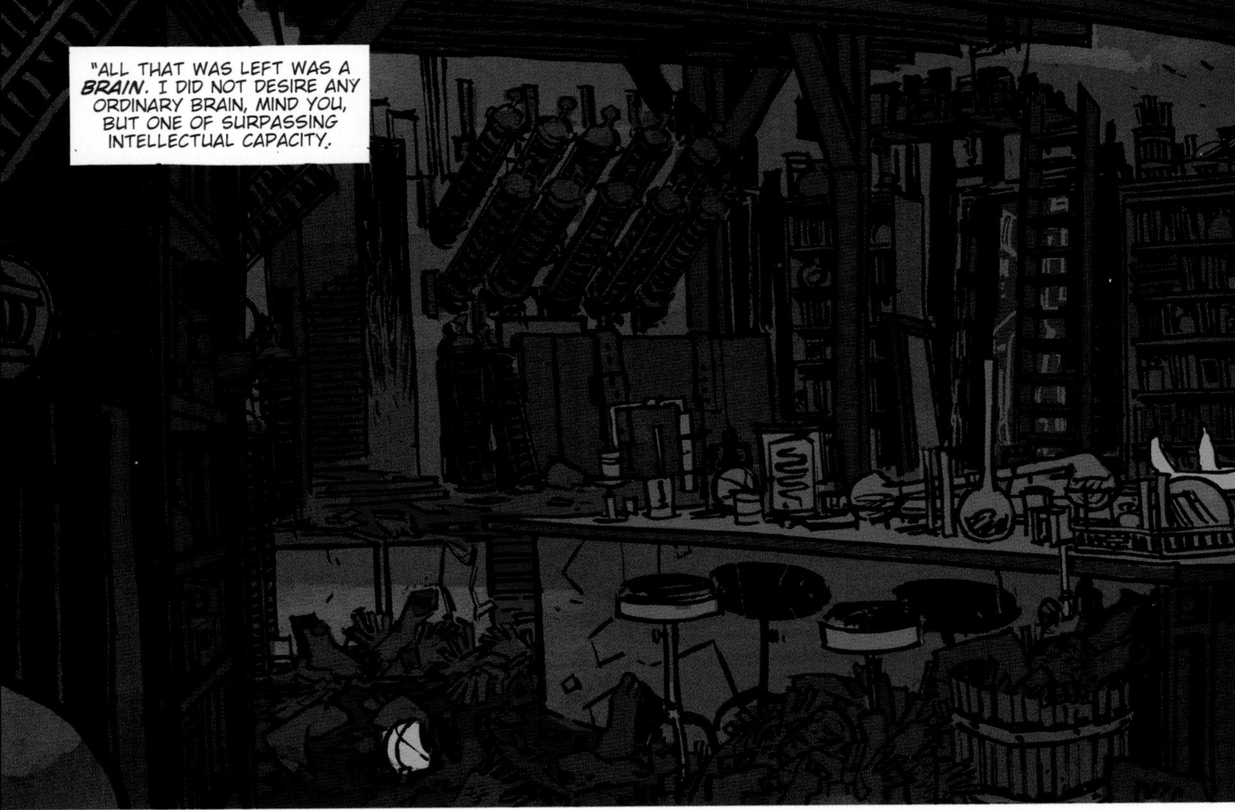
"ALL THAT WAS LEFT WAS A BRAIN. I DID NOT DESIRE ANY ORDINARY BRAIN, MIND YOU, BUT ONE OF SURPASSING INTELLECTUAL CAPACITY.

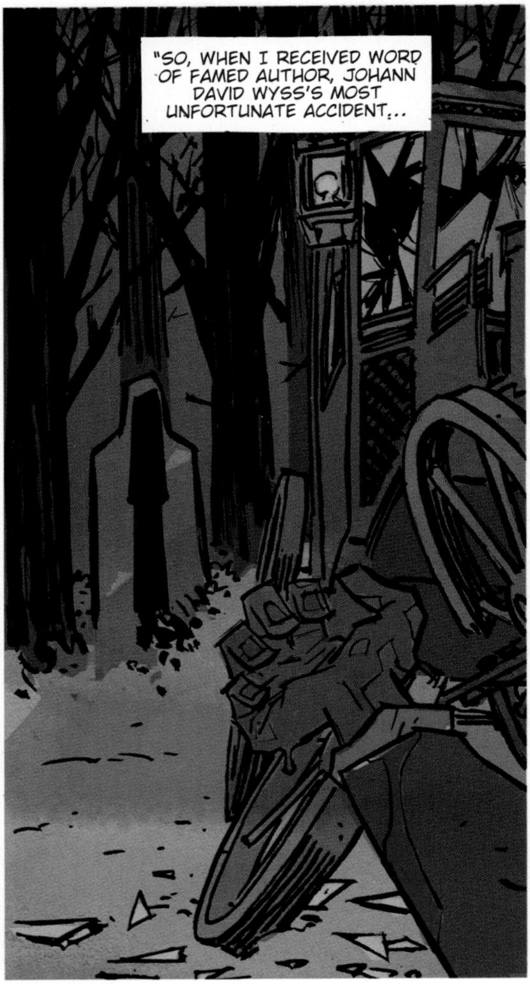
"SO, WHEN I RECEIVED WORD OF FAMED AUTHOR, JOHANN DAVID WYSS'S MOST UNFORTUNATE ACCIDENT...

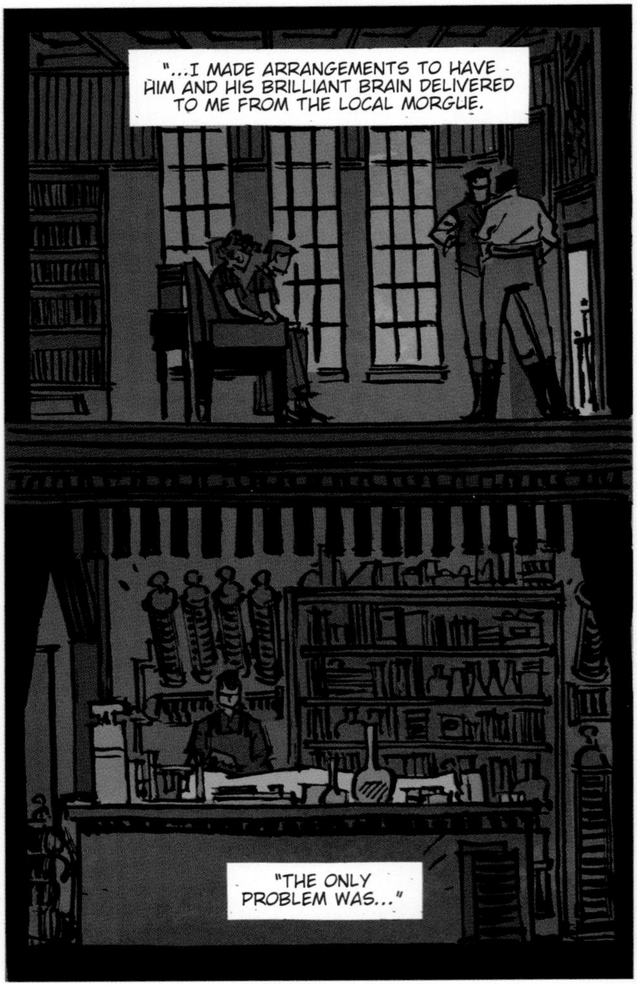
"...I MADE ARRANGEMENTS TO HAVE HIM AND HIS BRILLIANT BRAIN DELIVERED TO ME FROM THE LOCAL MORGUE.
"THE ONLY PROBLEM WAS..."

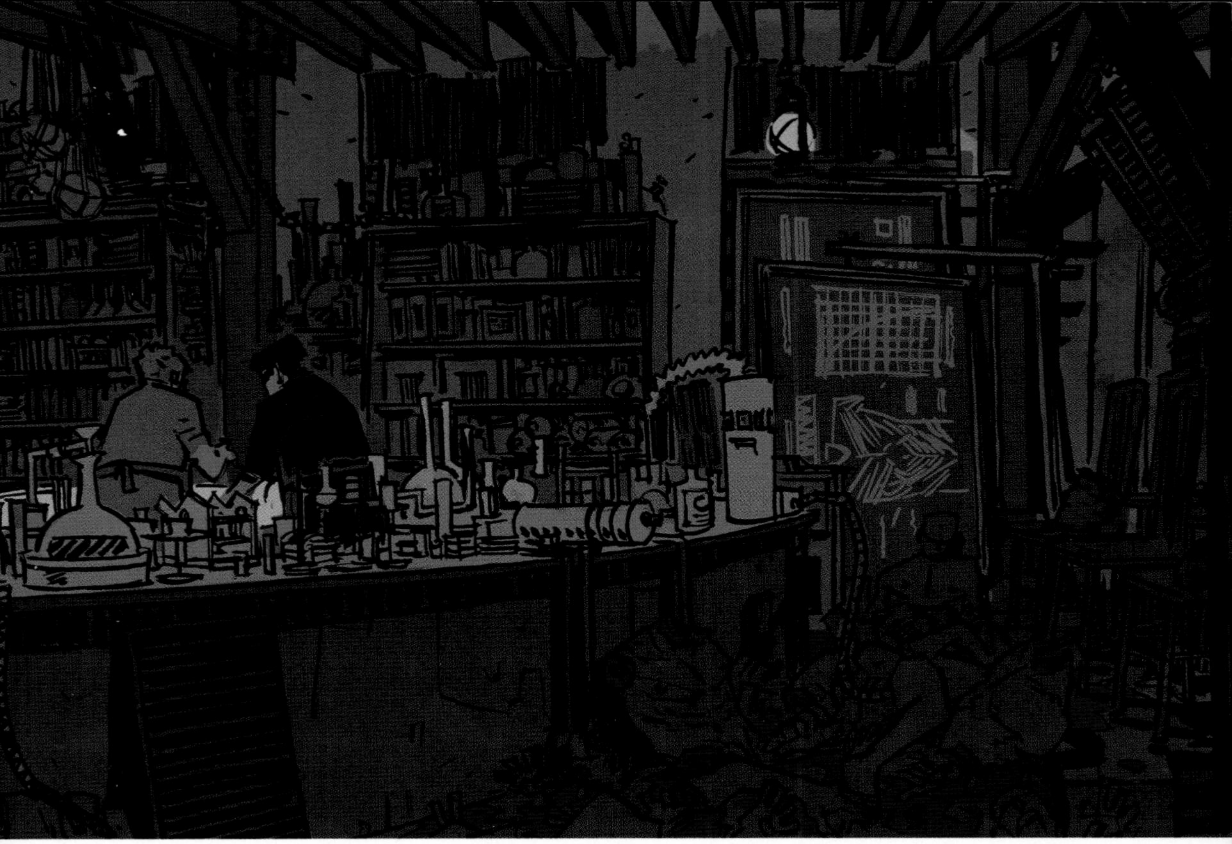

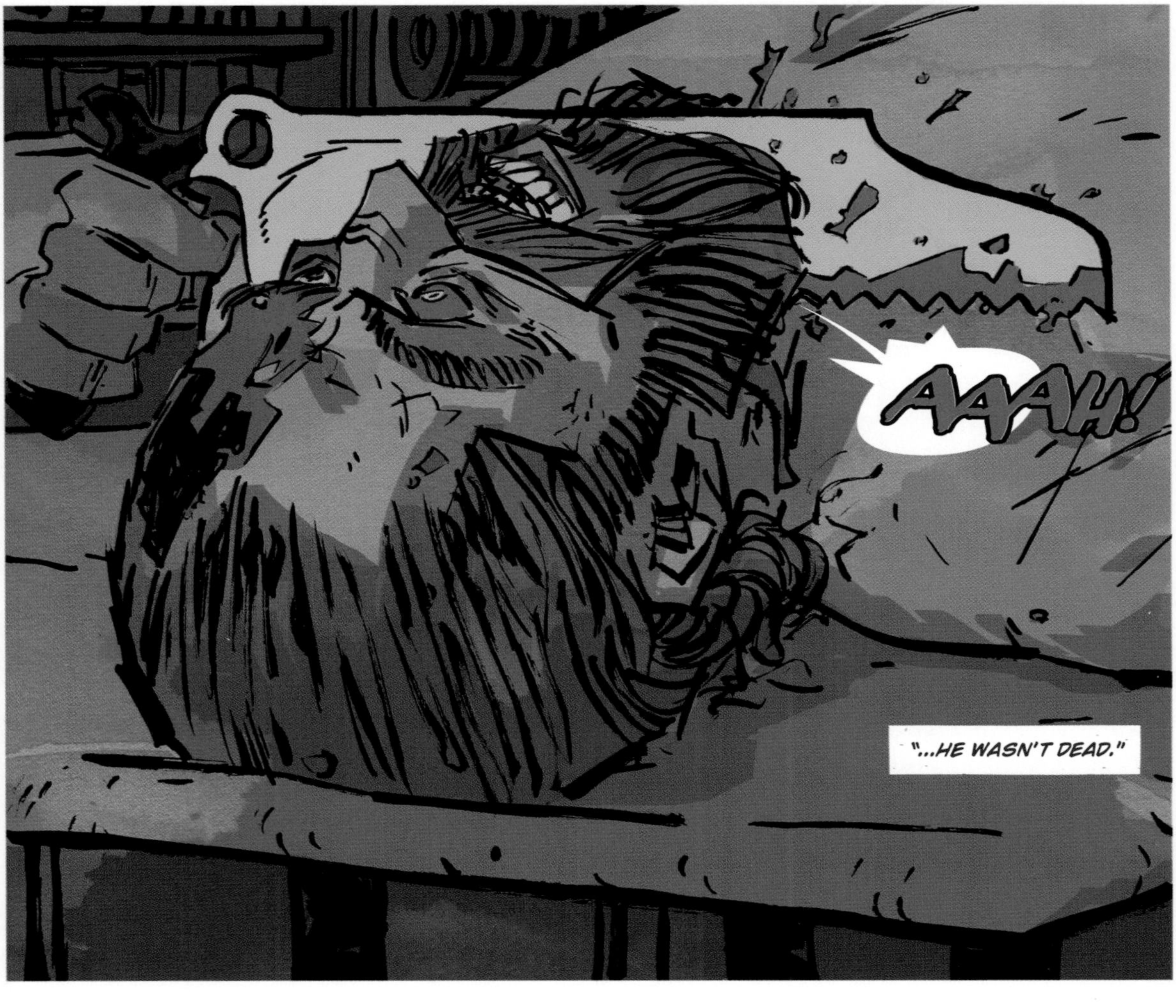
AAAH!
"...HE WASN'T DEAD."

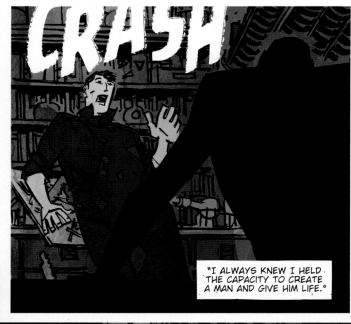

CRASH

I VON'T LET YOU KILL ME!

JOHANN?!

"I ALWAYS KNEW I HELD THE CAPACITY TO CREATE A MAN AND GIVE HIM LIFE."

"WHAT I DO NOT POSSESS IS THE DISCIPLINE OR PATIENCE TO EDUCATE MY CREATION.

"I WAS IN NEED OF A PARTNER. ONE SCHOOLED IN THE MOST FORWARD THINKING IDEOLOGY, AND VALUING THE HIGHEST OF ENLIGHTENED PRINCIPLES.

"SO, WHEN I HEARD *MARY GODWIN* HAD COME TO TOWN, THE DAUGHTER OF PROGRESSIVE PHILOSOPHER WILLIAM GODWIN, AND FAMED WOMEN'S LIBERATION WRITER *MARY WOLLSTONECRAFT*...

"...IT SEEMED MY PRAYERS HAD BEEN ANSWERED."

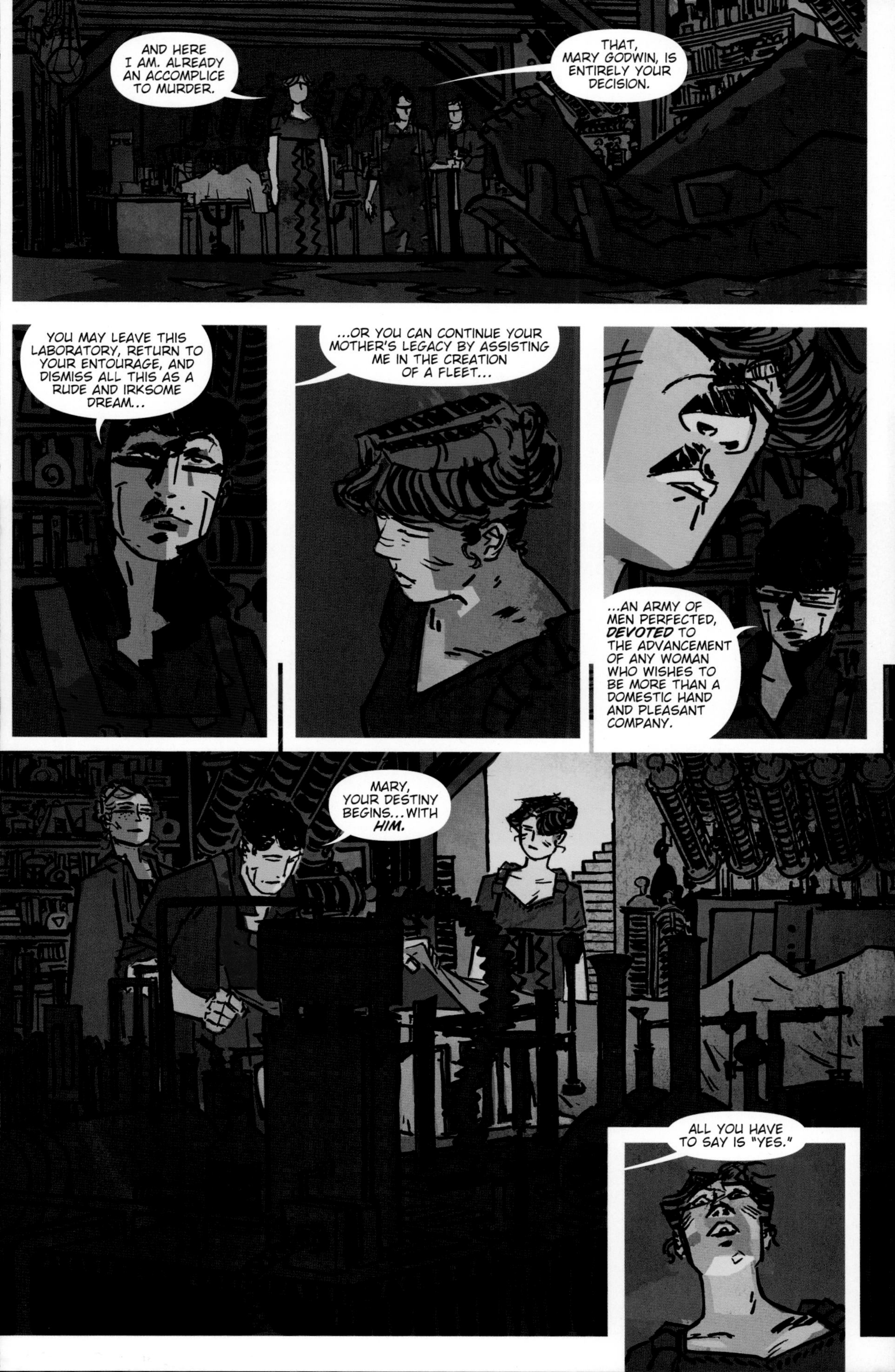
AND HERE I AM. ALREADY AN ACCOMPLICE TO MURDER.
THAT, MARY GODWIN, IS ENTIRELY YOUR DECISION.
YOU MAY LEAVE THIS LABORATORY, RETURN TO YOUR ENTOURAGE, AND DISMISS ALL THIS AS A RUDE AND IRKSOME DREAM...
...OR YOU CAN CONTINUE YOUR MOTHER'S LEGACY BY ASSISTING ME IN THE CREATION OF A FLEET...
...AN ARMY OF MEN PERFECTED, ***DEVOTED*** TO THE ADVANCEMENT OF ANY WOMAN WHO WISHES TO BE MORE THAN A DOMESTIC HAND AND PLEASANT COMPANY.
MARY, YOUR DESTINY BEGINS... WITH ***HIM.***
ALL YOU HAVE TO SAY IS "YES."

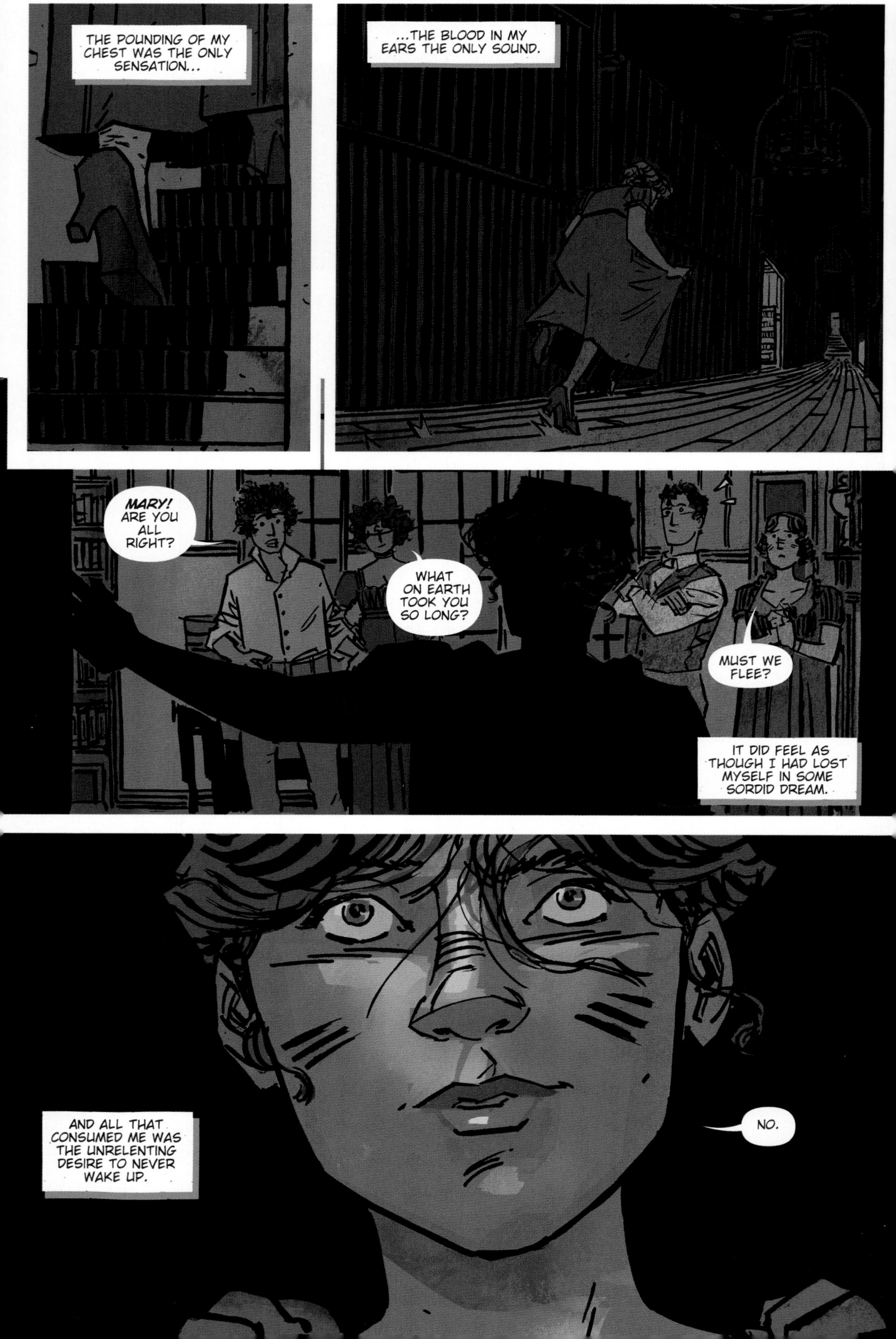
THE POUNDING OF MY CHEST WAS THE ONLY SENSATION...
...THE BLOOD IN MY EARS THE ONLY SOUND.
MARY! ARE YOU ALL RIGHT?
WHAT ON EARTH TOOK YOU SO LONG?
MUST WE FLEE?
IT DID FEEL AS THOUGH I HAD LOST MYSELF IN SOME SORDID DREAM.
AND ALL THAT CONSUMED ME WAS THE UNRELENTING DESIRE TO NEVER WAKE UP.
NO.

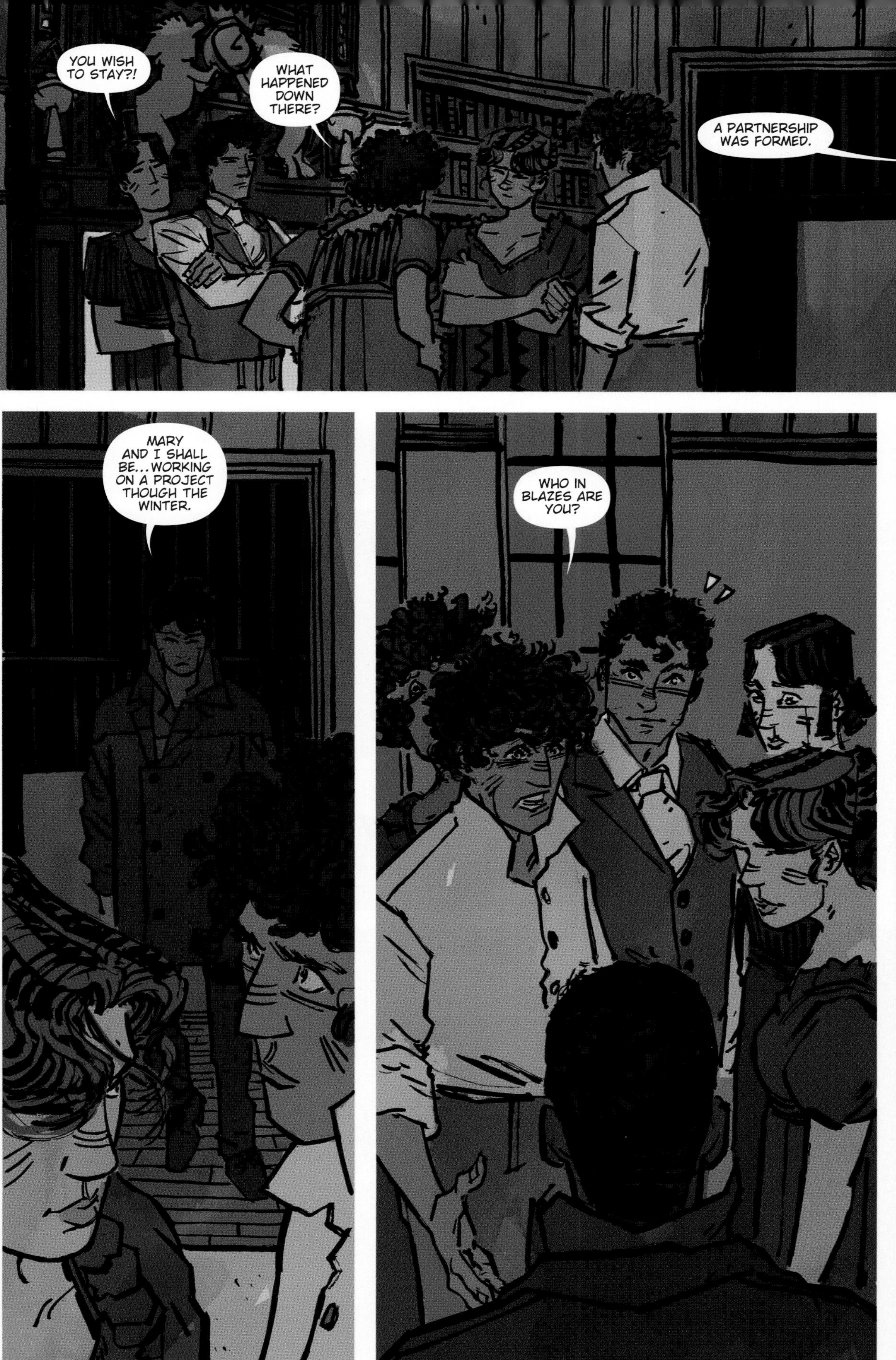
YOU WISH TO STAY?!
WHAT HAPPENED DOWN THERE?
A PARTNERSHIP WAS FORMED.
MARY AND I SHALL BE...WORKING ON A PROJECT THOUGH THE WINTER.
WHO IN BLAZES ARE YOU?

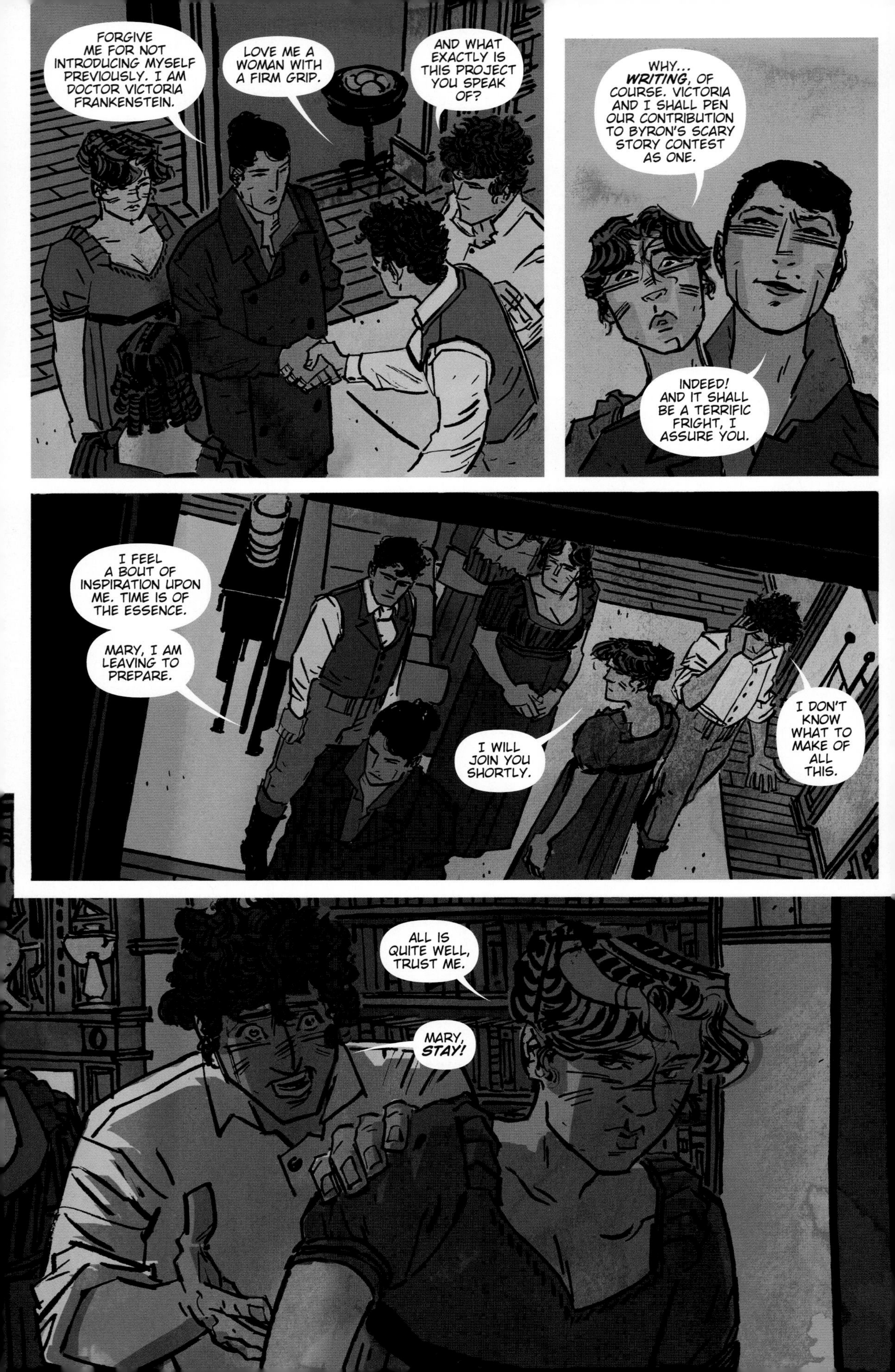
FORGIVE ME FOR NOT INTRODUCING MYSELF PREVIOUSLY. I AM DOCTOR VICTORIA FRANKENSTEIN.
LOVE ME A WOMAN WITH A FIRM GRIP.
AND WHAT EXACTLY IS THIS PROJECT YOU SPEAK OF?
WHY... WRITING, OF COURSE. VICTORIA AND I SHALL PEN OUR CONTRIBUTION TO BYRON'S SCARY STORY CONTEST AS ONE.
INDEED! AND IT SHALL BE A TERRIFIC FRIGHT, I ASSURE YOU.
I FEEL A BOUT OF INSPIRATION UPON ME. TIME IS OF THE ESSENCE.
MARY, I AM LEAVING TO PREPARE.
I WILL JOIN YOU SHORTLY.
I DON'T KNOW WHAT TO MAKE OF ALL THIS.
ALL IS QUITE WELL, TRUST ME.
MARY, STAY!

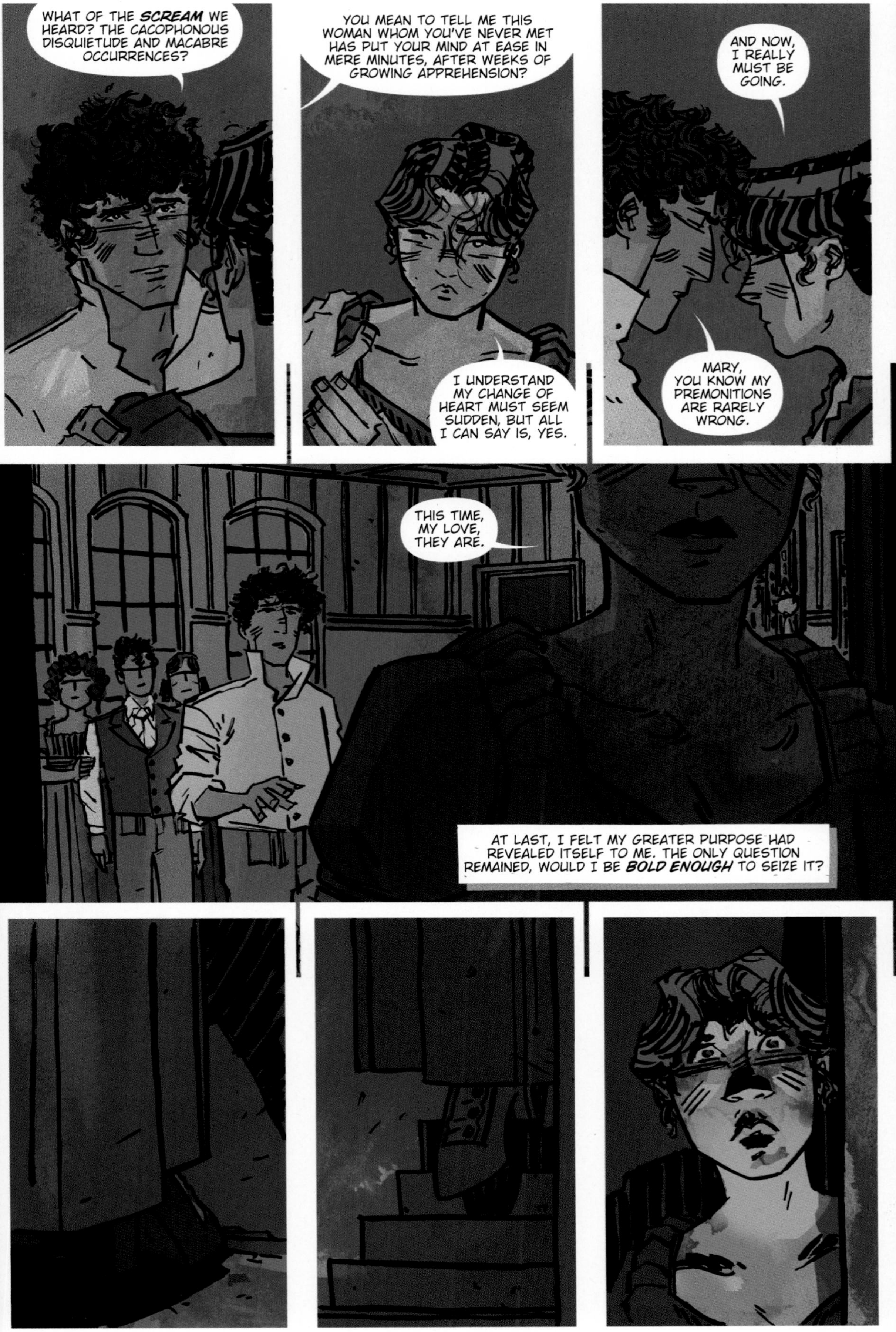
WHAT OF THE *SCREAM* WE HEARD? THE CACOPHONOUS DISQUIETUDE AND MACABRE OCCURRENCES?
YOU MEAN TO TELL ME THIS WOMAN WHOM YOU'VE NEVER MET HAS PUT YOUR MIND AT EASE IN MERE MINUTES, AFTER WEEKS OF GROWING APPREHENSION?
I UNDERSTAND MY CHANGE OF HEART MUST SEEM SUDDEN, BUT ALL I CAN SAY IS, YES.
AND NOW, I REALLY MUST BE GOING.
MARY, YOU KNOW MY PREMONITIONS ARE RARELY WRONG.
THIS TIME, MY LOVE, THEY ARE.
AT LAST, I FELT MY GREATER PURPOSE HAD REVEALED ITSELF TO ME. THE ONLY QUESTION REMAINED, WOULD I BE *BOLD ENOUGH* TO SEIZE IT?

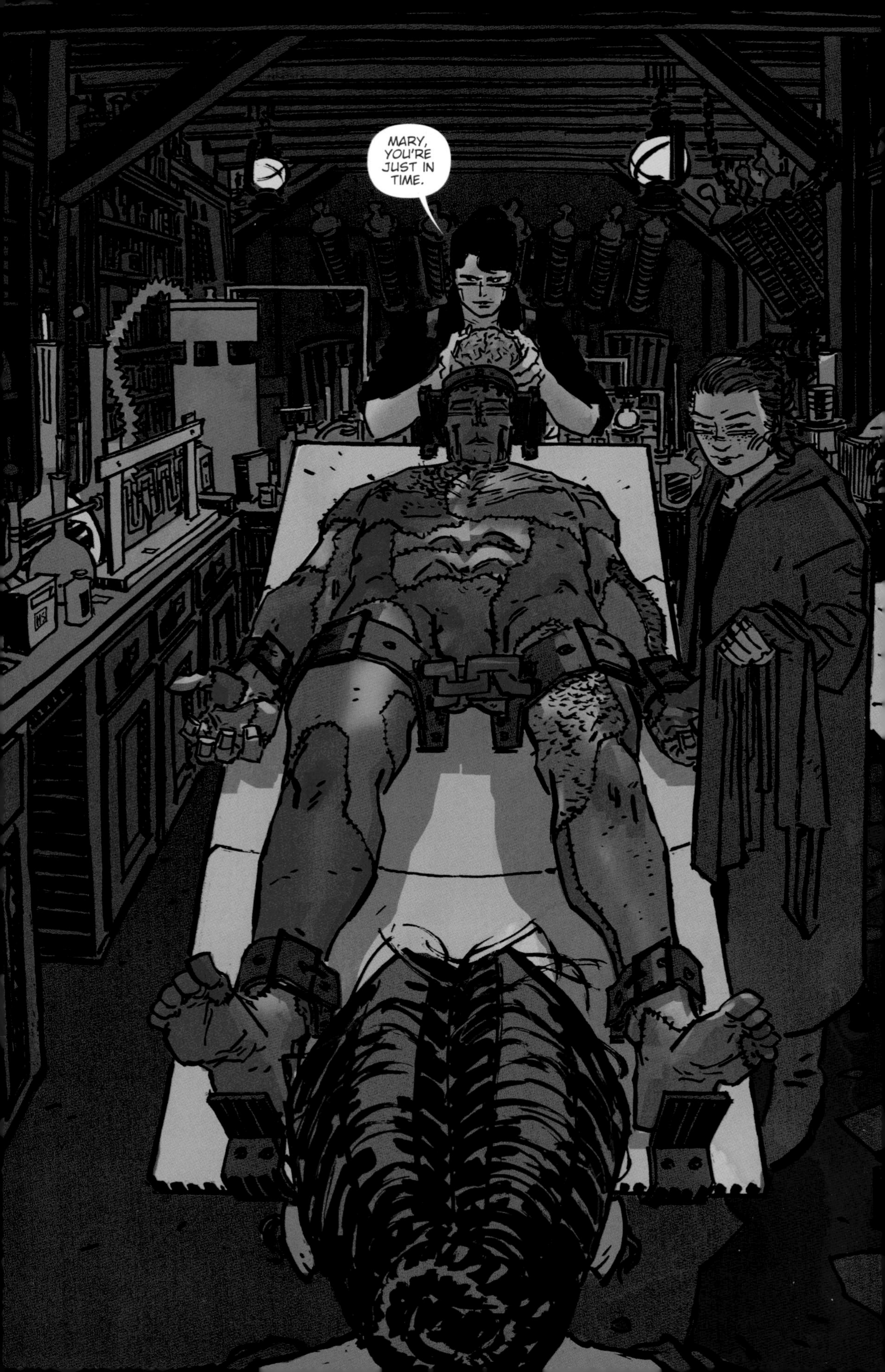
MARY, YOU'RE JUST IN TIME.

3

BIRTH OF A MONSTER

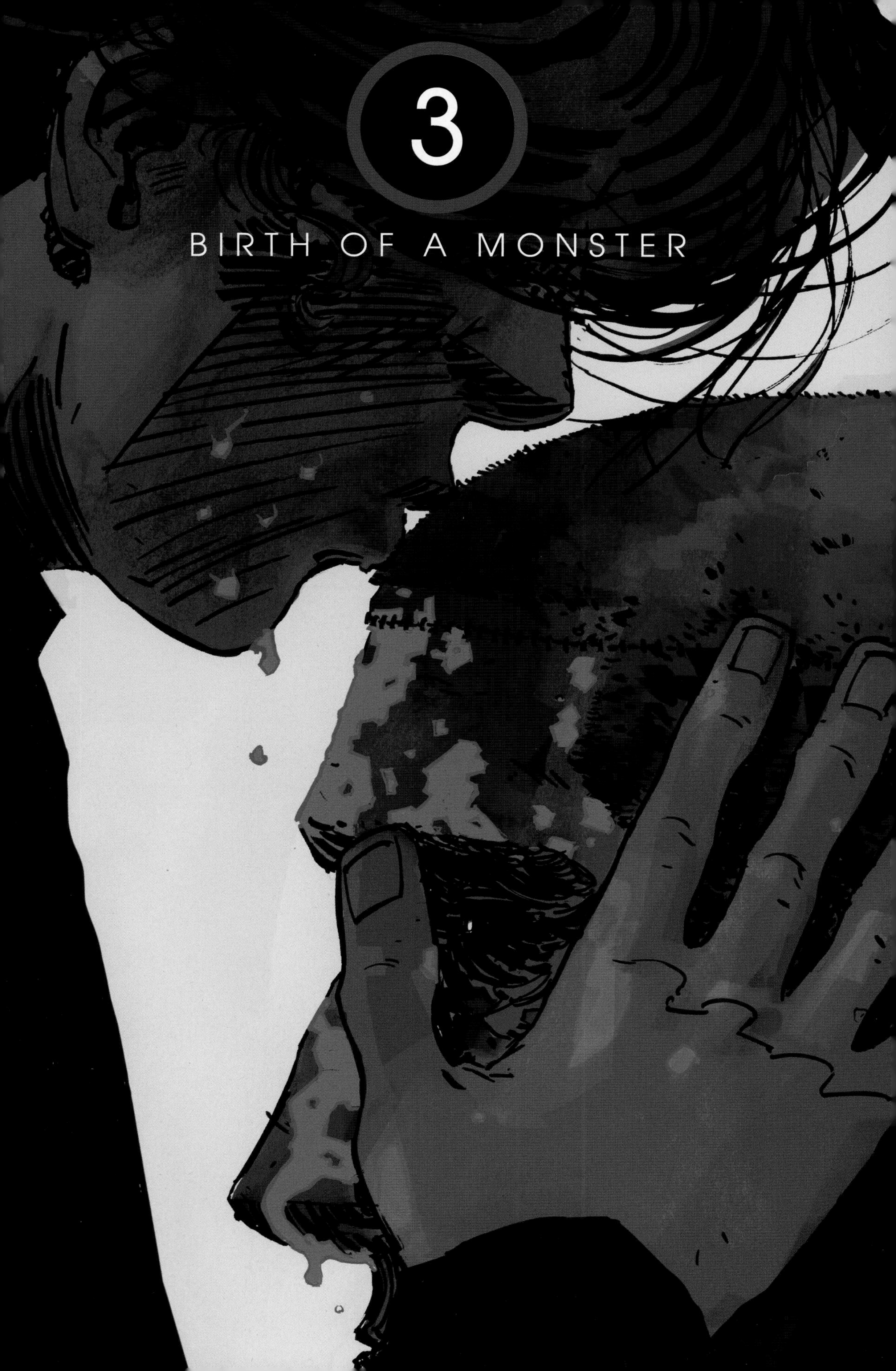

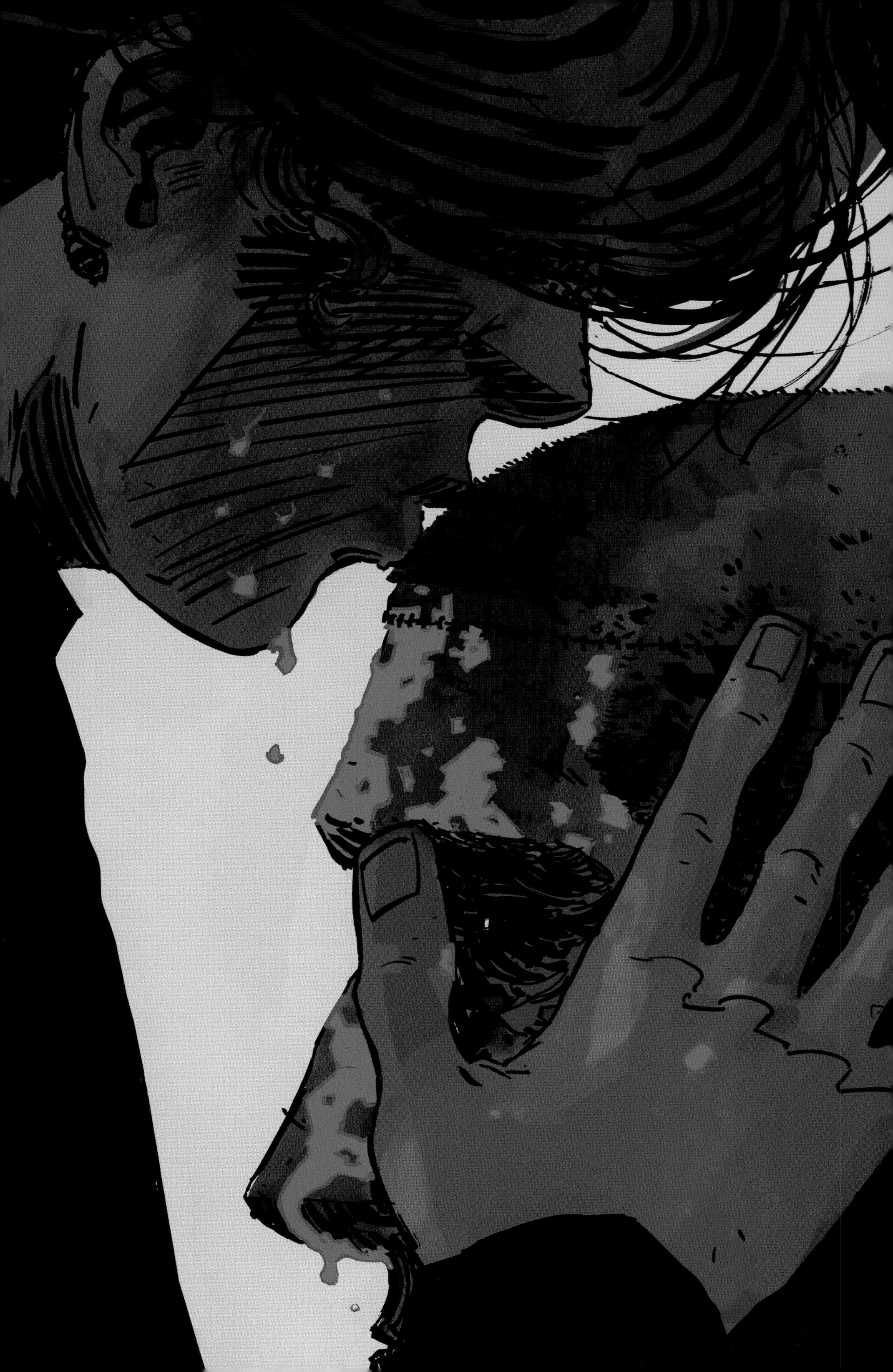

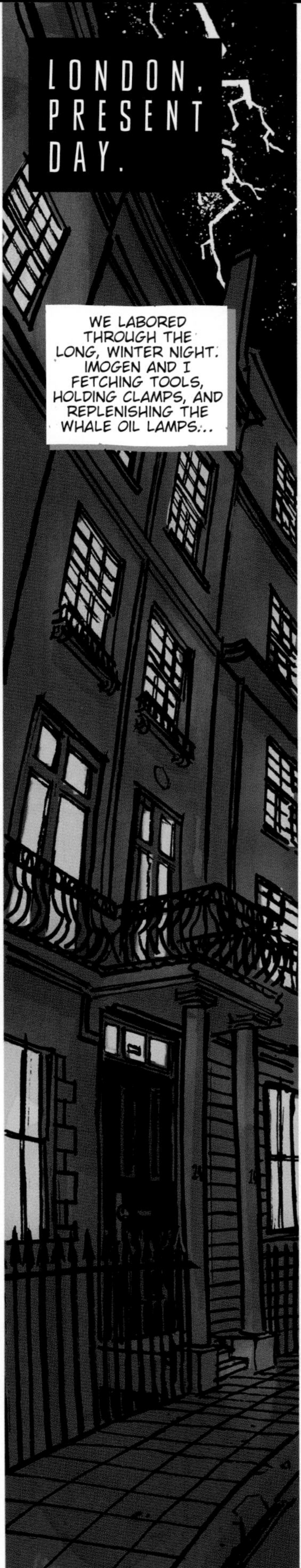
LONDON, PRESENT DAY.
WE LABORED THROUGH THE LONG, WINTER NIGHT. IMOGEN AND I FETCHING TOOLS, HOLDING CLAMPS, AND REPLENISHING THE WHALE OIL LAMPS...
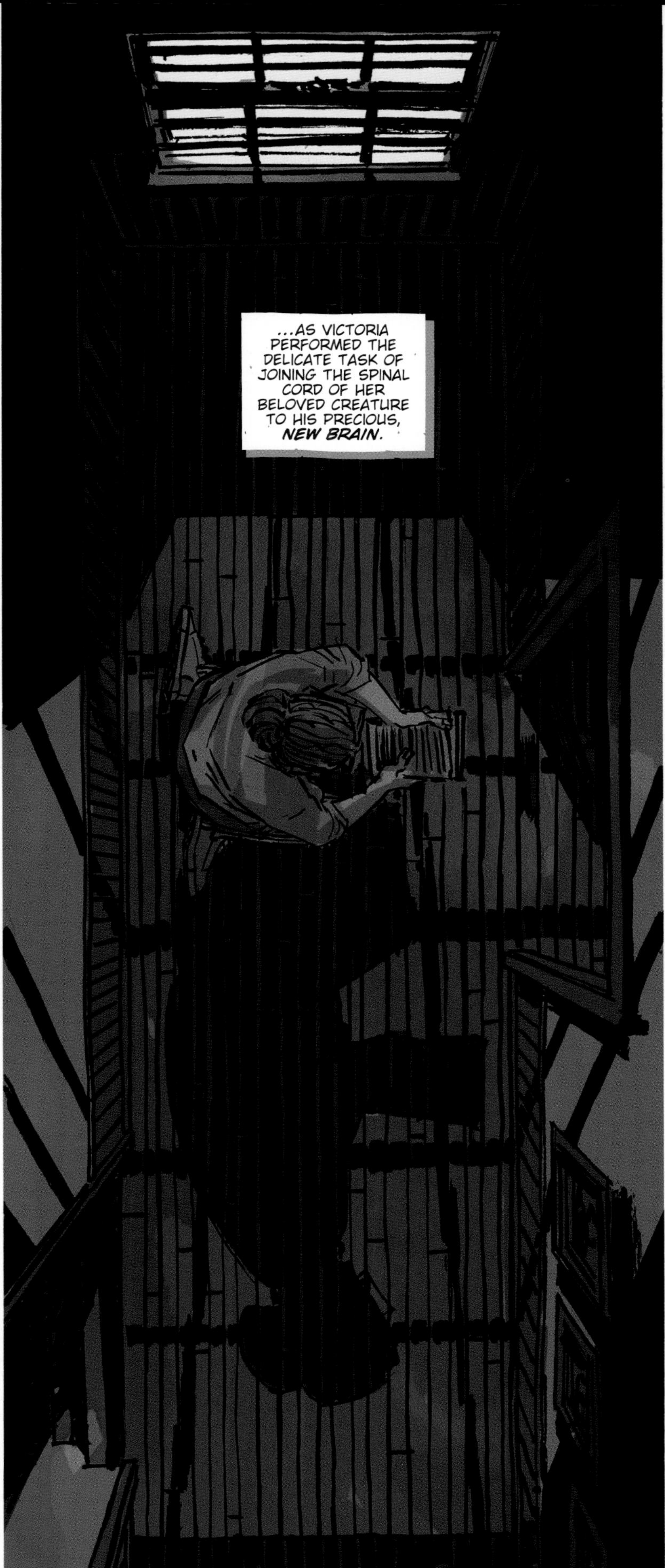
...AS VICTORIA PERFORMED THE DELICATE TASK OF JOINING THE SPINAL CORD OF HER BELOVED CREATURE TO HIS PRECIOUS, NEW BRAIN.

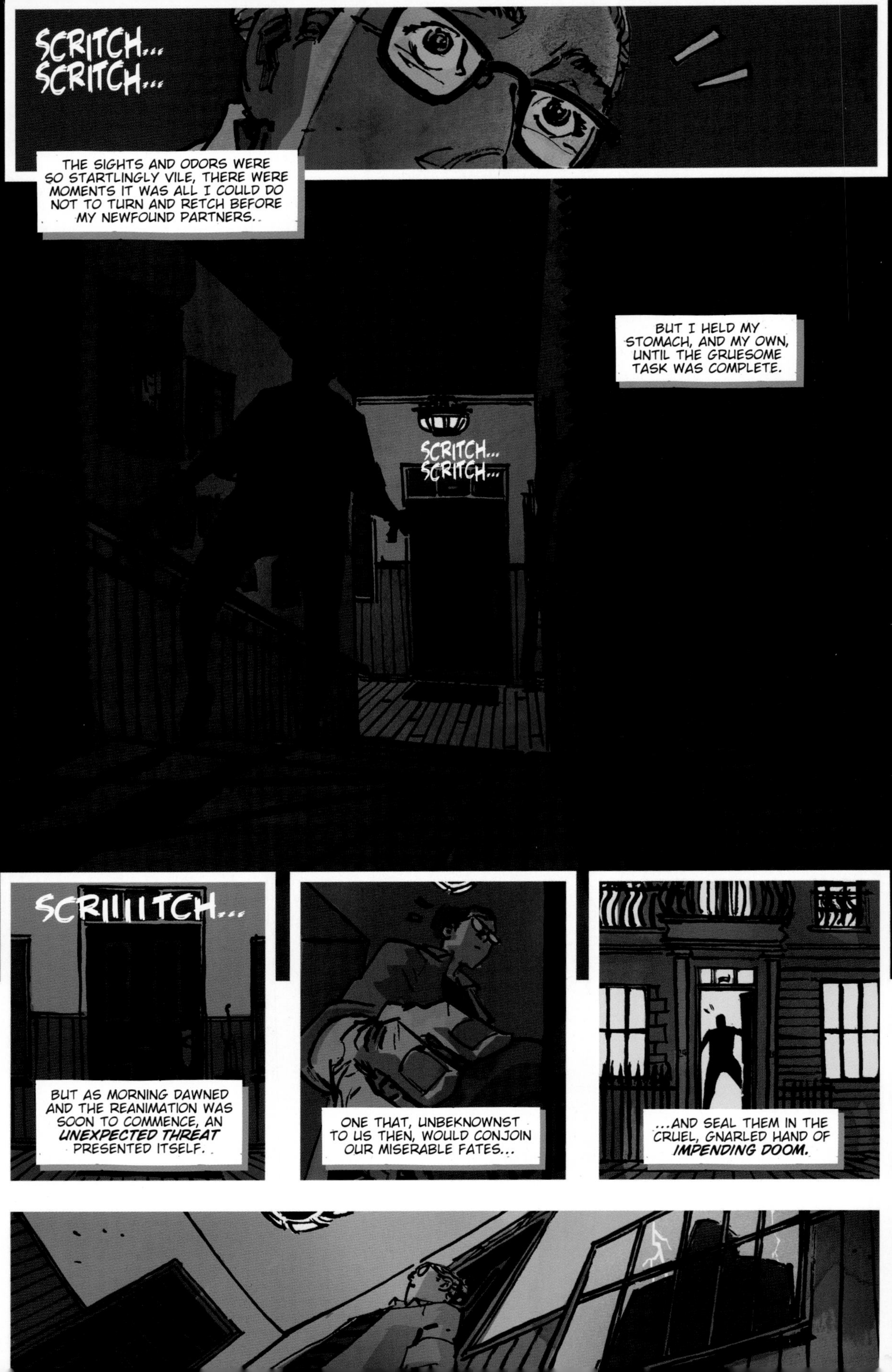
SCRITCH... SCRITCH...
THE SIGHTS AND ODORS WERE SO STARTLINGLY VILE, THERE WERE MOMENTS IT WAS ALL I COULD DO NOT TO TURN AND RETCH BEFORE MY NEWFOUND PARTNERS.
BUT I HELD MY STOMACH, AND MY OWN, UNTIL THE GRUESOME TASK WAS COMPLETE.
SCRITCH... SCRITCH...
SCRIIIITCH...
BUT AS MORNING DAWNED AND THE REANIMATION WAS SOON TO COMMENCE, AN UNEXPECTED THREAT PRESENTED ITSELF.
ONE THAT, UNBEKNOWNST TO US THEN, WOULD CONJOIN OUR MISERABLE FATES...
...AND SEAL THEM IN THE CRUEL, GNARLED HAND OF IMPENDING DOOM.

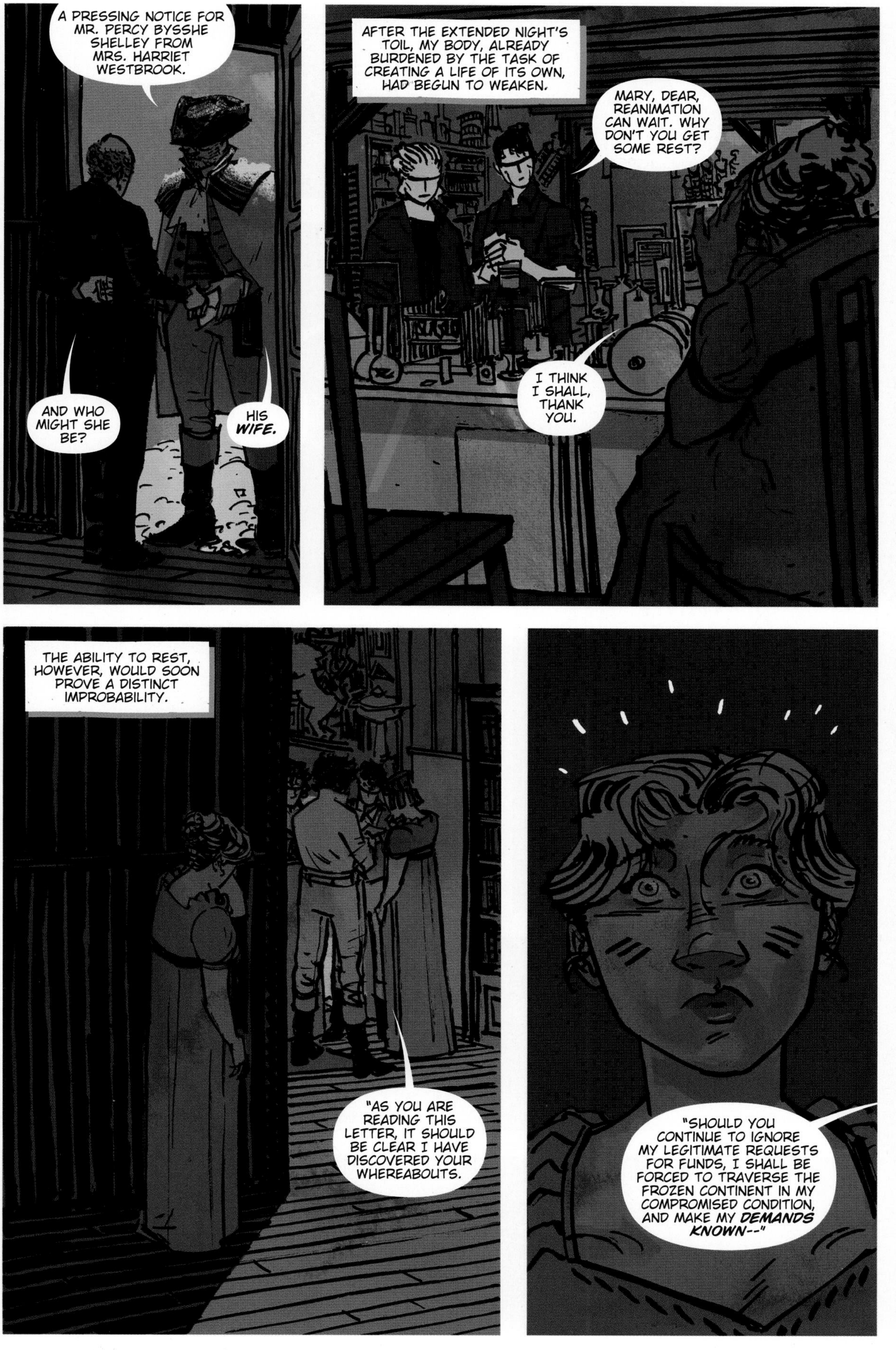

A PRESSING NOTICE FOR MR. PERCY BYSSHE SHELLEY FROM MRS. HARRIET WESTBROOK.
AND WHO MIGHT SHE BE?
HIS *WIFE.*
AFTER THE EXTENDED NIGHT'S TOIL, MY BODY, ALREADY BURDENED BY THE TASK OF CREATING A LIFE OF ITS OWN, HAD BEGUN TO WEAKEN.
MARY, DEAR, REANIMATION CAN WAIT. WHY DON'T YOU GET SOME REST?
I THINK I SHALL, THANK YOU.
THE ABILITY TO REST, HOWEVER, WOULD SOON PROVE A DISTINCT IMPROBABILITY.
"AS YOU ARE READING THIS LETTER, IT SHOULD BE CLEAR I HAVE DISCOVERED YOUR WHEREABOUTS.
"SHOULD YOU CONTINUE TO IGNORE MY LEGITIMATE REQUESTS FOR FUNDS, I SHALL BE FORCED TO TRAVERSE THE FROZEN CONTINENT IN MY COMPROMISED CONDITION, AND MAKE MY *DEMANDS KNOWN--"*

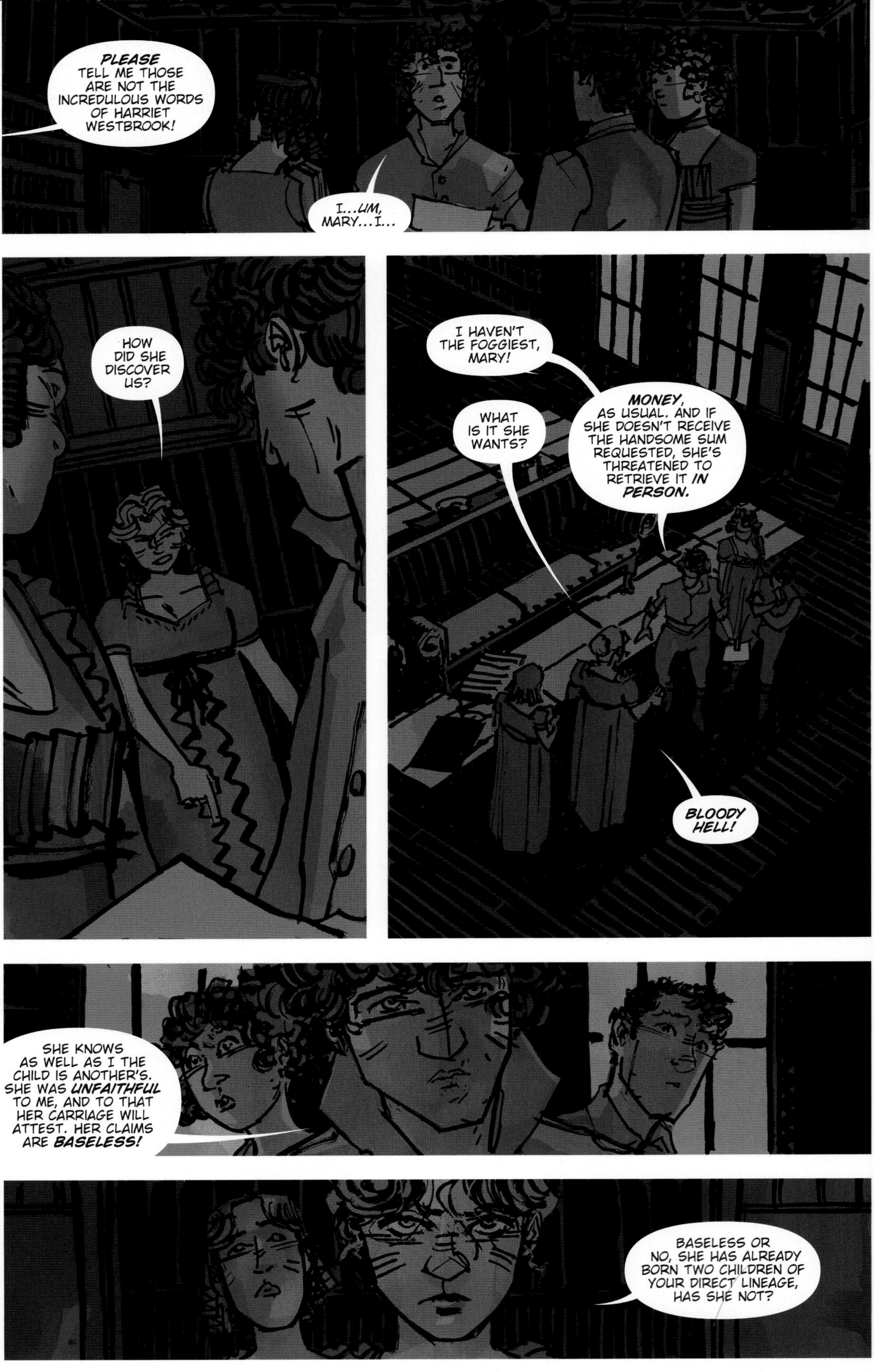
PLEASE TELL ME THOSE ARE NOT THE INCREDULOUS WORDS OF HARRIET WESTBROOK!
I...UM, MARY...I...
HOW DID SHE DISCOVER US?
I HAVEN'T THE FOGGIEST, MARY!
WHAT IS IT SHE WANTS?
MONEY, AS USUAL. AND IF SHE DOESN'T RECEIVE THE HANDSOME SUM REQUESTED, SHE'S THREATENED TO RETRIEVE IT IN PERSON.
BLOODY HELL!
SHE KNOWS AS WELL AS I THE CHILD IS ANOTHER'S. SHE WAS UNFAITHFUL TO ME, AND TO THAT HER CARRIAGE WILL ATTEST. HER CLAIMS ARE BASELESS!
BASELESS OR NO, SHE HAS ALREADY BORN TWO CHILDREN OF YOUR DIRECT LINEAGE, HAS SHE NOT?

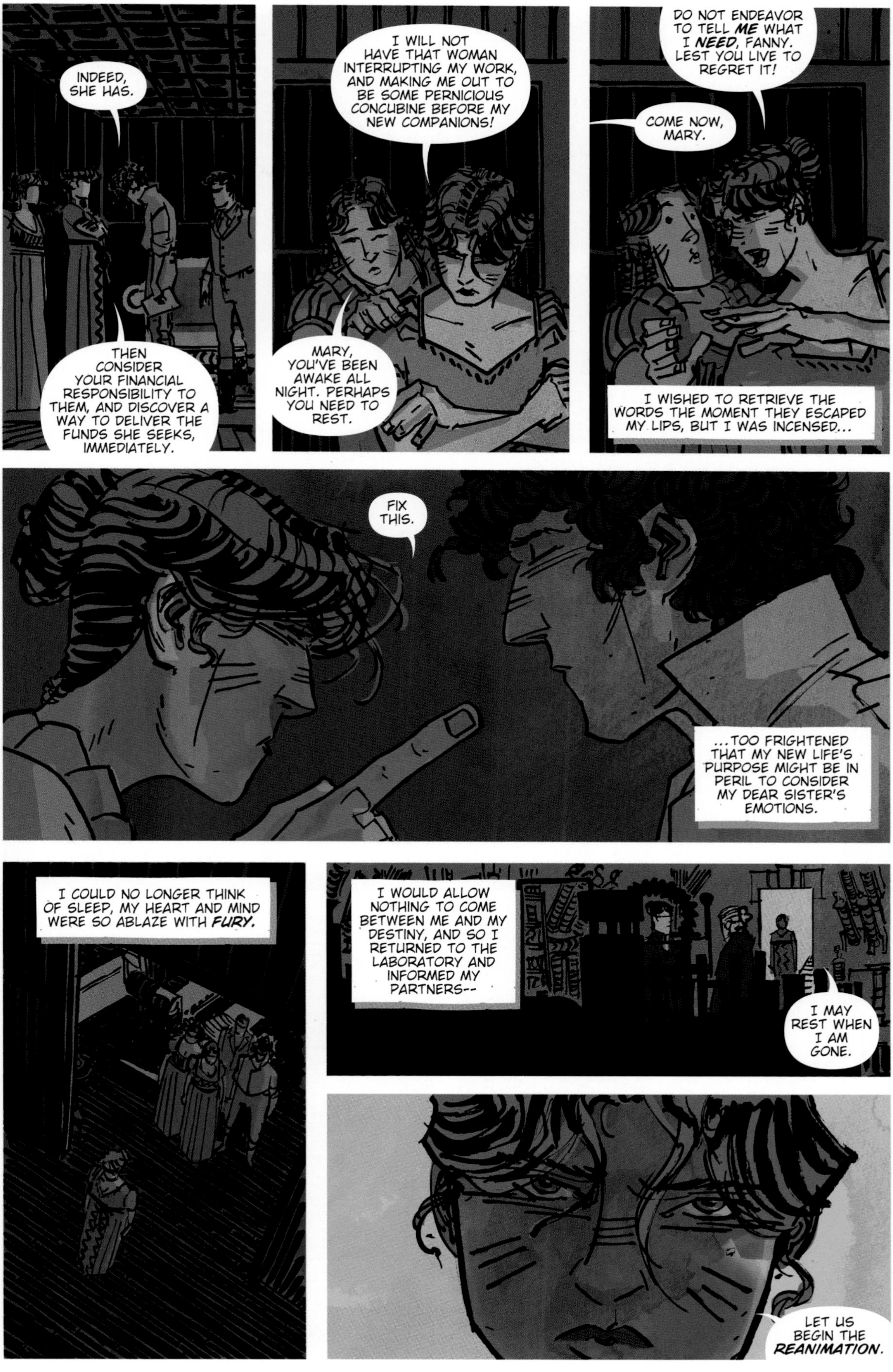
INDEED, SHE HAS.
THEN CONSIDER YOUR FINANCIAL RESPONSIBILITY TO THEM, AND DISCOVER A WAY TO DELIVER THE FUNDS SHE SEEKS, IMMEDIATELY.
I WILL NOT HAVE THAT WOMAN INTERRUPTING MY WORK, AND MAKING ME OUT TO BE SOME PERNICIOUS CONCUBINE BEFORE MY NEW COMPANIONS!
MARY, YOU'VE BEEN AWAKE ALL NIGHT. PERHAPS YOU NEED TO REST.
DO NOT ENDEAVOR TO TELL ME WHAT I NEED, FANNY. LEST YOU LIVE TO REGRET IT!
COME NOW, MARY.
I WISHED TO RETRIEVE THE WORDS THE MOMENT THEY ESCAPED MY LIPS, BUT I WAS INCENSED...
FIX THIS.
...TOO FRIGHTENED THAT MY NEW LIFE'S PURPOSE MIGHT BE IN PERIL TO CONSIDER MY DEAR SISTER'S EMOTIONS.
I COULD NO LONGER THINK OF SLEEP, MY HEART AND MIND WERE SO ABLAZE WITH FURY.
I WOULD ALLOW NOTHING TO COME BETWEEN ME AND MY DESTINY, AND SO I RETURNED TO THE LABORATORY AND INFORMED MY PARTNERS--
I MAY REST WHEN I AM GONE.
LET US BEGIN THE REANIMATION.

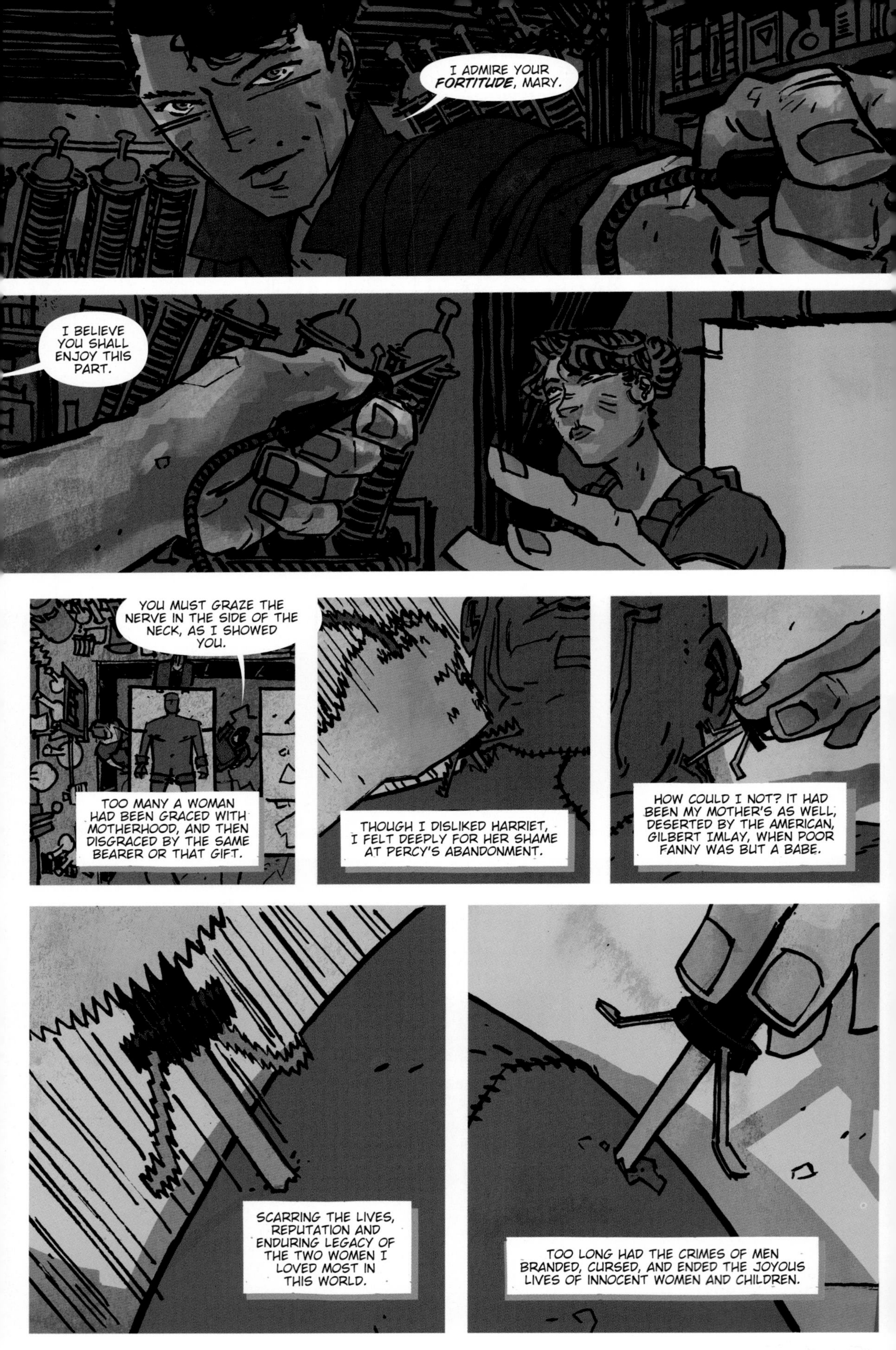
I ADMIRE YOUR FORTITUDE, MARY.
I BELIEVE YOU SHALL ENJOY THIS PART.
YOU MUST GRAZE THE NERVE IN THE SIDE OF THE NECK, AS I SHOWED YOU.
TOO MANY A WOMAN HAD BEEN GRACED WITH MOTHERHOOD, AND THEN DISGRACED BY THE SAME BEARER OR THAT GIFT.
THOUGH I DISLIKED HARRIET, I FELT DEEPLY FOR HER SHAME AT PERCY'S ABANDONMENT.
HOW COULD I NOT? IT HAD BEEN MY MOTHER'S AS WELL, DESERTED BY THE AMERICAN, GILBERT IMLAY, WHEN POOR FANNY WAS BUT A BABE.
SCARRING THE LIVES, REPUTATION AND ENDURING LEGACY OF THE TWO WOMEN I LOVED MOST IN THIS WORLD.
TOO LONG HAD THE CRIMES OF MEN BRANDED, CURSED, AND ENDED THE JOYOUS LIVES OF INNOCENT WOMEN AND CHILDREN.

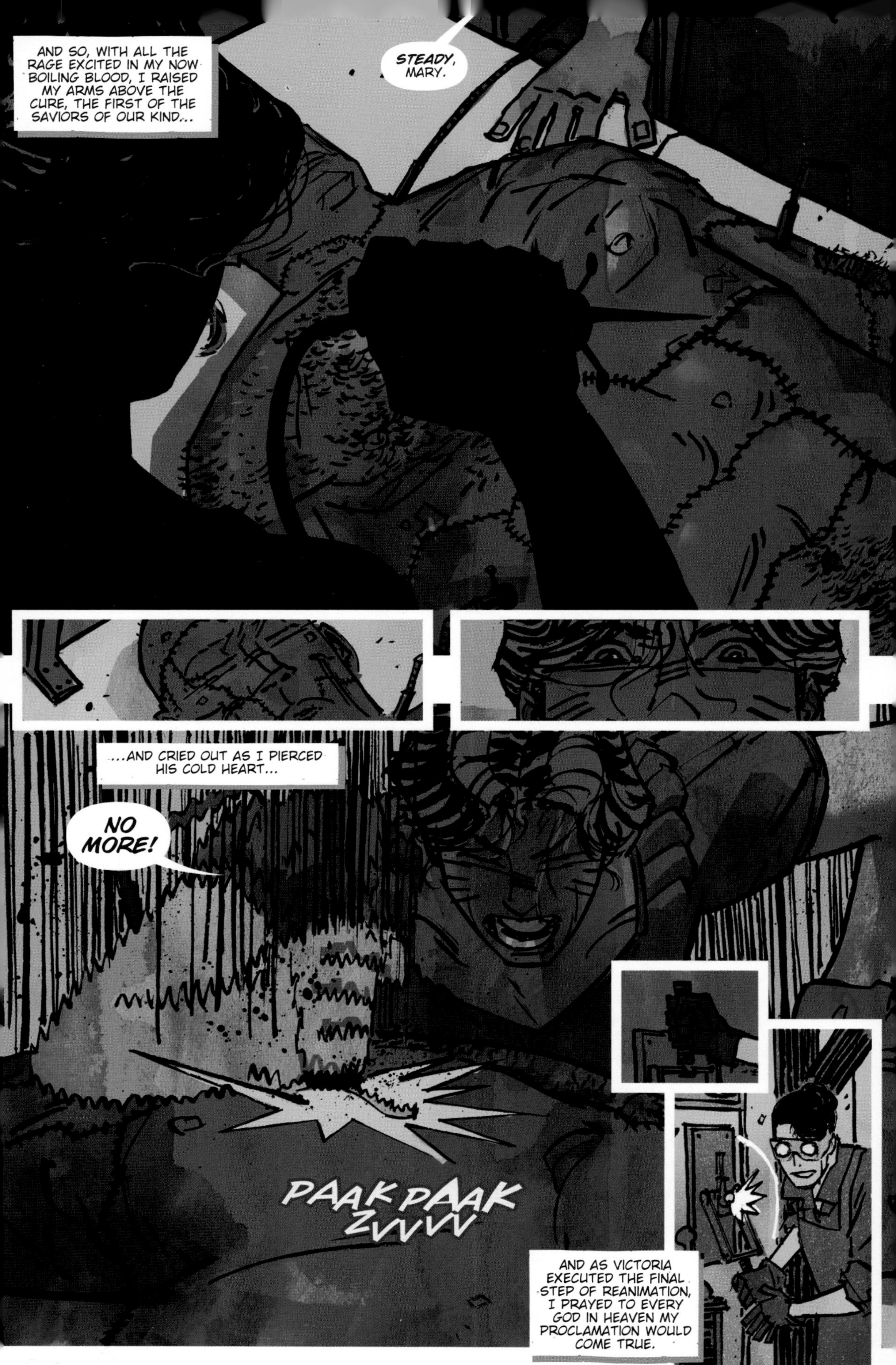
AND SO, WITH ALL THE RAGE EXCITED IN MY NOW BOILING BLOOD, I RAISED MY ARMS ABOVE THE CURE, THE FIRST OF THE SAVIORS OF OUR KIND...
STEADY, MARY.
...AND CRIED OUT AS I PIERCED HIS COLD HEART...
NO MORE!
PAAK PAAK
ZVVVV
AND AS VICTORIA EXECUTED THE FINAL STEP OF REANIMATION, I PRAYED TO EVERY GOD IN HEAVEN MY PROCLAMATION WOULD COME TRUE.

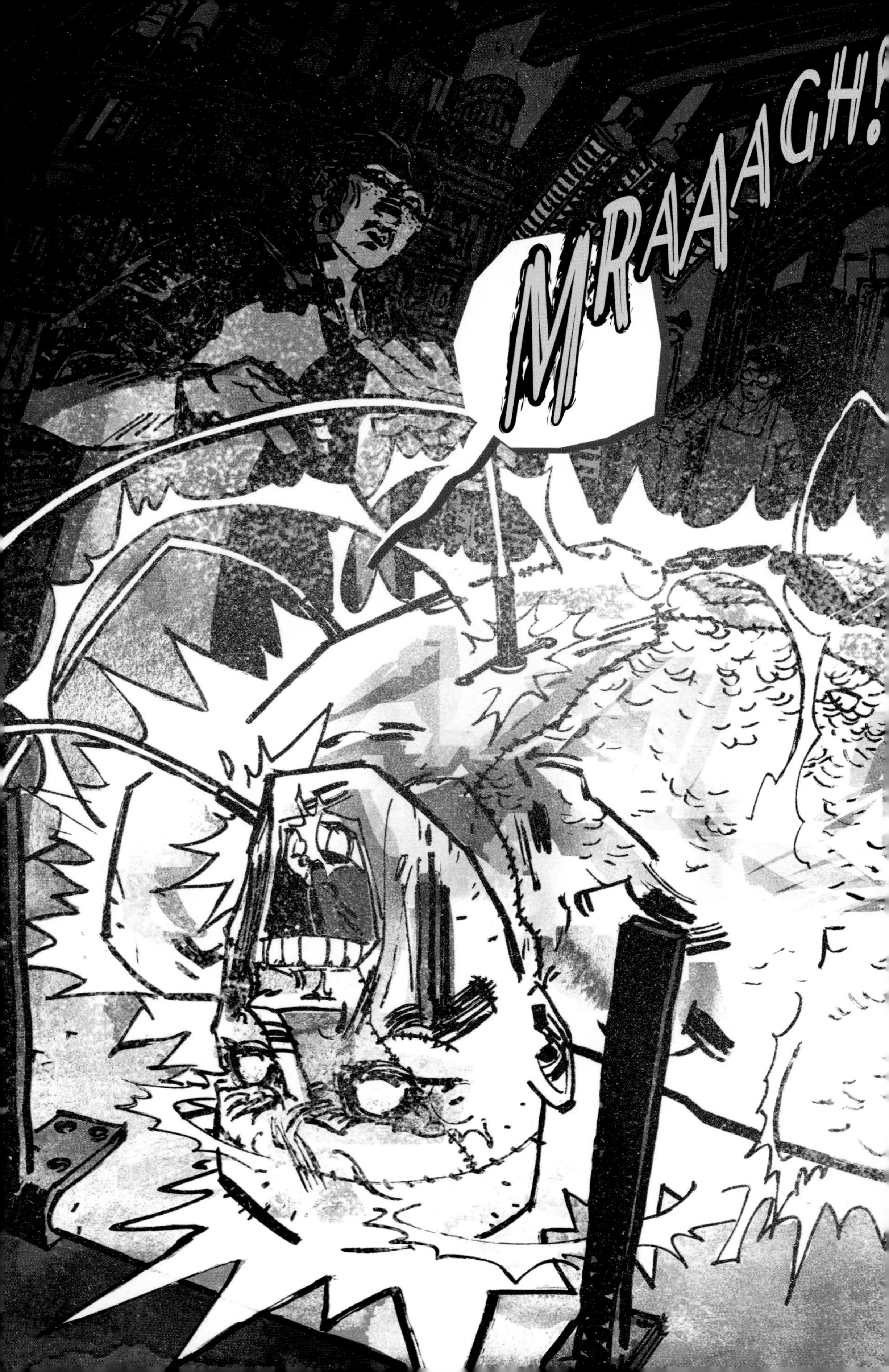
MRAAAGH!

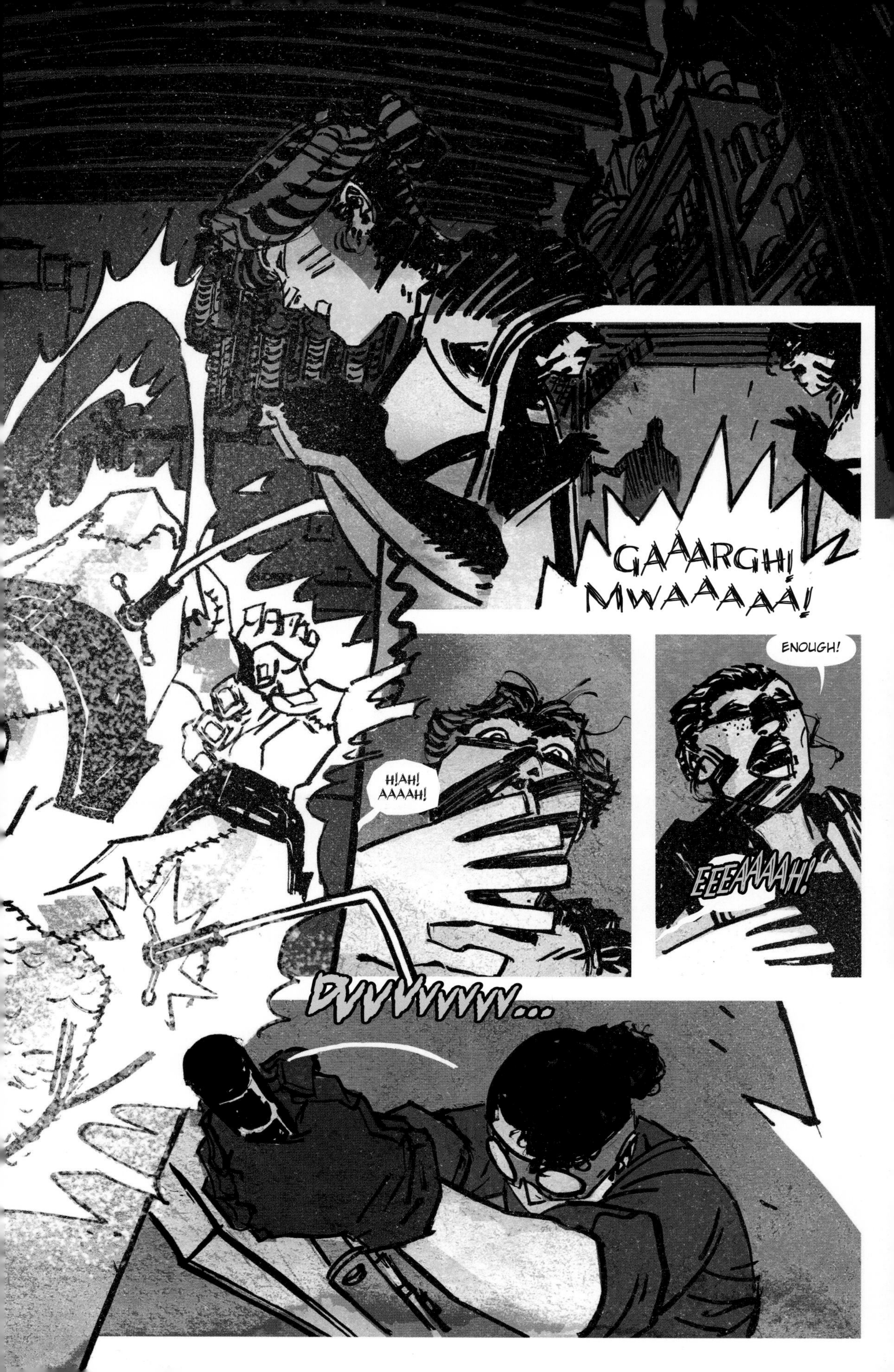
GAAARGH! MWAAAAAA!
HIAH! AAAAH!
ENOUGH!
EEEAAAAH!
DVVVVVVV...

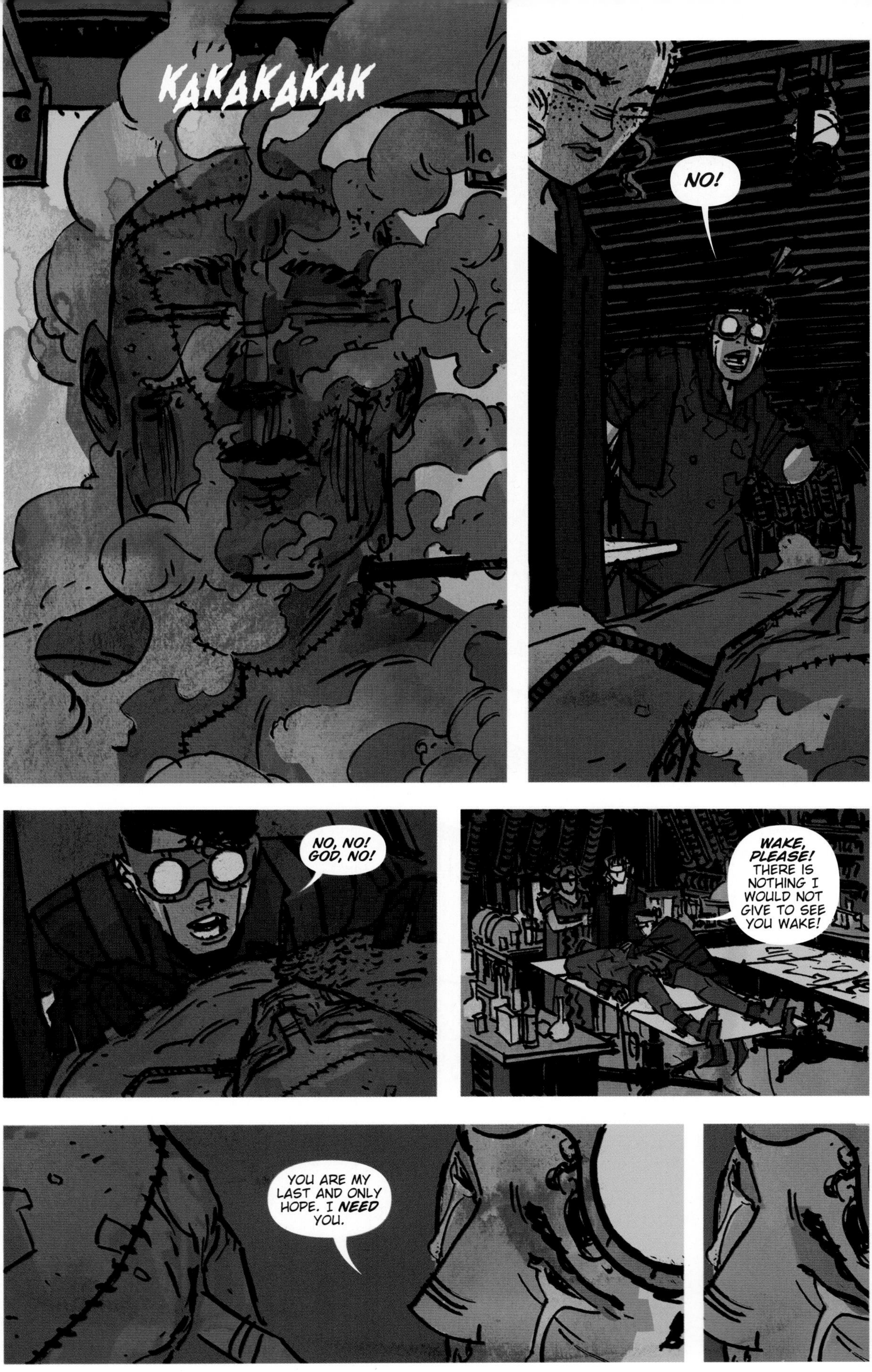
KAKAKAKAK
NO!
NO, NO! GOD, NO!
WAKE, PLEASE! THERE IS NOTHING I WOULD NOT GIVE TO SEE YOU WAKE!
YOU ARE MY LAST AND ONLY HOPE. I NEED YOU.

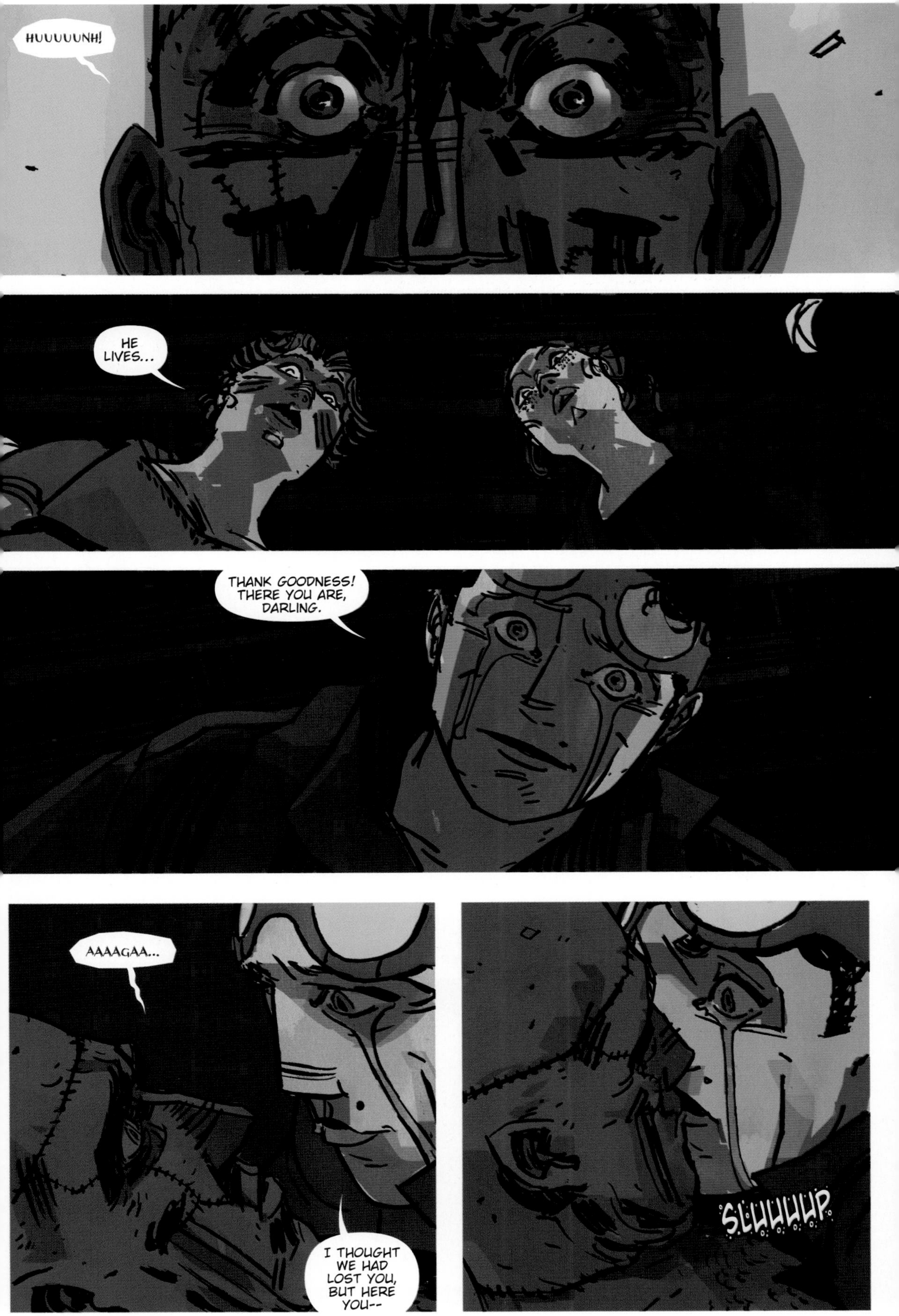
HUUUUUNH!
HE LIVES...
THANK GOODNESS! THERE YOU ARE, DARLING.
AAAAGAA...
I THOUGHT WE HAD LOST YOU, BUT HERE YOU--
SLUUUUUP

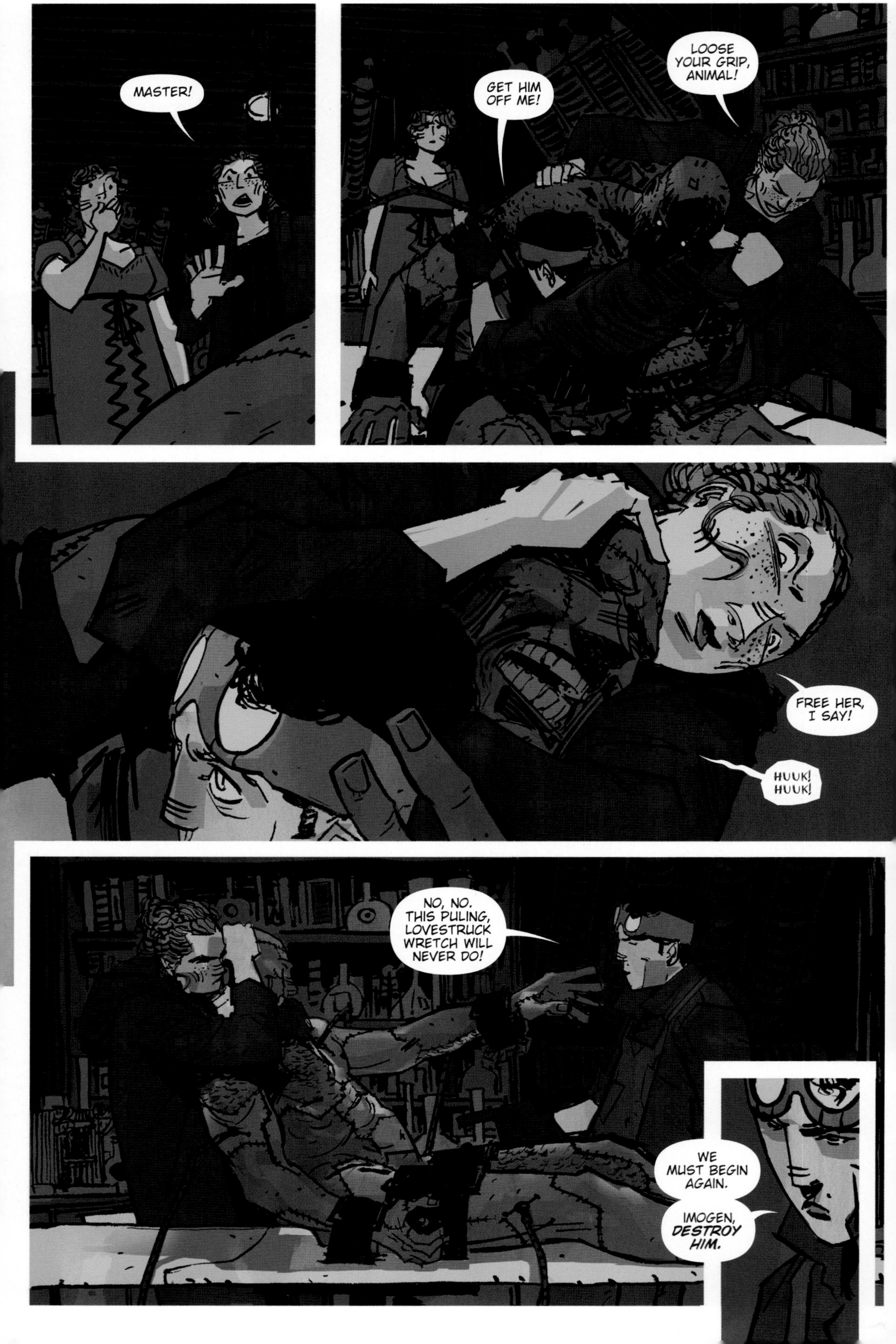
MASTER!
GET HIM OFF ME!
LOOSE YOUR GRIP, ANIMAL!
FREE HER, I SAY!
HUUK! HUUK!
NO, NO. THIS PULING, LOVESTRUCK WRETCH WILL NEVER DO!
WE MUST BEGIN AGAIN.
IMOGEN, *DESTROY HIM.*

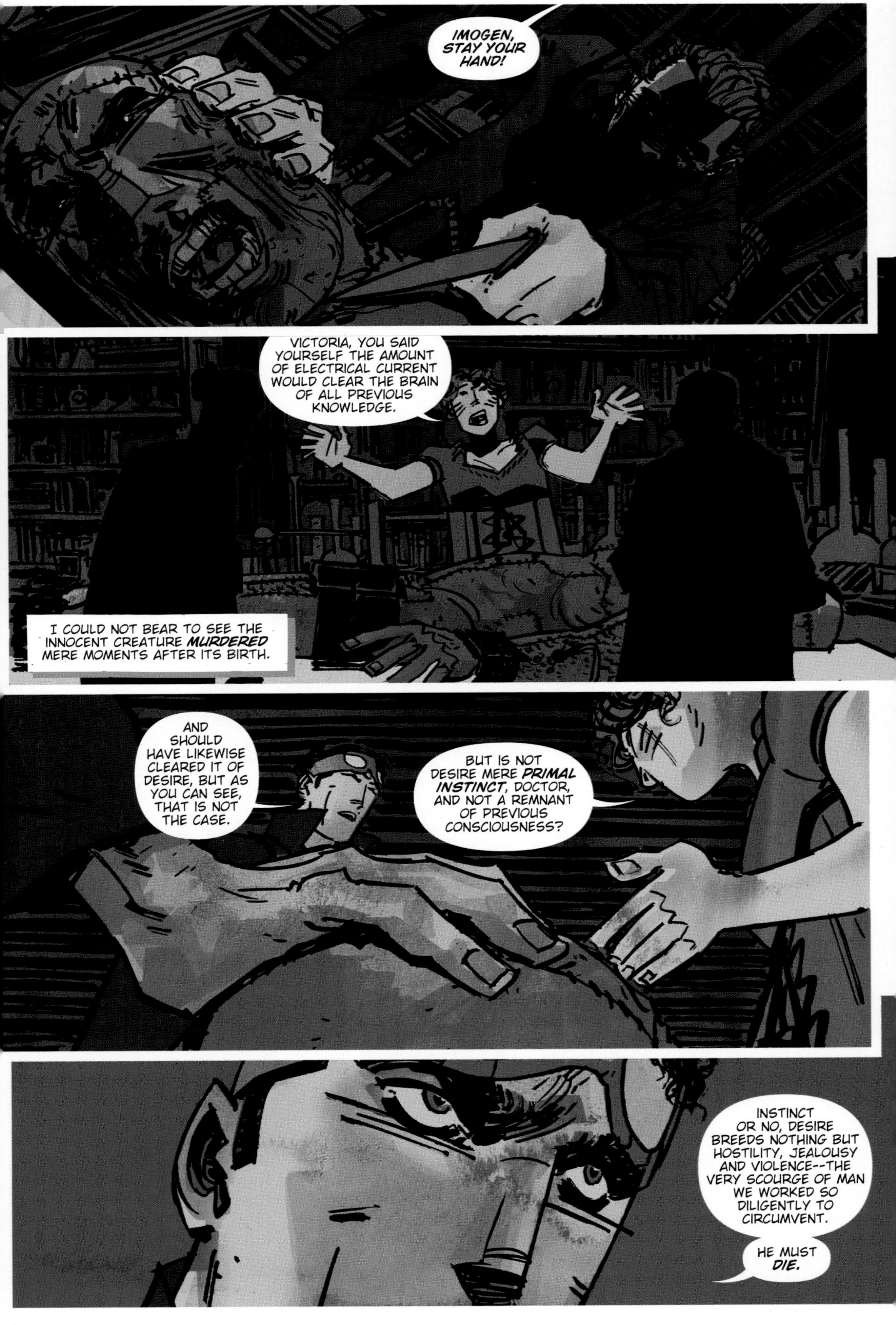
IMOGEN, STAY YOUR HAND!
VICTORIA, YOU SAID YOURSELF THE AMOUNT OF ELECTRICAL CURRENT WOULD CLEAR THE BRAIN OF ALL PREVIOUS KNOWLEDGE.
I COULD NOT BEAR TO SEE THE INNOCENT CREATURE MURDERED MERE MOMENTS AFTER ITS BIRTH.
AND SHOULD HAVE LIKEWISE CLEARED IT OF DESIRE, BUT AS YOU CAN SEE, THAT IS NOT THE CASE.
BUT IS NOT DESIRE MERE PRIMAL INSTINCT, DOCTOR, AND NOT A REMNANT OF PREVIOUS CONSCIOUSNESS?
INSTINCT OR NO, DESIRE BREEDS NOTHING BUT HOSTILITY, JEALOUSY AND VIOLENCE--THE VERY SCOURGE OF MAN WE WORKED SO DILIGENTLY TO CIRCUMVENT.
HE MUST DIE.

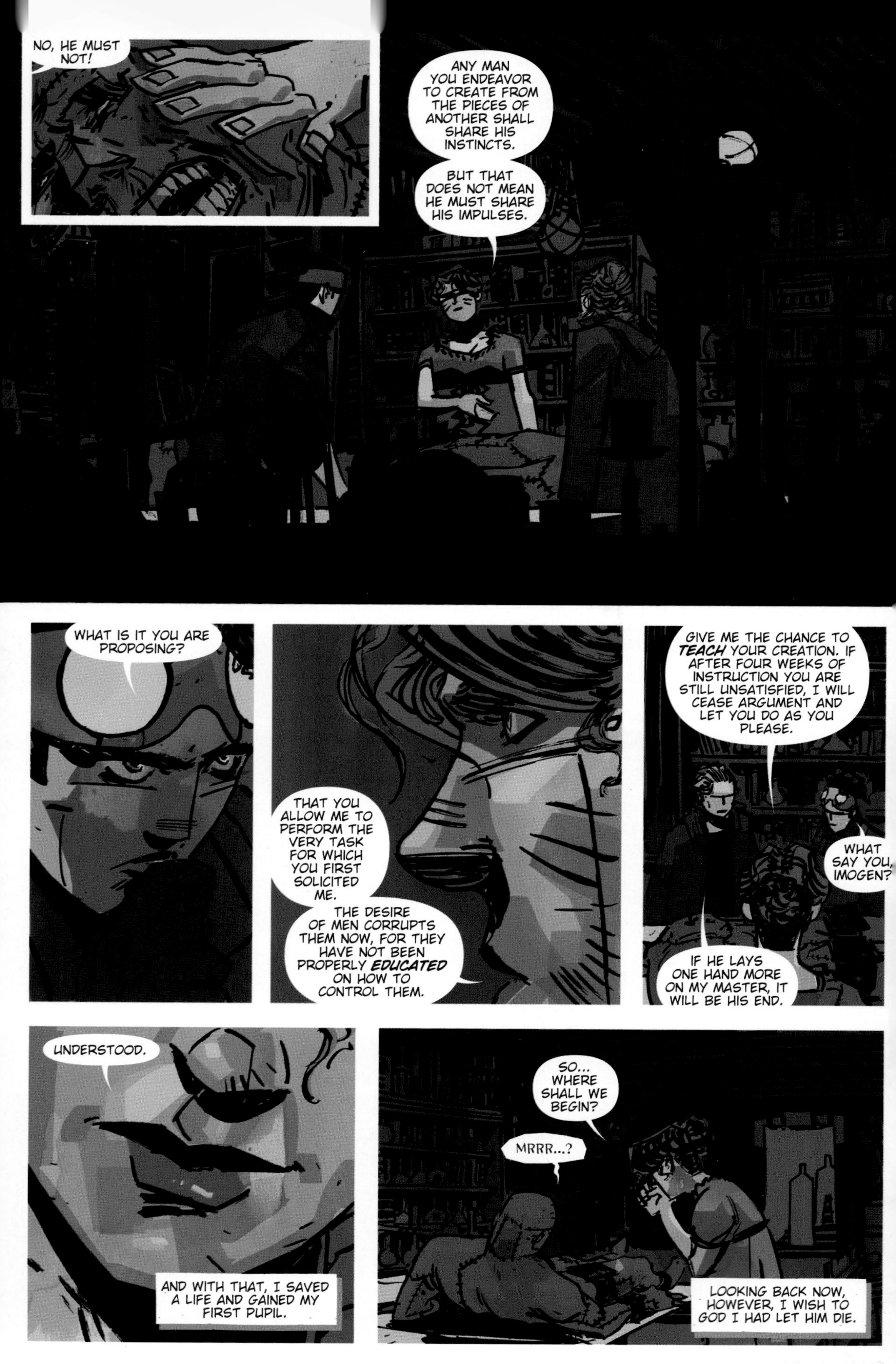
NO, HE MUST NOT!
ANY MAN YOU ENDEAVOR TO CREATE FROM THE PIECES OF ANOTHER SHALL SHARE HIS INSTINCTS.
BUT THAT DOES NOT MEAN HE MUST SHARE HIS IMPULSES.
WHAT IS IT YOU ARE PROPOSING?
THAT YOU ALLOW ME TO PERFORM THE VERY TASK FOR WHICH YOU FIRST SOLICITED ME.
THE DESIRE OF MEN CORRUPTS THEM NOW, FOR THEY HAVE NOT BEEN PROPERLY EDUCATED ON HOW TO CONTROL THEM.
GIVE ME THE CHANCE TO TEACH YOUR CREATION. IF AFTER FOUR WEEKS OF INSTRUCTION YOU ARE STILL UNSATISFIED, I WILL CEASE ARGUMENT AND LET YOU DO AS YOU PLEASE.
WHAT SAY YOU, IMOGEN?
IF HE LAYS ONE HAND MORE ON MY MASTER, IT WILL BE HIS END.
UNDERSTOOD.
AND WITH THAT, I SAVED A LIFE AND GAINED MY FIRST PUPIL.
SO... WHERE SHALL WE BEGIN?
MRRR...?
LOOKING BACK NOW, HOWEVER, I WISH TO GOD I HAD LET HIM DIE.

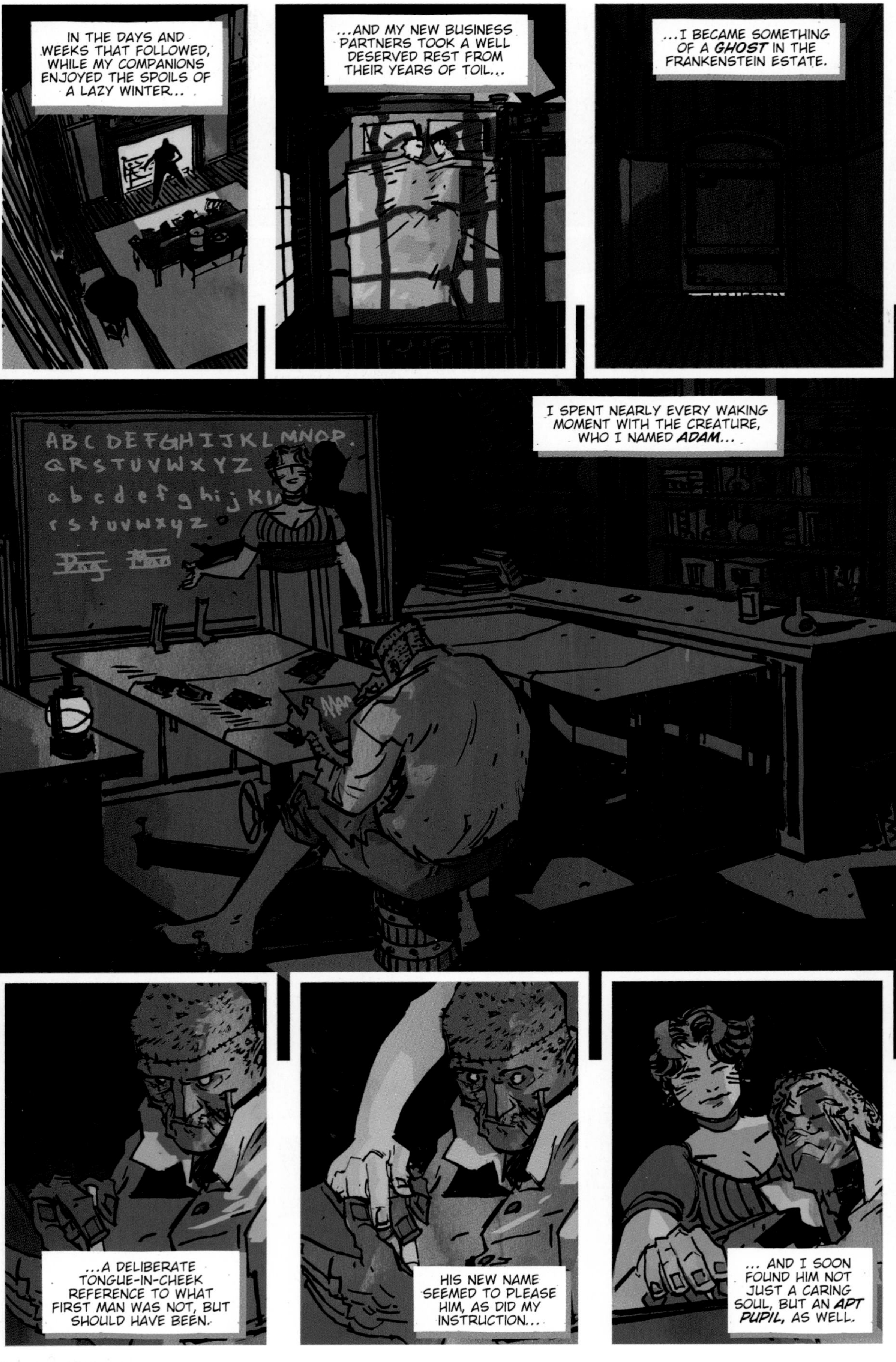
IN THE DAYS AND WEEKS THAT FOLLOWED, WHILE MY COMPANIONS ENJOYED THE SPOILS OF A LAZY WINTER...
...AND MY NEW BUSINESS PARTNERS TOOK A WELL DESERVED REST FROM THEIR YEARS OF TOIL...
...I BECAME SOMETHING OF A GHOST IN THE FRANKENSTEIN ESTATE.
I SPENT NEARLY EVERY WAKING MOMENT WITH THE CREATURE, WHO I NAMED ADAM...
...A DELIBERATE TONGUE-IN-CHEEK REFERENCE TO WHAT FIRST MAN WAS NOT, BUT SHOULD HAVE BEEN.
HIS NEW NAME SEEMED TO PLEASE HIM, AS DID MY INSTRUCTION...
... AND I SOON FOUND HIM NOT JUST A CARING SOUL, BUT AN APT PUPIL, AS WELL.

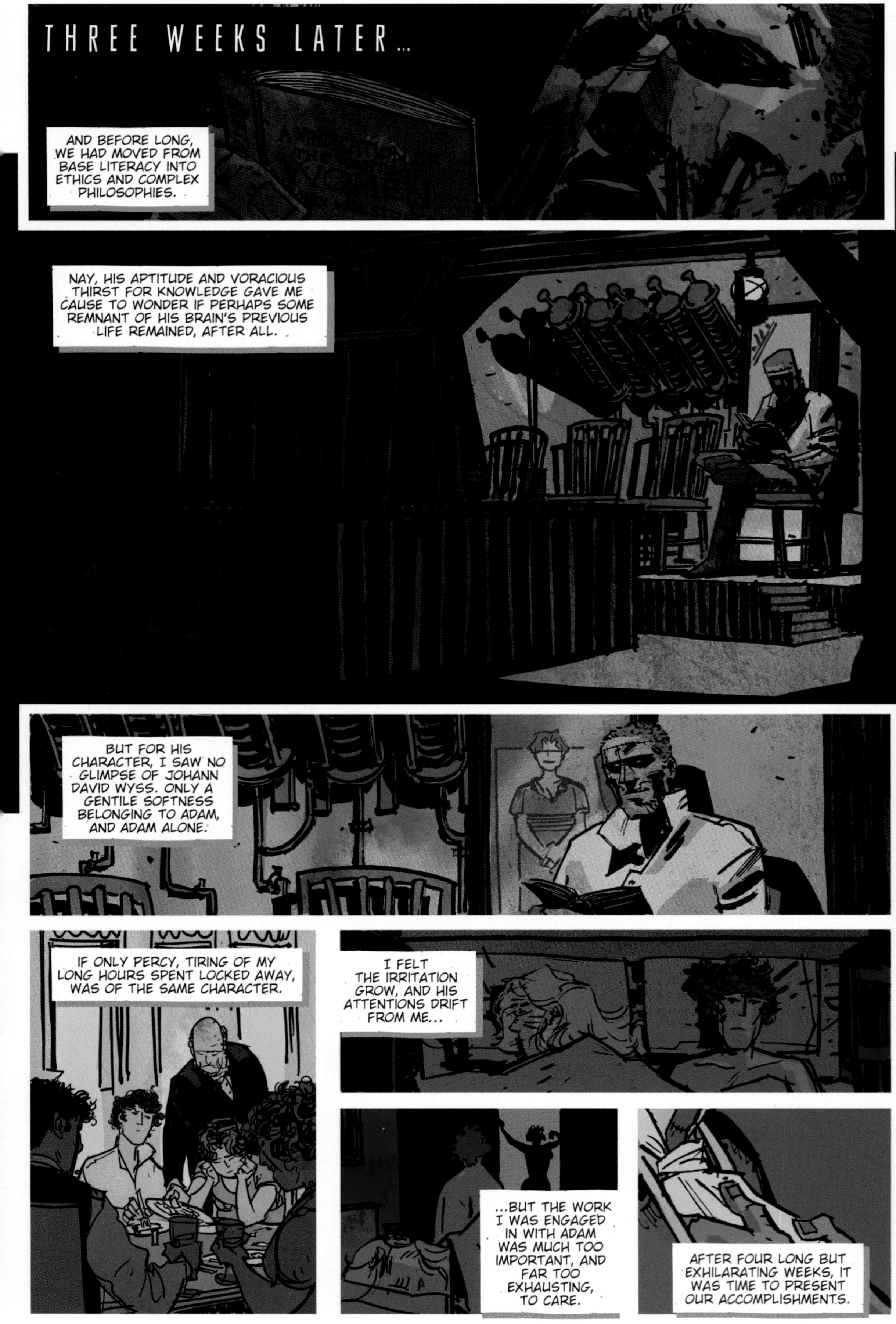
THREE WEEKS LATER...
AND BEFORE LONG, WE HAD MOVED FROM BASE LITERACY INTO ETHICS AND COMPLEX PHILOSOPHIES.
NAY, HIS APTITUDE AND VORACIOUS THIRST FOR KNOWLEDGE GAVE ME CAUSE TO WONDER IF PERHAPS SOME REMNANT OF HIS BRAIN'S PREVIOUS LIFE REMAINED, AFTER ALL.
BUT FOR HIS CHARACTER, I SAW NO GLIMPSE OF JOHANN DAVID WYSS. ONLY A GENTILE SOFTNESS BELONGING TO ADAM, AND ADAM ALONE.
IF ONLY PERCY, TIRING OF MY LONG HOURS SPENT LOCKED AWAY, WAS OF THE SAME CHARACTER.
I FELT THE IRRITATION GROW, AND HIS ATTENTIONS DRIFT FROM ME...
...BUT THE WORK I WAS ENGAGED IN WITH ADAM WAS MUCH TOO IMPORTANT, AND FAR TOO EXHAUSTING, TO CARE.
AFTER FOUR LONG BUT EXHILARATING WEEKS, IT WAS TIME TO PRESENT OUR ACCOMPLISHMENTS.

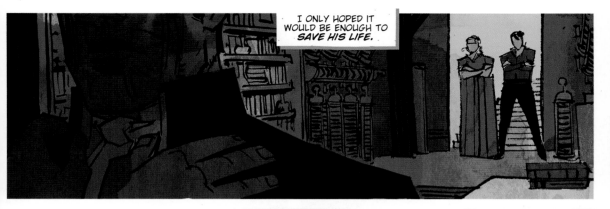

I ONLY HOPED IT WOULD BE ENOUGH TO *SAVE HIS LIFE.*

DR. FRANKENSTEIN AND MISS GULL, A PLEASURE TO SEE YOU BOTH.

YOU MUST FORGIVE ME, WHEN LAST WE MET I WAS BUT A SIMPLE, PRIMITIVE MAN.

AND WHAT ARE YOU NOW, PRAY TELL?

I AM A DUTIFUL SERVANT OF WOMANKIND, DEDICATED TO HER LIBERATION FROM THE CONSTRAINTS OF OUR OPPRESSIVE MODERN SOCIETY.

AND MY SOLE, ENDURING MISSION BEGINS WITH YOU, DR. VICTORIA FRANKENSTEIN.

YOU SWEAR TO BOTH SERVE AND PROTECT ME?

UNTIL THE END OF MY DAYS.

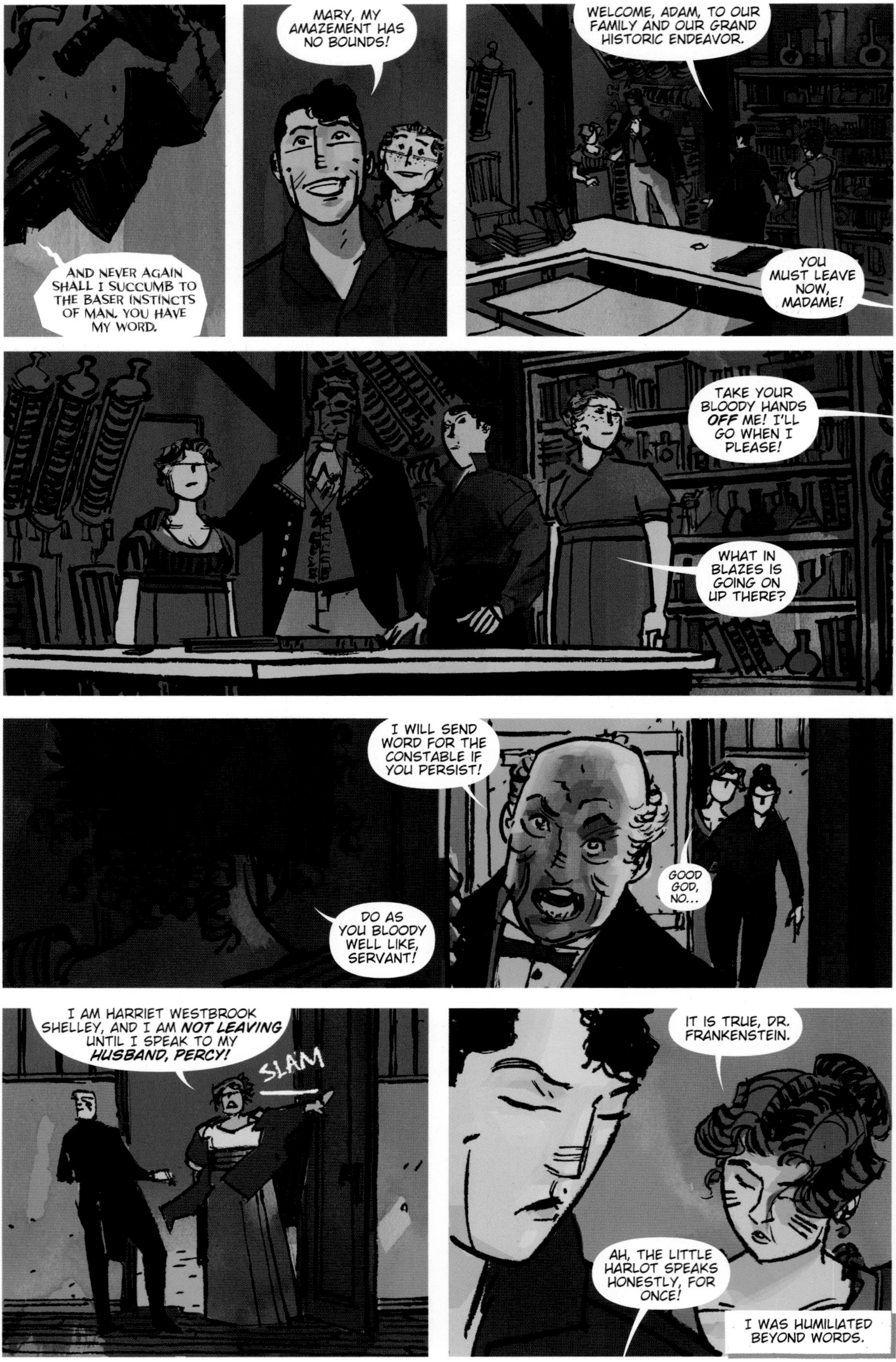
AND NEVER AGAIN SHALL I SUCCUMB TO THE BASER INSTINCTS OF MAN. YOU HAVE MY WORD.
MARY, MY AMAZEMENT HAS NO BOUNDS!
WELCOME, ADAM, TO OUR FAMILY AND OUR GRAND HISTORIC ENDEAVOR.
YOU MUST LEAVE NOW, MADAME!
TAKE YOUR BLOODY HANDS OFF ME! I'LL GO WHEN I PLEASE!
WHAT IN BLAZES IS GOING ON UP THERE?
DO AS YOU BLOODY WELL LIKE, SERVANT!
I WILL SEND WORD FOR THE CONSTABLE IF YOU PERSIST!
GOOD GOD, NO...
I AM HARRIET WESTBROOK SHELLEY, AND I AM NOT LEAVING UNTIL I SPEAK TO MY HUSBAND, PERCY!
SLAM
IT IS TRUE, DR. FRANKENSTEIN.
AH, THE LITTLE HARLOT SPEAKS HONESTLY, FOR ONCE!
I WAS HUMILIATED BEYOND WORDS.

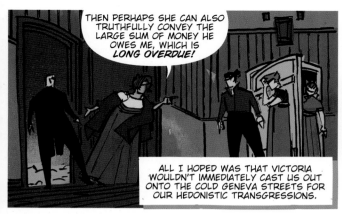

THEN PERHAPS SHE CAN ALSO TRUTHFULLY CONVEY THE LARGE SUM OF MONEY HE OWES ME, WHICH IS *LONG OVERDUE!*

ALL I HOPED WAS THAT VICTORIA WOULDN'T IMMEDIATELY CAST US OUT ONTO THE COLD GENEVA STREETS FOR OUR HEDONISTIC TRANSGRESSIONS.

YOU MEAN TO TELL ME YOU HAVE TRAVELED ALL THE WAY FROM LONDON IN THE DEAD OF WINTER TO CONFRONT A MAN WHO DOESN'T LOVE YOU AND TO FORCEFULLY TAKE FROM HIS PURSE?

I WAS PLEASANTLY MISTAKEN.

I BORE HIS CHILDREN! FEELINGS OR NO, THAT MONEY IS *DUE TO ME!*

THOUGH NOTHING COULD HAVE PREPARED ME FOR WHAT WOULD TRANSPIRE NEXT.

HOW *DARE* YOU SPEAK TO ME THAT WAY!

THWACK!

AAH!

UNHAND ME, MADMAN!

ADAM?!

YOU LAID YOUR HAND ON MY MASTER. AS SUCH, SHE WILL BE THE LAST THING YOU TOUCH.

AH! AAAH! AAAAH!

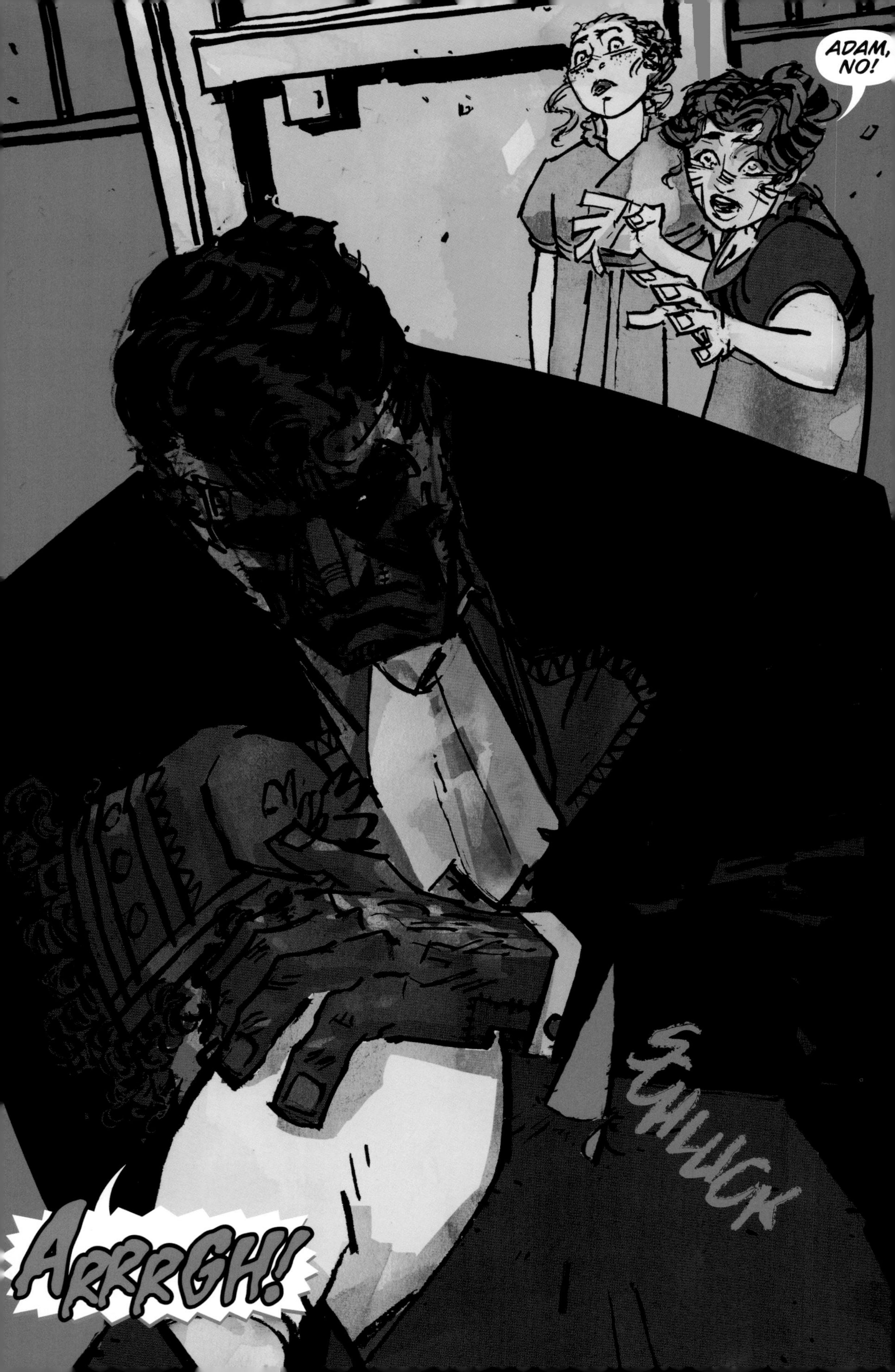
ADAM, NO!
SCHLUCK
ARRRGH!

4

BETRAYAL

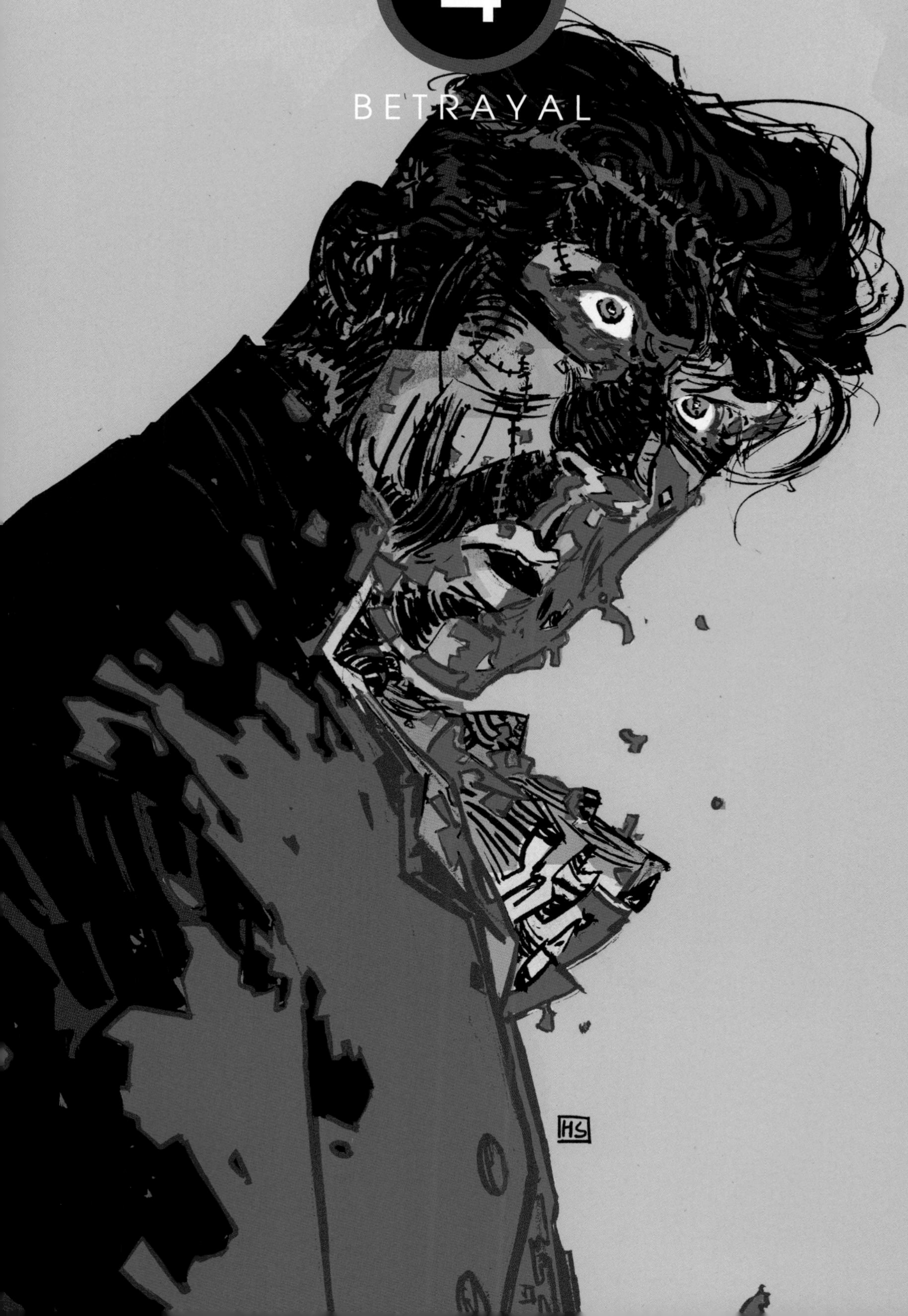
HS

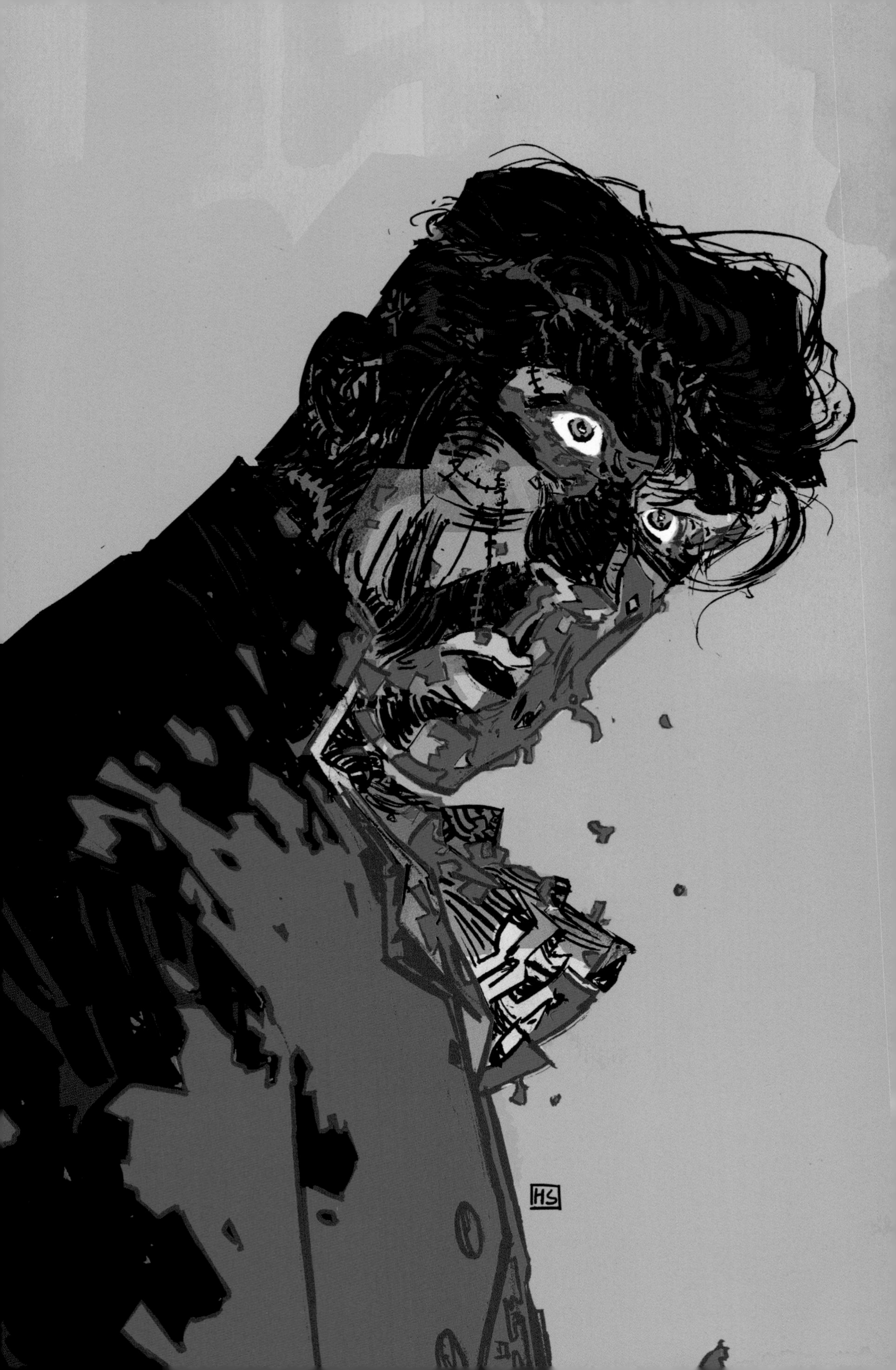

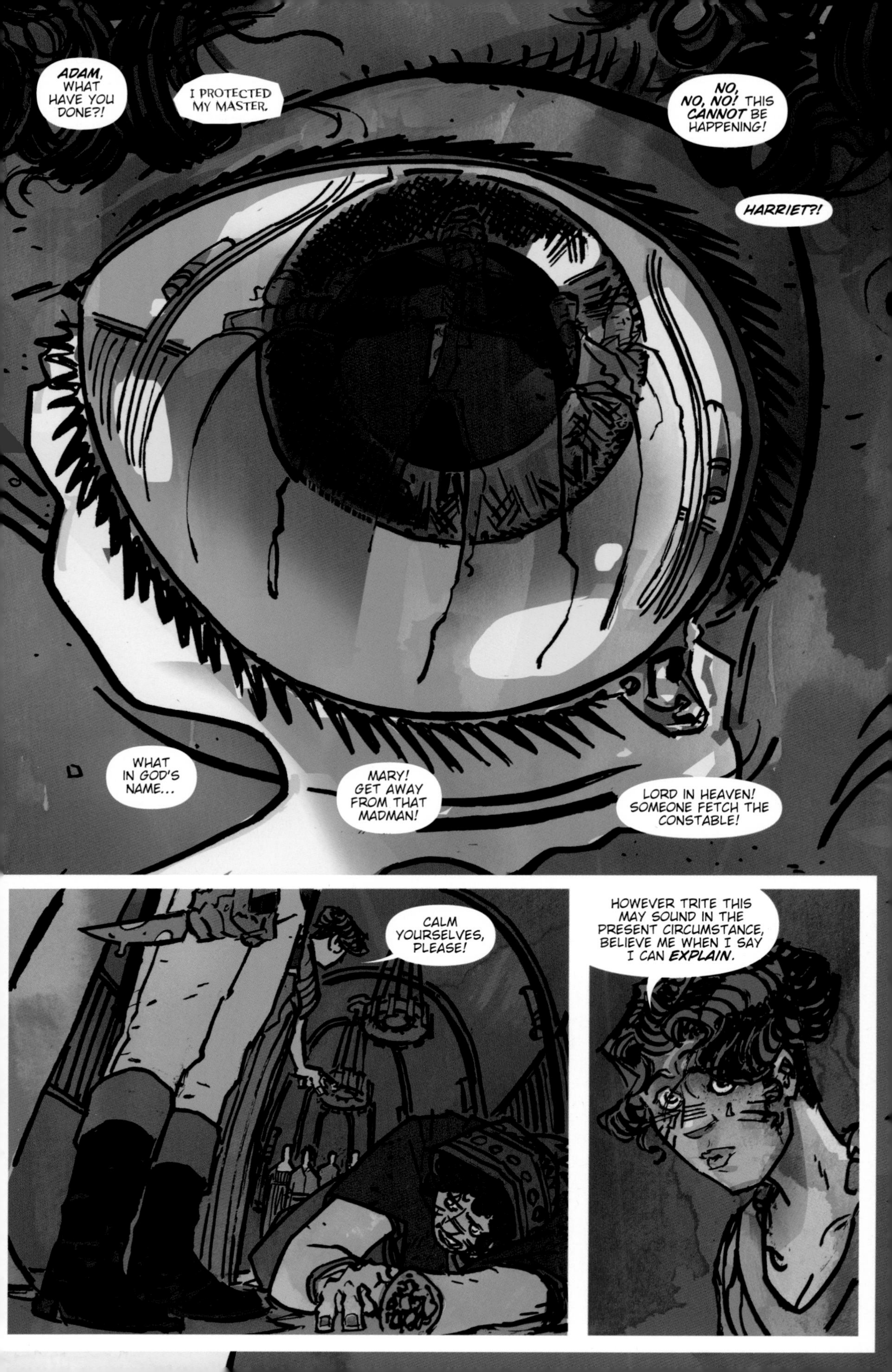

ADAM, WHAT HAVE YOU DONE?!
I PROTECTED MY MASTER.
NO, NO, NO! THIS CANNOT BE HAPPENING!
HARRIET?!
WHAT IN GOD'S NAME...
MARY! GET AWAY FROM THAT MADMAN!
LORD IN HEAVEN! SOMEONE FETCH THE CONSTABLE!
CALM YOURSELVES, PLEASE!
HOWEVER TRITE THIS MAY SOUND IN THE PRESENT CIRCUMSTANCE, BELIEVE ME WHEN I SAY I CAN EXPLAIN.

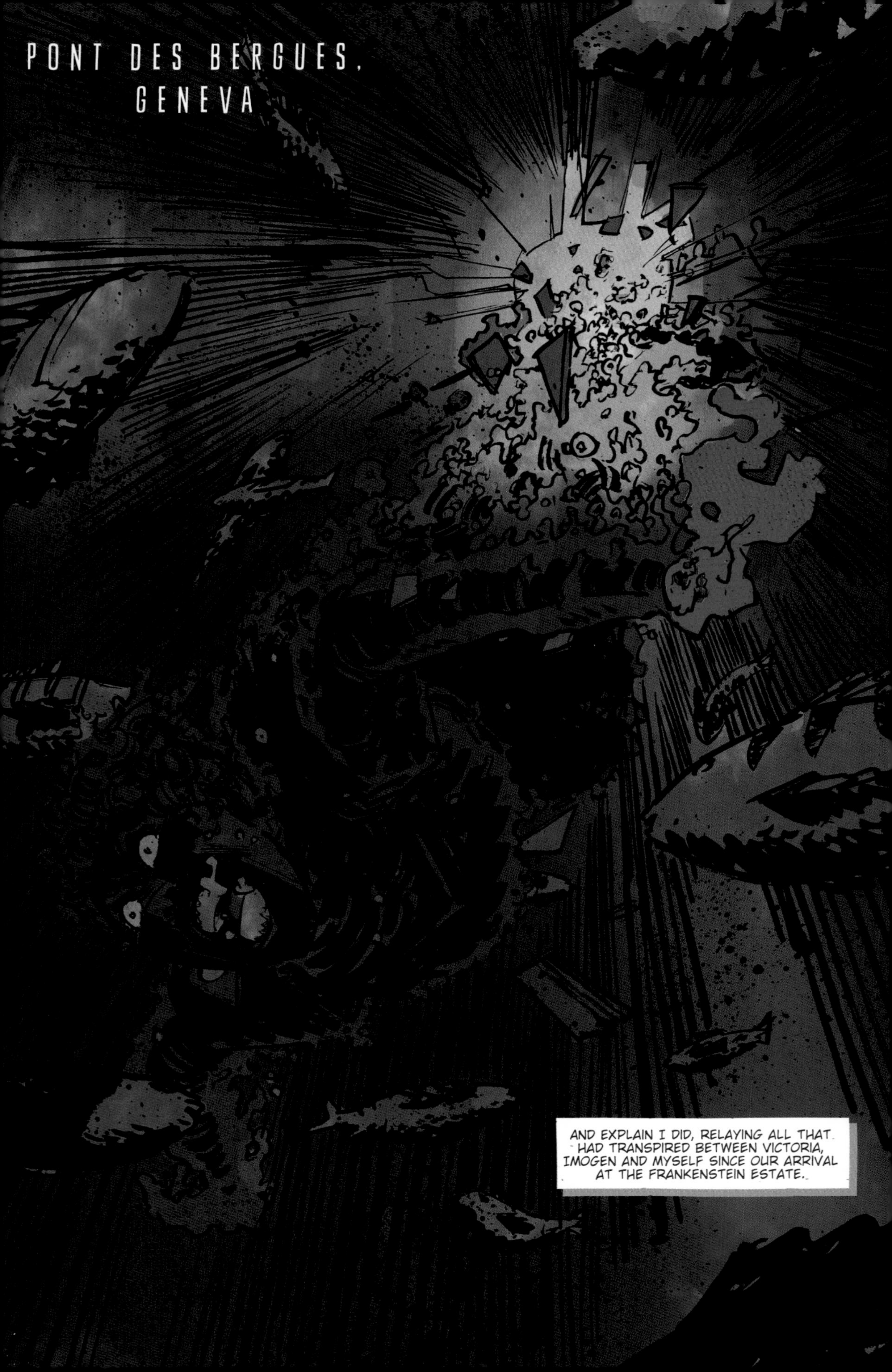
PONT DES BERGUES, GENEVA
AND EXPLAIN I DID, RELAYING ALL THAT HAD TRANSPIRED BETWEEN VICTORIA, IMOGEN AND MYSELF SINCE OUR ARRIVAL AT THE FRANKENSTEIN ESTATE.

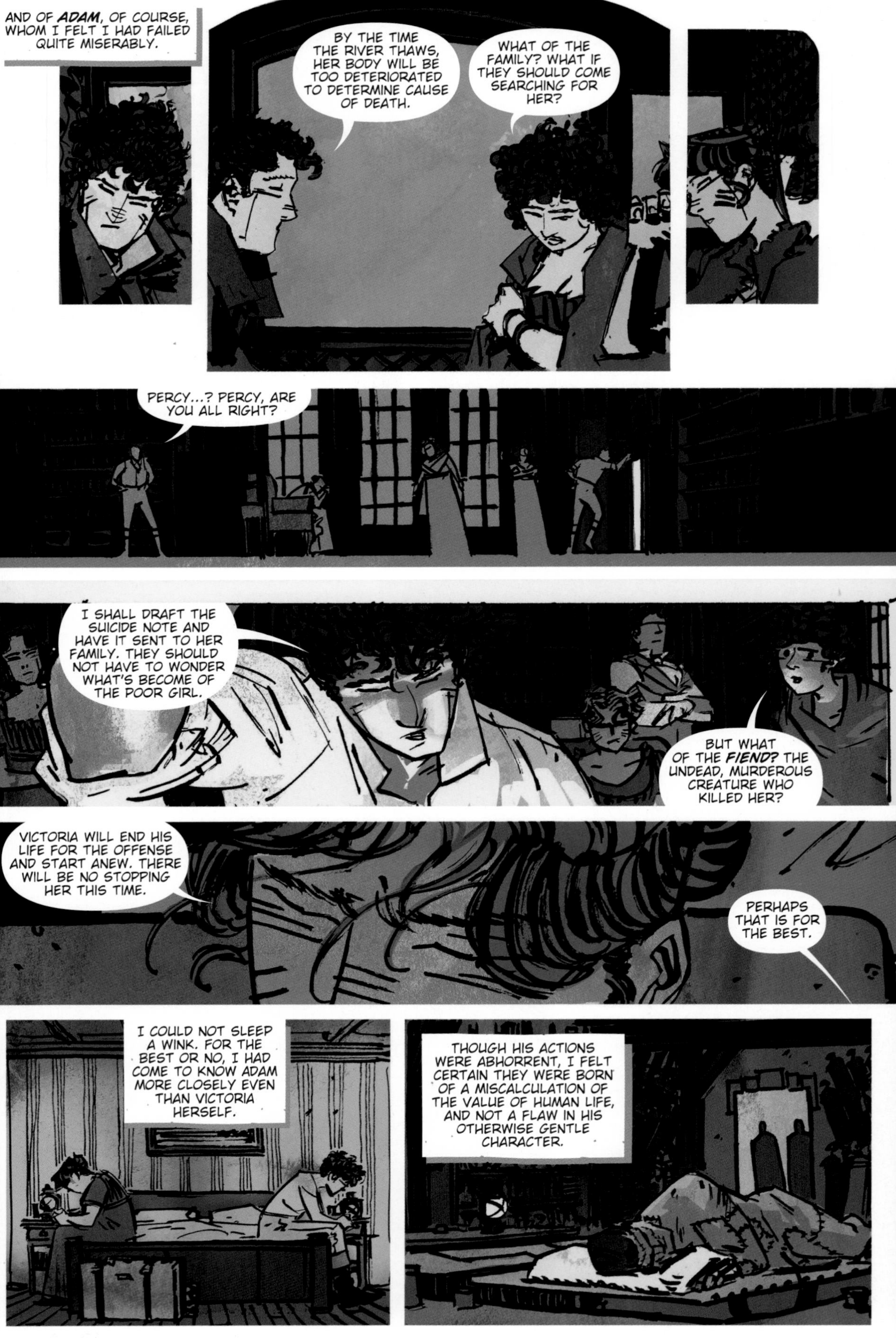

AND OF ***ADAM***, OF COURSE, WHOM I FELT I HAD FAILED QUITE MISERABLY.
BY THE TIME THE RIVER THAWS, HER BODY WILL BE TOO DETERIORATED TO DETERMINE CAUSE OF DEATH.
WHAT OF THE FAMILY? WHAT IF THEY SHOULD COME SEARCHING FOR HER?
PERCY...? PERCY, ARE YOU ALL RIGHT?
I SHALL DRAFT THE SUICIDE NOTE AND HAVE IT SENT TO HER FAMILY. THEY SHOULD NOT HAVE TO WONDER WHAT'S BECOME OF THE POOR GIRL.
BUT WHAT OF THE ***FIEND?*** THE UNDEAD, MURDEROUS CREATURE WHO KILLED HER?
VICTORIA WILL END HIS LIFE FOR THE OFFENSE AND START ANEW. THERE WILL BE NO STOPPING HER THIS TIME.
PERHAPS THAT IS FOR THE BEST.
I COULD NOT SLEEP A WINK. FOR THE BEST OR NO, I HAD COME TO KNOW ADAM MORE CLOSELY EVEN THAN VICTORIA HERSELF.
THOUGH HIS ACTIONS WERE ABHORRENT, I FELT CERTAIN THEY WERE BORN OF A MISCALCULATION OF THE VALUE OF HUMAN LIFE, AND NOT A FLAW IN HIS OTHERWISE GENTLE CHARACTER.

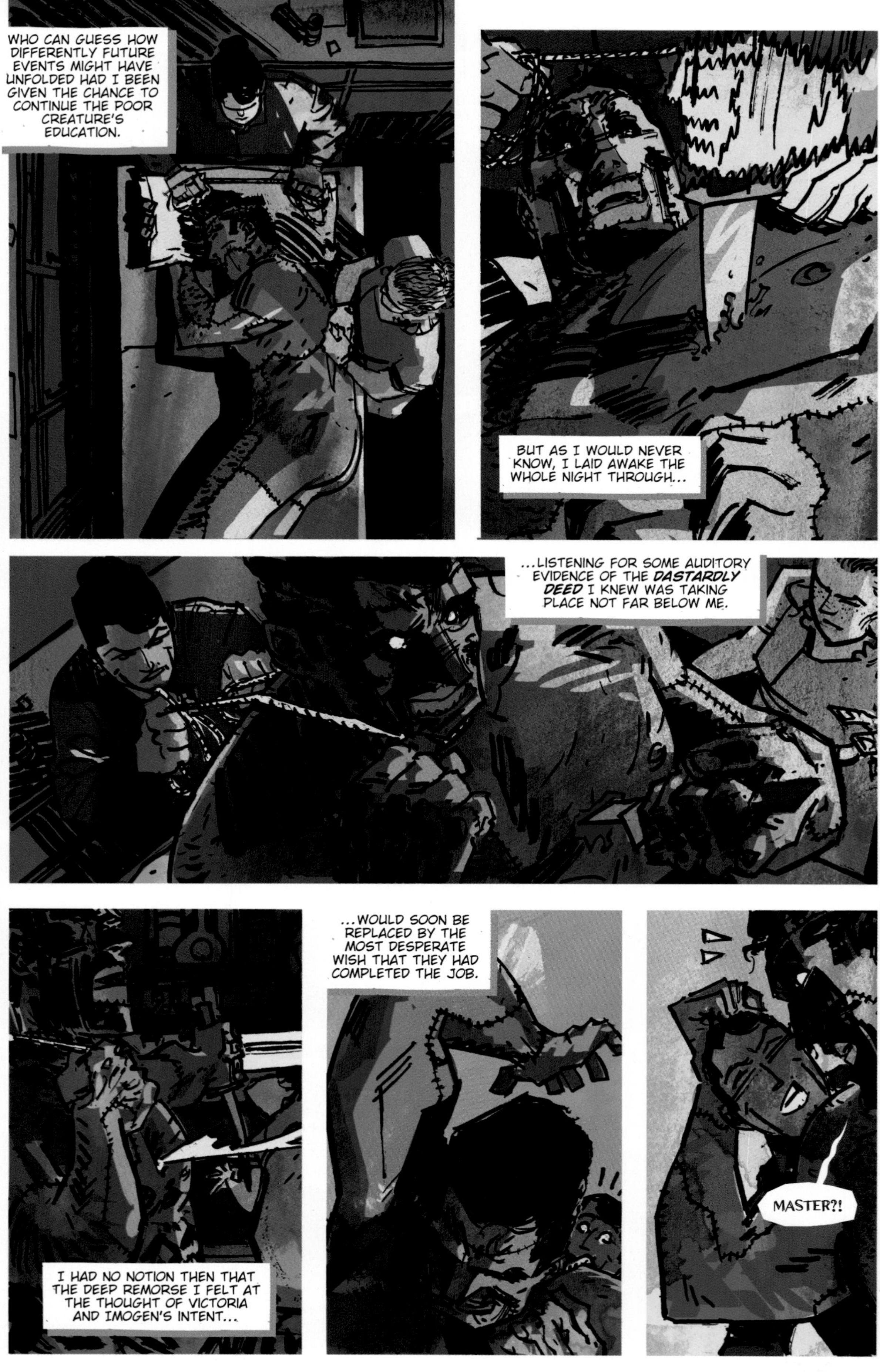
WHO CAN GUESS HOW DIFFERENTLY FUTURE EVENTS MIGHT HAVE UNFOLDED HAD I BEEN GIVEN THE CHANCE TO CONTINUE THE POOR CREATURE'S EDUCATION.
BUT AS I WOULD NEVER KNOW, I LAID AWAKE THE WHOLE NIGHT THROUGH...
...LISTENING FOR SOME AUDITORY EVIDENCE OF THE DASTARDLY DEED I KNEW WAS TAKING PLACE NOT FAR BELOW ME.
I HAD NO NOTION THEN THAT THE DEEP REMORSE I FELT AT THE THOUGHT OF VICTORIA AND IMOGEN'S INTENT...
...WOULD SOON BE REPLACED BY THE MOST DESPERATE WISH THAT THEY HAD COMPLETED THE JOB.
MASTER?!

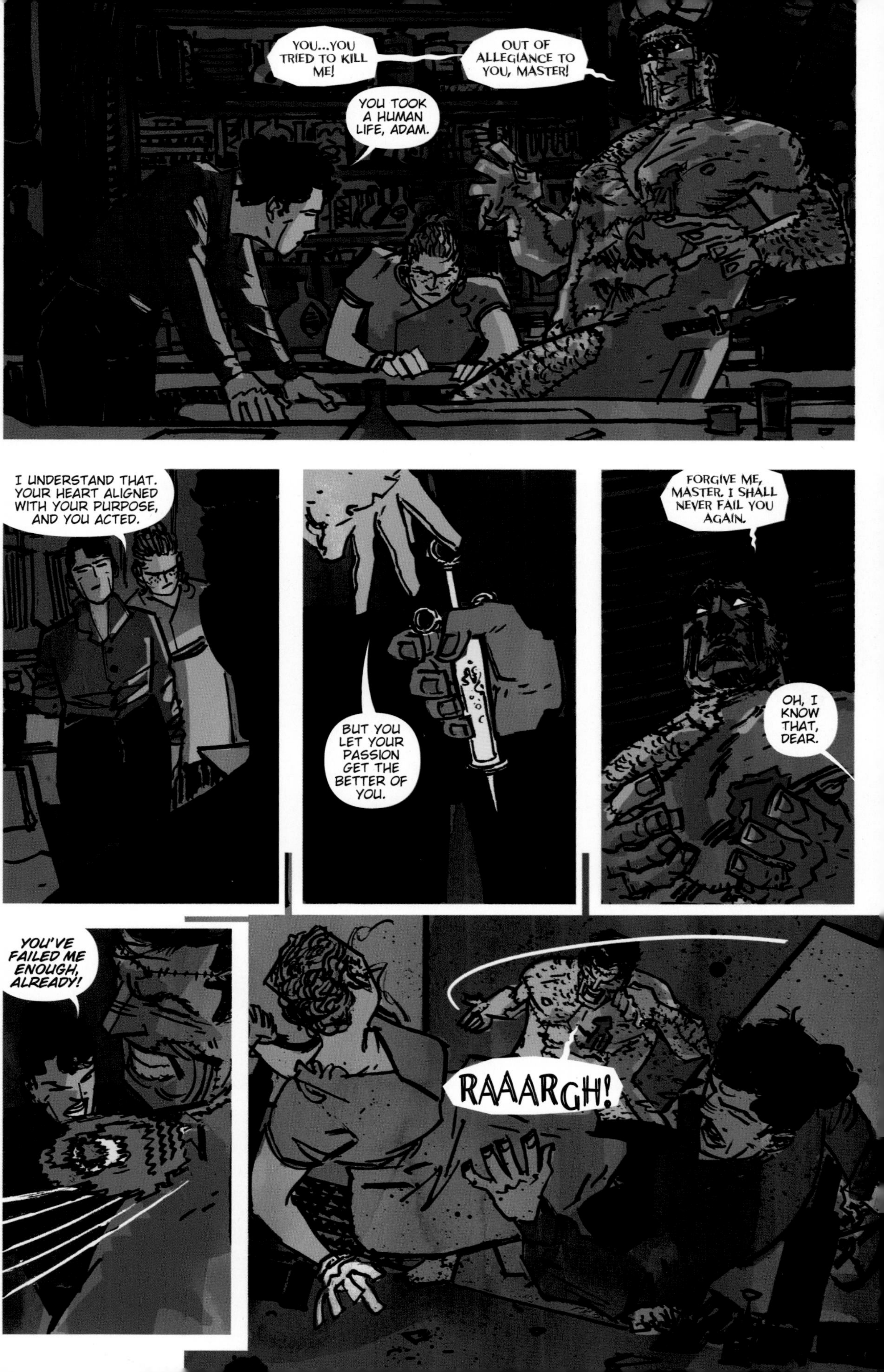
YOU...YOU TRIED TO KILL ME!
OUT OF ALLEGIANCE TO YOU, MASTER!
YOU TOOK A HUMAN LIFE, ADAM.
I UNDERSTAND THAT. YOUR HEART ALIGNED WITH YOUR PURPOSE, AND YOU ACTED.
BUT YOU LET YOUR PASSION GET THE BETTER OF YOU.
FORGIVE ME, MASTER. I SHALL NEVER FAIL YOU AGAIN.
OH, I KNOW THAT, DEAR.
YOU'VE FAILED ME ENOUGH, ALREADY!
RAAARGH!

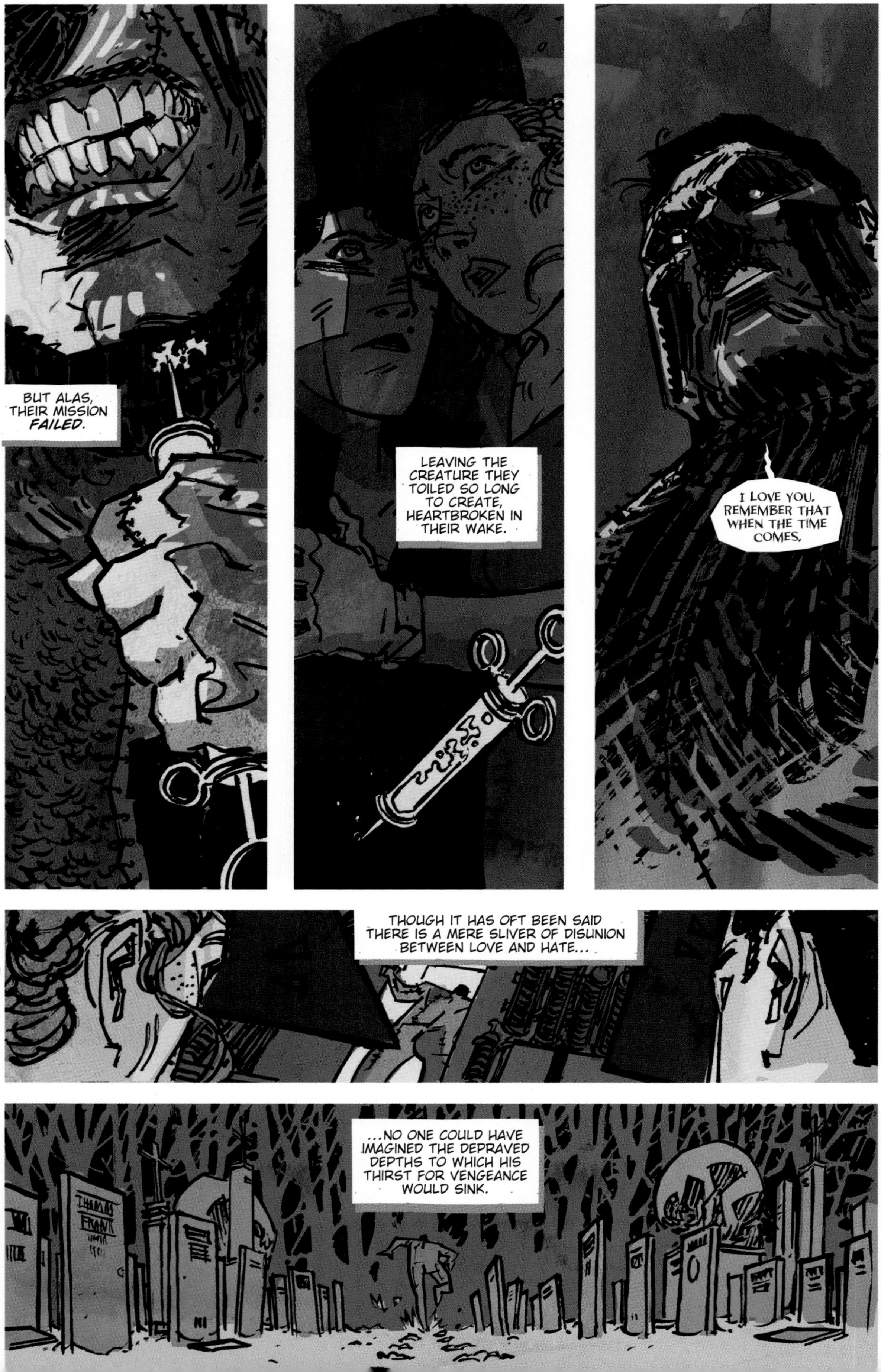
BUT ALAS, THEIR MISSION *FAILED.*
LEAVING THE CREATURE THEY TOILED SO LONG TO CREATE, HEARTBROKEN IN THEIR WAKE.
I LOVE YOU. REMEMBER THAT WHEN THE TIME COMES.
THOUGH IT HAS OFT BEEN SAID THERE IS A MERE SLIVER OF DISUNION BETWEEN LOVE AND HATE...
...NO ONE COULD HAVE IMAGINED THE DEPRAVED DEPTHS TO WHICH HIS THIRST FOR VENGEANCE WOULD SINK.

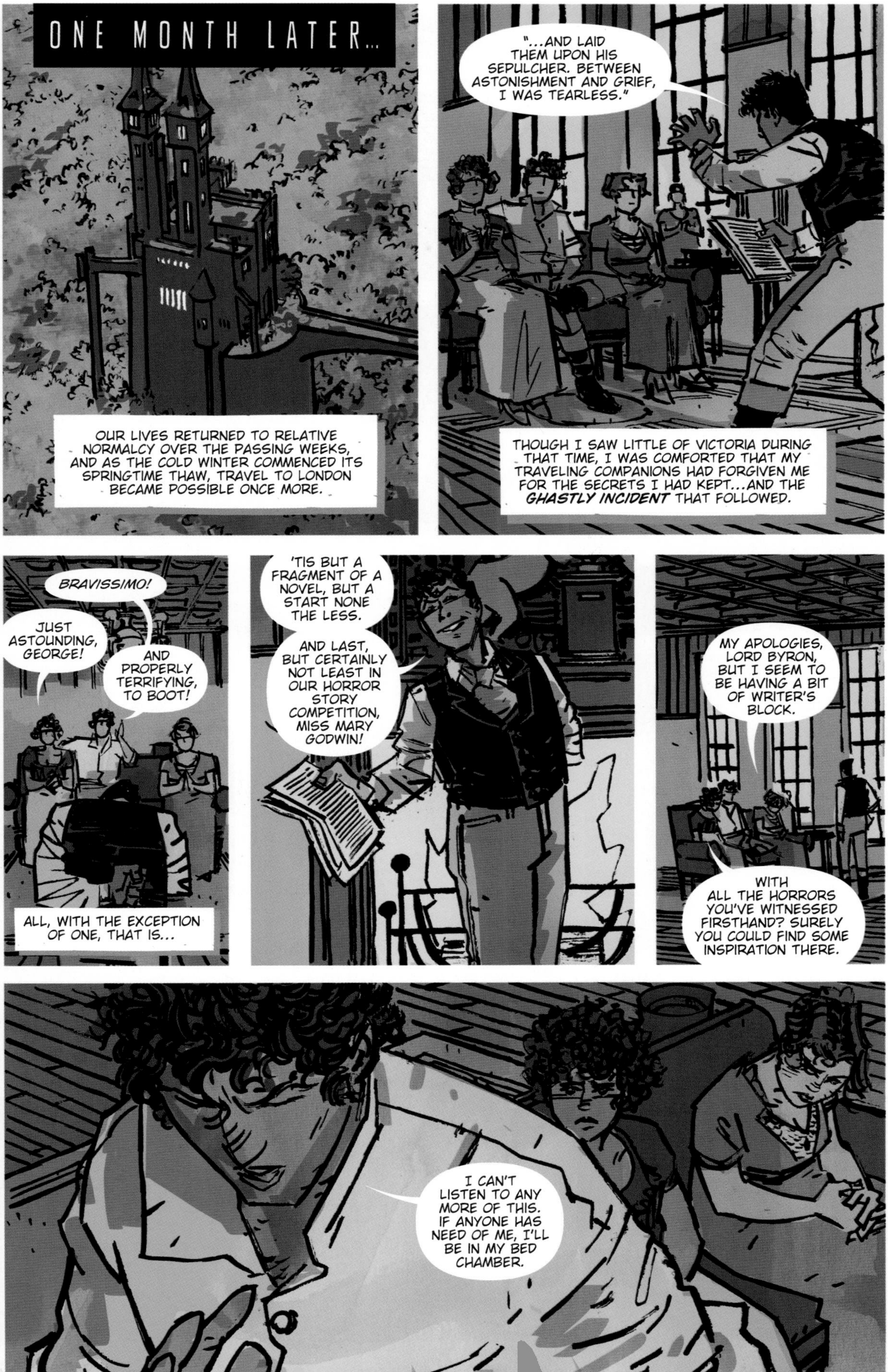
ONE MONTH LATER...
OUR LIVES RETURNED TO RELATIVE NORMALCY OVER THE PASSING WEEKS, AND AS THE COLD WINTER COMMENCED ITS SPRINGTIME THAW, TRAVEL TO LONDON BECAME POSSIBLE ONCE MORE.
"...AND LAID THEM UPON HIS SEPULCHER. BETWEEN ASTONISHMENT AND GRIEF, I WAS TEARLESS."
THOUGH I SAW LITTLE OF VICTORIA DURING THAT TIME, I WAS COMFORTED THAT MY TRAVELING COMPANIONS HAD FORGIVEN ME FOR THE SECRETS I HAD KEPT...AND THE *GHASTLY INCIDENT* THAT FOLLOWED.
BRAVISSIMO!
JUST ASTOUNDING, GEORGE!
AND PROPERLY TERRIFYING, TO BOOT!
ALL, WITH THE EXCEPTION OF ONE, THAT IS...
'TIS BUT A FRAGMENT OF A NOVEL, BUT A START NONE THE LESS.
AND LAST, BUT CERTAINLY NOT LEAST IN OUR HORROR STORY COMPETITION, MISS MARY GODWIN!
MY APOLOGIES, LORD BYRON, BUT I SEEM TO BE HAVING A BIT OF WRITER'S BLOCK.
WITH ALL THE HORRORS YOU'VE WITNESSED FIRSTHAND? SURELY YOU COULD FIND SOME INSPIRATION THERE.
I CAN'T LISTEN TO ANY MORE OF THIS. IF ANYONE HAS NEED OF ME, I'LL BE IN MY BED CHAMBER.

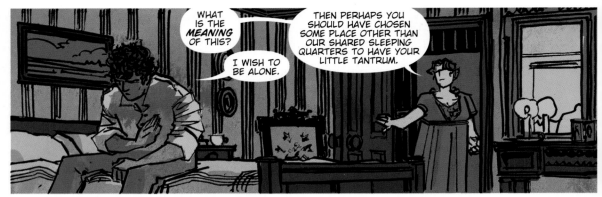

WHAT IS THE *MEANING* OF THIS?

I WISH TO BE ALONE.

THEN PERHAPS YOU SHOULD HAVE CHOSEN SOME PLACE OTHER THAN OUR SHARED SLEEPING QUARTERS TO HAVE YOUR LITTLE TANTRUM.

WHAT IS IT YOU *WANT* FROM ME?

TO TALK THINGS THROUGH. YOU'RE CLEARLY STILL ANGRY WITH ME.

I'VE SAID NO SUCH THING.

YOU EXPECT ME TO BELIEVE YOU'VE AVOIDED ME AT ALL COSTS, AND TURNED TO *CLAIRE* OF ALL PEOPLE, BECAUSE YOU'RE SO DELIGHTFULLY *PLEASED WITH ME?* OUT WITH IT, MR. SHELLEY!

FINE, MARY! IT ISN'T ENOUGH THAT THE MOTHER OF MY CHILDREN IS DEAD, VEXING AS SHE WAS, BUT YOU HAVE MADE ME AN *ACCOMPLICE* TO HER *MURDER!* NOT TO MENTION THE FACT THAT THE *CULPRIT* IS STILL *OUT THERE!*

AS I TOLD YOU, ADAM IS DEAD AND GONE. VICTORIA INFORMED ME OF THAT HERSELF!

I'VE SEEN HIM IN MY *VISIONS*, MARY, AND HE IS ANYTHING BUT "DEAD" OR "GONE".

EITHER YOUR NEW CONFIDANTE VICTORIA IS LYING TO YOU, OR YOU ARE ONCE MORE LYING TO ME!

SO THAT'S IT, *EH?* YOU'RE IRATE BECAUSE I DIDN'T TELL YOU OF VICTORIA'S PLAN?

OR YOUR INVOLVEMENT IN IT, THE HOURS UPON HOURS YOU SPENT WITH THAT MAN, ALL THE WHILE LEADING ME TO BELIEVE YOU WERE WITH VICTORIA, WRITING.

FROM THE MOMENT WE MET THOSE THREE MARVELOUS YEARS AGO IN YOUR FATHER'S DRAWING ROOM, WE HAVE SHARED *EVERYTHING* WITH ONE ANOTHER.

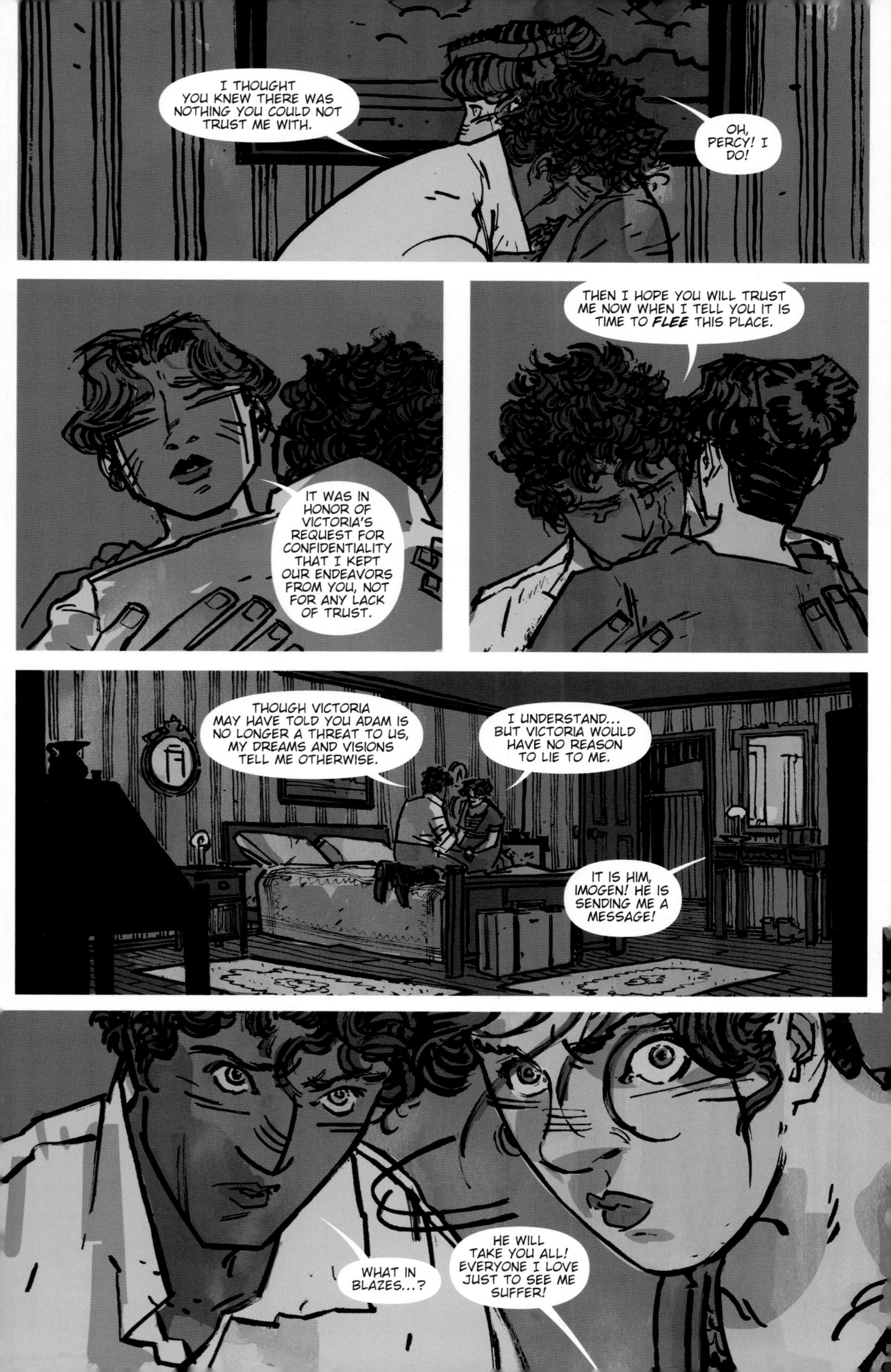
I THOUGHT YOU KNEW THERE WAS NOTHING YOU COULD NOT TRUST ME WITH.
OH, PERCY! I DO!
IT WAS IN HONOR OF VICTORIA'S REQUEST FOR CONFIDENTIALITY THAT I KEPT OUR ENDEAVORS FROM YOU, NOT FOR ANY LACK OF TRUST.
THEN I HOPE YOU WILL TRUST ME NOW WHEN I TELL YOU IT IS TIME TO FLEE THIS PLACE.
THOUGH VICTORIA MAY HAVE TOLD YOU ADAM IS NO LONGER A THREAT TO US, MY DREAMS AND VISIONS TELL ME OTHERWISE.
I UNDERSTAND... BUT VICTORIA WOULD HAVE NO REASON TO LIE TO ME.
IT IS HIM, IMOGEN! HE IS SENDING ME A MESSAGE!
WHAT IN BLAZES...?
HE WILL TAKE YOU ALL! EVERYONE I LOVE JUST TO SEE ME SUFFER!

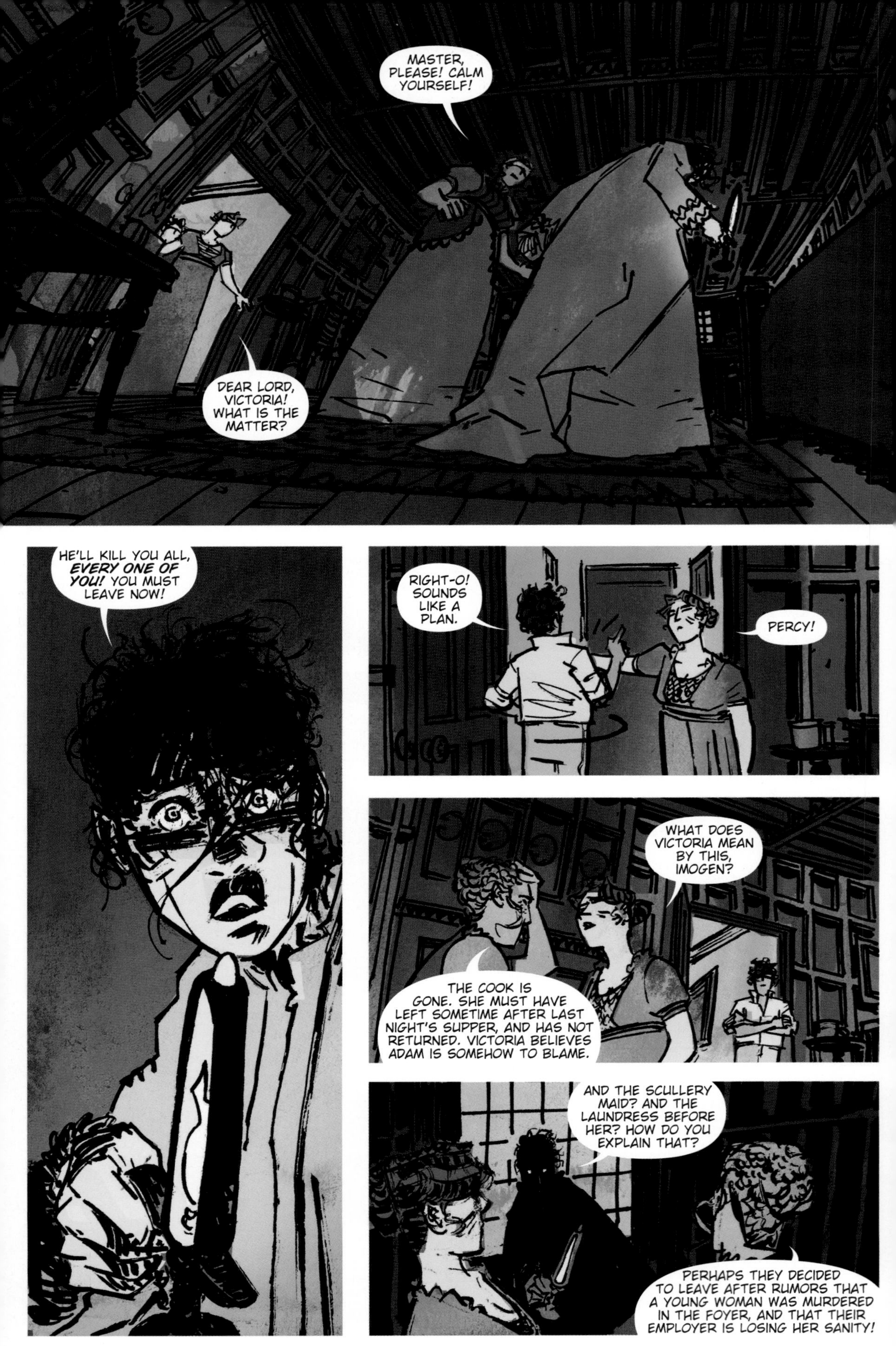
MASTER, PLEASE! CALM YOURSELF!
DEAR LORD, VICTORIA! WHAT IS THE MATTER?
HE'LL KILL YOU ALL, *EVERY ONE OF YOU!* YOU MUST LEAVE NOW!
RIGHT-O! SOUNDS LIKE A PLAN.
PERCY!
WHAT DOES VICTORIA MEAN BY THIS, IMOGEN?
THE COOK IS GONE. SHE MUST HAVE LEFT SOMETIME AFTER LAST NIGHT'S SUPPER, AND HAS NOT RETURNED. VICTORIA BELIEVES ADAM IS SOMEHOW TO BLAME.
AND THE SCULLERY MAID? AND THE LAUNDRESS BEFORE HER? HOW DO YOU EXPLAIN THAT?
PERHAPS THEY DECIDED TO LEAVE AFTER RUMORS THAT A YOUNG WOMAN WAS MURDERED IN THE FOYER, AND THAT THEIR EMPLOYER IS LOSING HER SANITY!

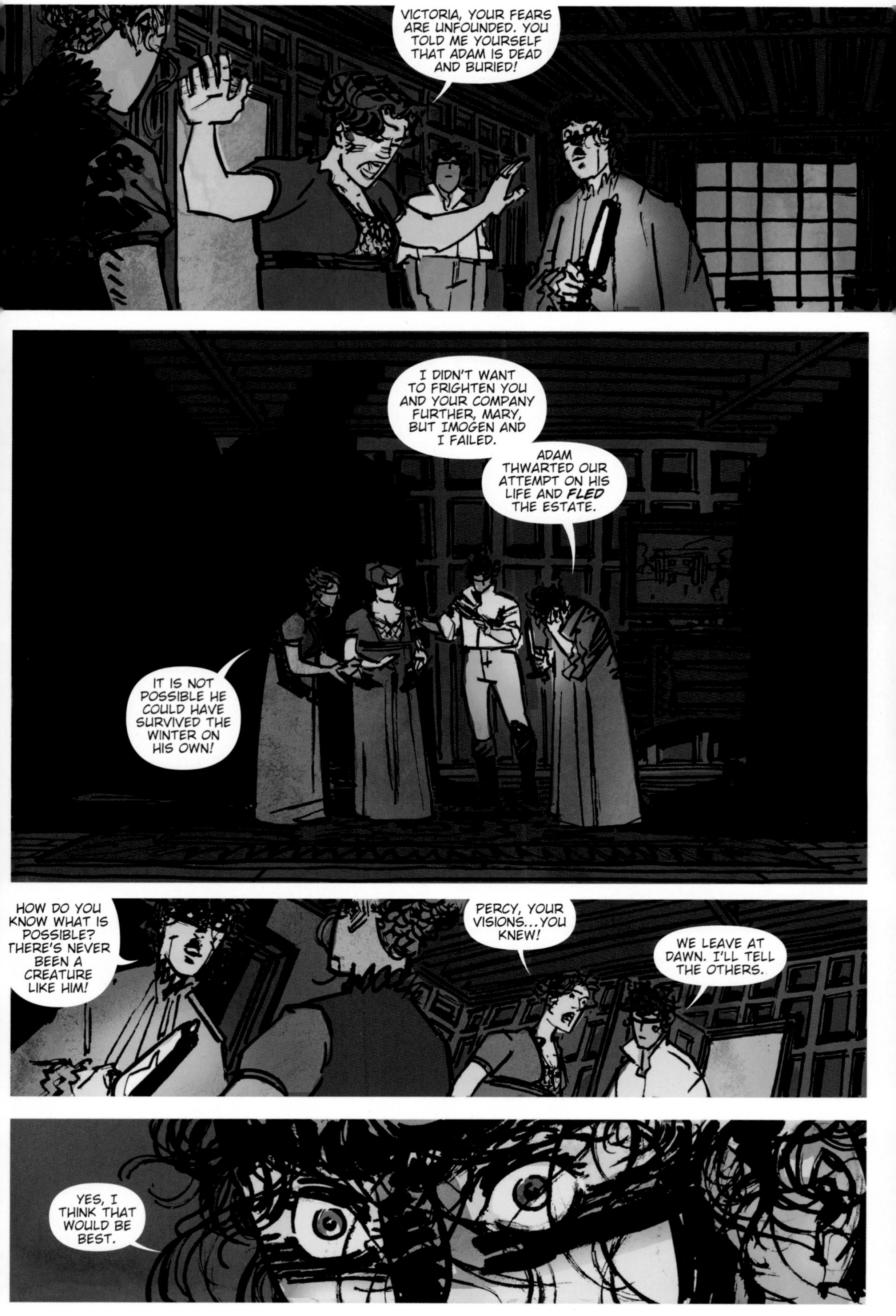
VICTORIA, YOUR FEARS ARE UNFOUNDED. YOU TOLD ME YOURSELF THAT ADAM IS DEAD AND BURIED!
I DIDN'T WANT TO FRIGHTEN YOU AND YOUR COMPANY FURTHER, MARY, BUT IMOGEN AND I FAILED.
ADAM THWARTED OUR ATTEMPT ON HIS LIFE AND *FLED* THE ESTATE.
IT IS NOT POSSIBLE HE COULD HAVE SURVIVED THE WINTER ON HIS OWN!
HOW DO YOU KNOW WHAT IS POSSIBLE? THERE'S NEVER BEEN A CREATURE LIKE HIM!
PERCY, YOUR VISIONS...YOU KNEW!
WE LEAVE AT DAWN. I'LL TELL THE OTHERS.
YES, I THINK THAT WOULD BE BEST.

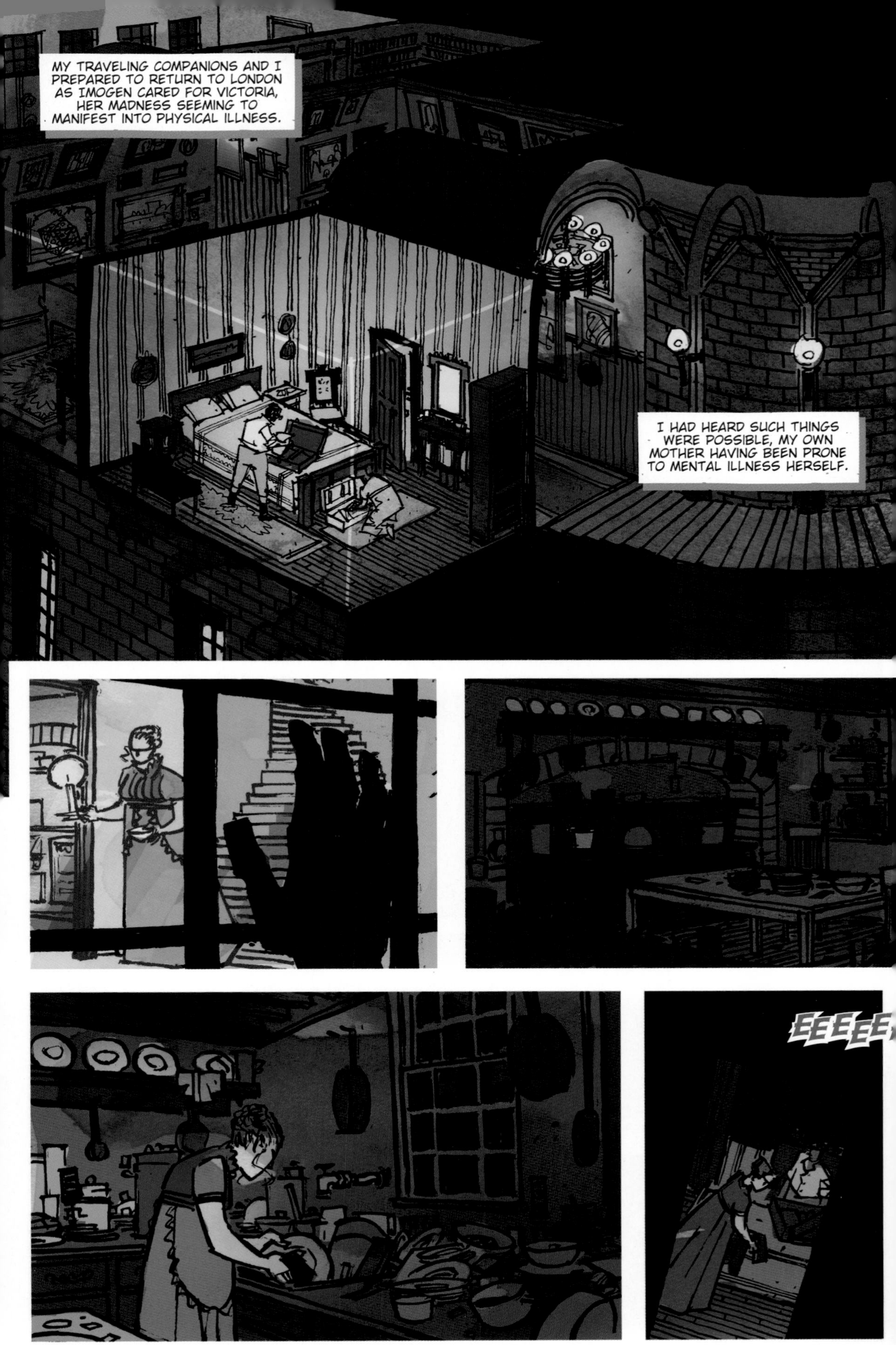
MY TRAVELING COMPANIONS AND I PREPARED TO RETURN TO LONDON AS IMOGEN CARED FOR VICTORIA, HER MADNESS SEEMING TO MANIFEST INTO PHYSICAL ILLNESS.
I HAD HEARD SUCH THINGS WERE POSSIBLE, MY OWN MOTHER HAVING BEEN PRONE TO MENTAL ILLNESS HERSELF.
EEEEE

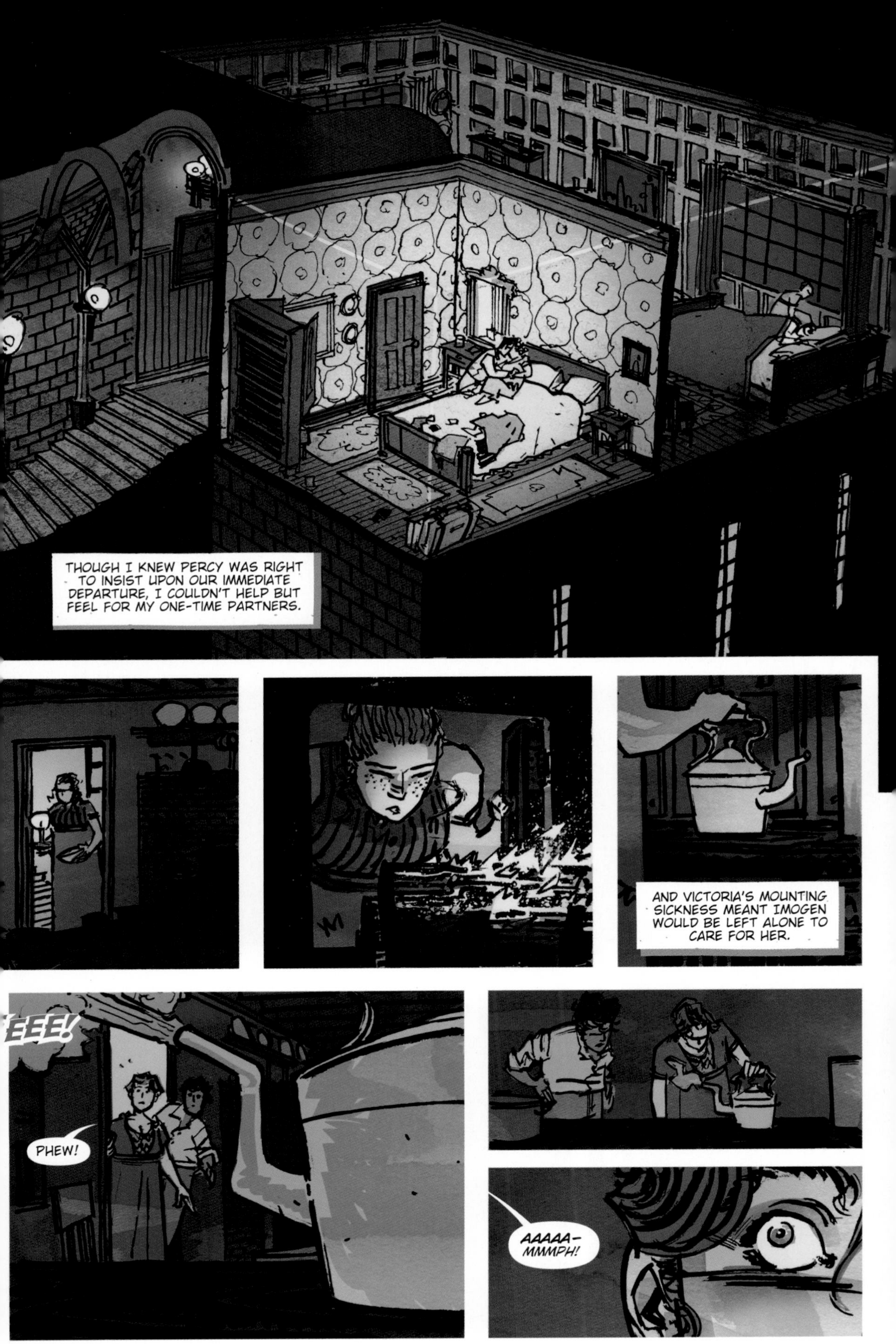
THOUGH I KNEW PERCY WAS RIGHT TO INSIST UPON OUR IMMEDIATE DEPARTURE, I COULDN'T HELP BUT FEEL FOR MY ONE-TIME PARTNERS.
AND VICTORIA'S MOUNTING SICKNESS MEANT IMOGEN WOULD BE LEFT ALONE TO CARE FOR HER.
EEE!
PHEW!
AAAAA-MMMPH!

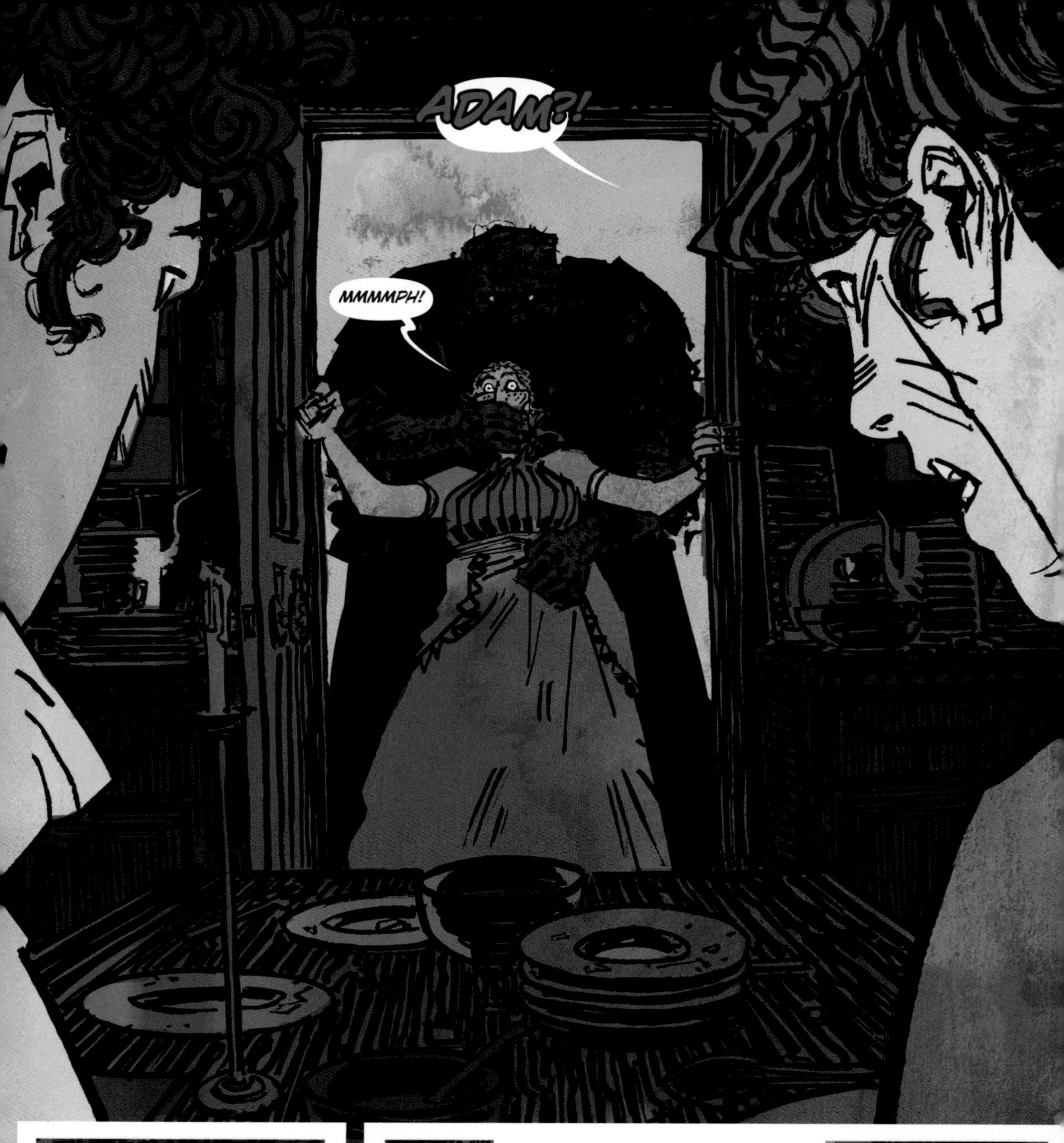
ADAM?!
MMMMPH!

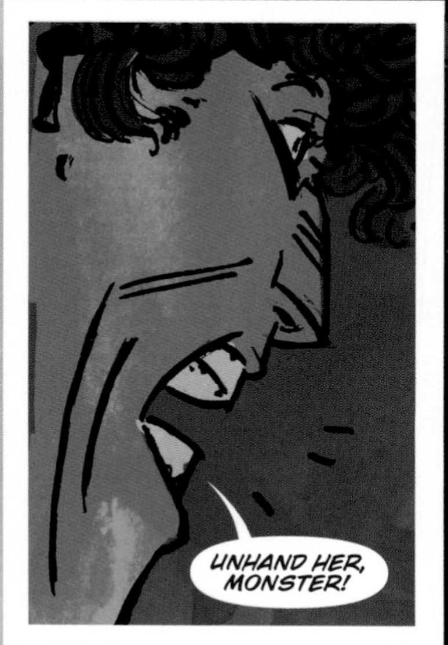
UNHAND HER, MONSTER!

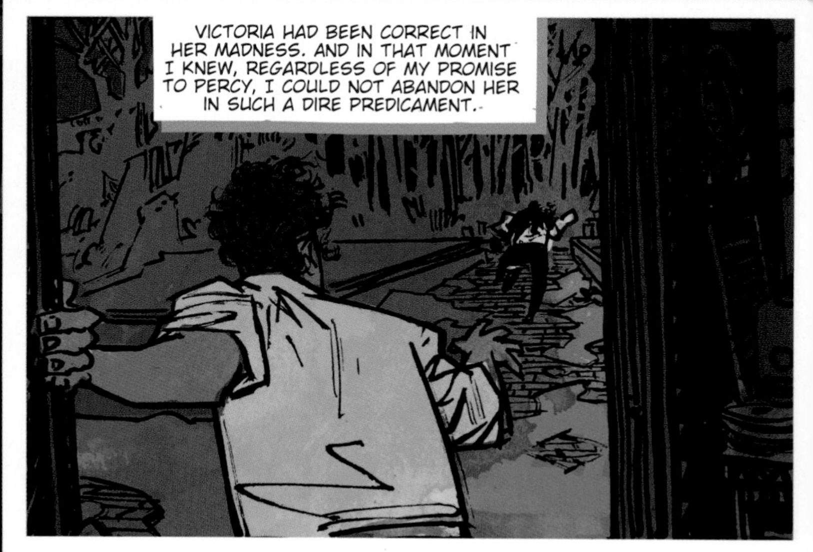
VICTORIA HAD BEEN CORRECT IN HER MADNESS. AND IN THAT MOMENT I KNEW, REGARDLESS OF MY PROMISE TO PERCY, I COULD NOT ABANDON HER IN SUCH A DIRE PREDICAMENT.

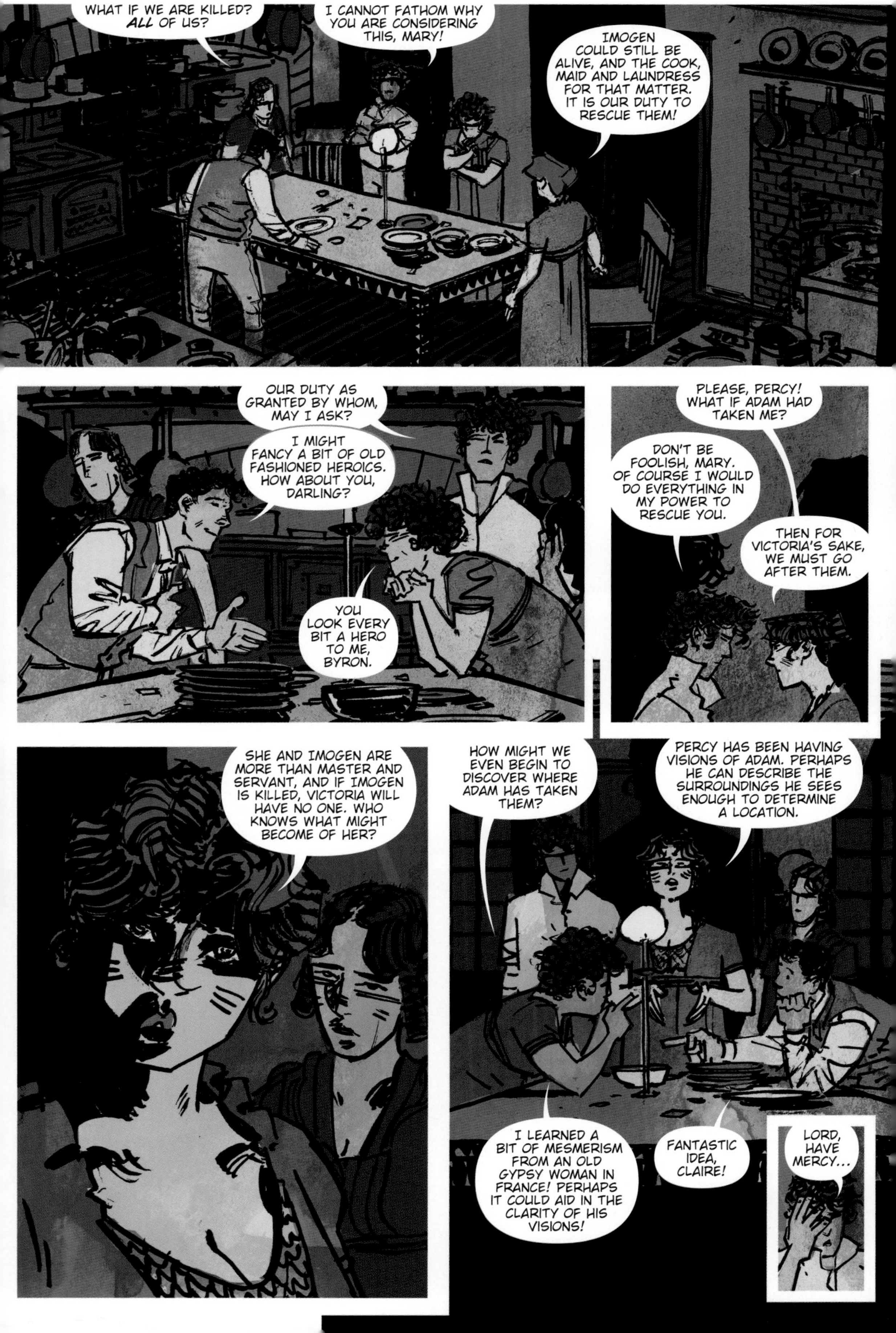
WHAT IF WE ARE KILLED? ***ALL*** OF US?
I CANNOT FATHOM WHY YOU ARE CONSIDERING THIS, MARY!
IMOGEN COULD STILL BE ALIVE, AND THE COOK, MAID AND LAUNDRESS FOR THAT MATTER. IT IS OUR DUTY TO RESCUE THEM!
OUR DUTY AS GRANTED BY WHOM, MAY I ASK?
I MIGHT FANCY A BIT OF OLD FASHIONED HEROICS. HOW ABOUT YOU, DARLING?
YOU LOOK EVERY BIT A HERO TO ME, BYRON.
PLEASE, PERCY! WHAT IF ADAM HAD TAKEN ME?
DON'T BE FOOLISH, MARY. OF COURSE I WOULD DO EVERYTHING IN MY POWER TO RESCUE YOU.
THEN FOR VICTORIA'S SAKE, WE MUST GO AFTER THEM.
SHE AND IMOGEN ARE MORE THAN MASTER AND SERVANT, AND IF IMOGEN IS KILLED, VICTORIA WILL HAVE NO ONE. WHO KNOWS WHAT MIGHT BECOME OF HER?
HOW MIGHT WE EVEN BEGIN TO DISCOVER WHERE ADAM HAS TAKEN THEM?
PERCY HAS BEEN HAVING VISIONS OF ADAM. PERHAPS HE CAN DESCRIBE THE SURROUNDINGS HE SEES ENOUGH TO DETERMINE A LOCATION.
I LEARNED A BIT OF MESMERISM FROM AN OLD GYPSY WOMAN IN FRANCE! PERHAPS IT COULD AID IN THE CLARITY OF HIS VISIONS!
FANTASTIC IDEA, CLAIRE!
LORD, HAVE MERCY...

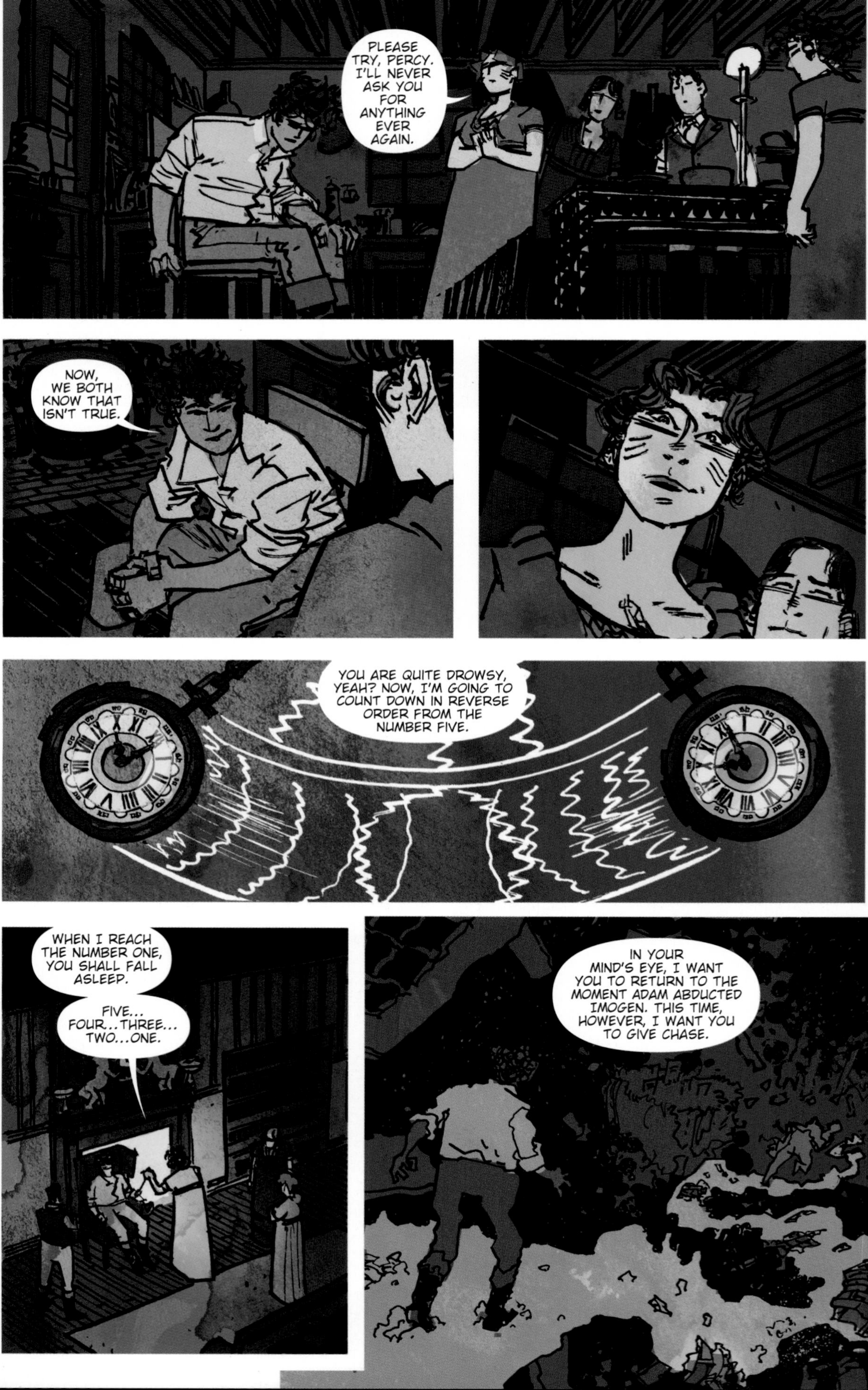
PLEASE TRY, PERCY. I'LL NEVER ASK YOU FOR ANYTHING EVER AGAIN.
NOW, WE BOTH KNOW THAT ISN'T TRUE.
YOU ARE QUITE DROWSY, YEAH? NOW, I'M GOING TO COUNT DOWN IN REVERSE ORDER FROM THE NUMBER FIVE.
WHEN I REACH THE NUMBER ONE, YOU SHALL FALL ASLEEP.
FIVE... FOUR...THREE... TWO...ONE.
IN YOUR MIND'S EYE, I WANT YOU TO RETURN TO THE MOMENT ADAM ABDUCTED IMOGEN. THIS TIME, HOWEVER, I WANT YOU TO GIVE CHASE.

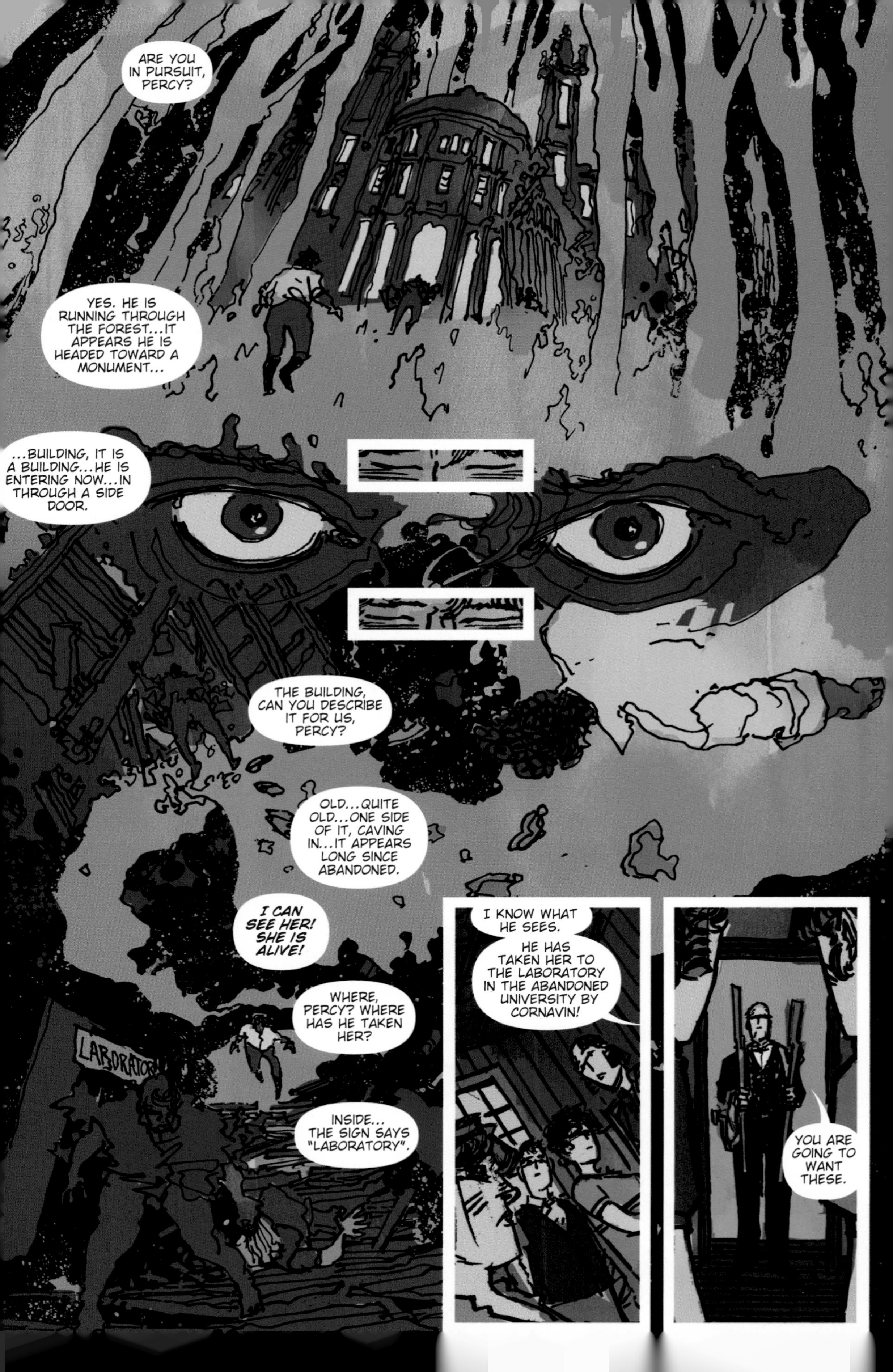
ARE YOU IN PURSUIT, PERCY?
YES. HE IS RUNNING THROUGH THE FOREST...IT APPEARS HE IS HEADED TOWARD A MONUMENT...
...BUILDING, IT IS A BUILDING...HE IS ENTERING NOW...IN THROUGH A SIDE DOOR.
THE BUILDING, CAN YOU DESCRIBE IT FOR US, PERCY?
OLD...QUITE OLD...ONE SIDE OF IT, CAVING IN...IT APPEARS LONG SINCE ABANDONED.
I CAN SEE HER! SHE IS ALIVE!
WHERE, PERCY? WHERE HAS HE TAKEN HER?
LABORATOR
INSIDE... THE SIGN SAYS "LABORATORY".
I KNOW WHAT HE SEES.
HE HAS TAKEN HER TO THE LABORATORY IN THE ABANDONED UNIVERSITY BY CORNAVIN!
YOU ARE GOING TO WANT THESE.

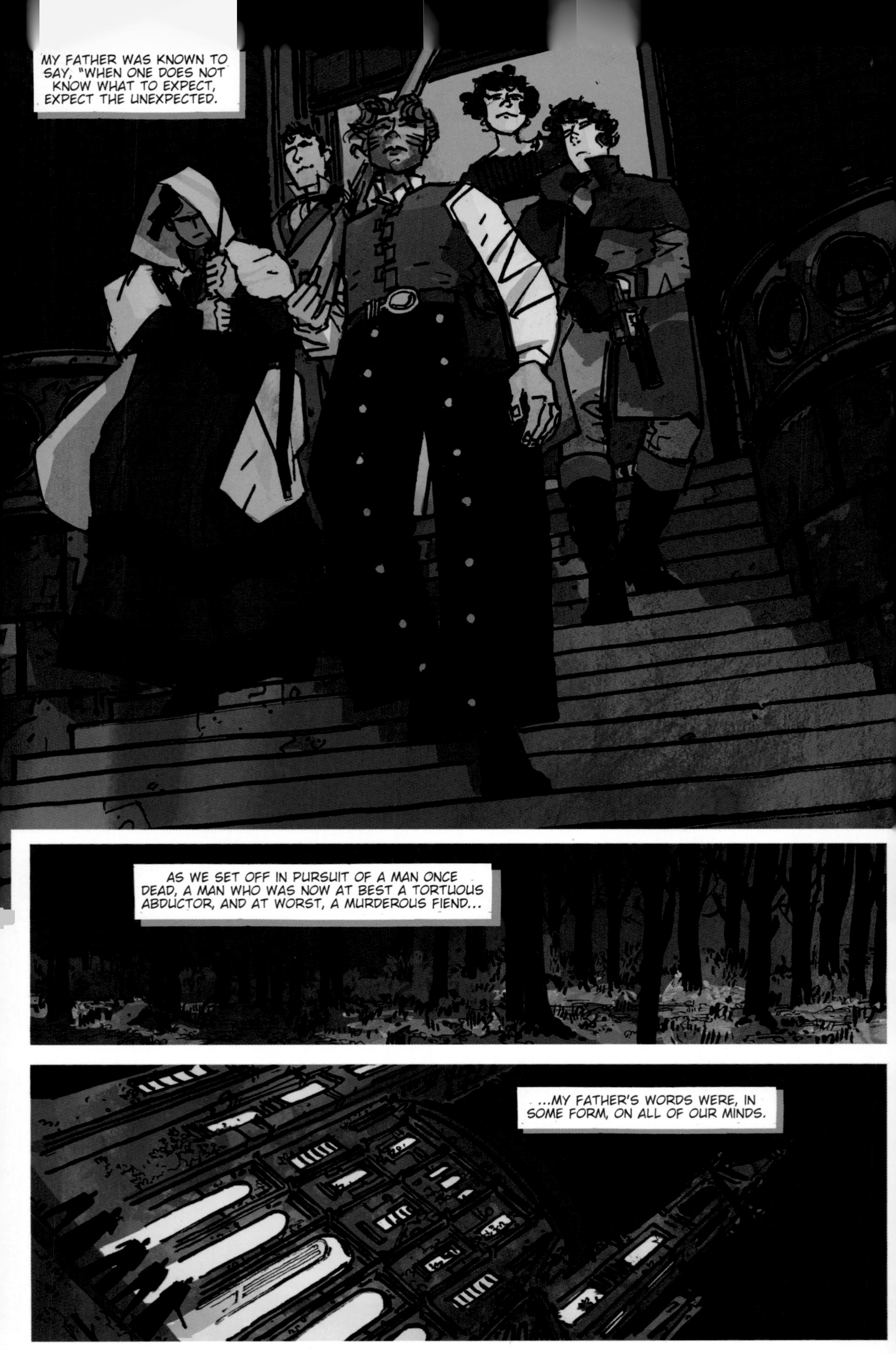
MY FATHER WAS KNOWN TO SAY, "WHEN ONE DOES NOT KNOW WHAT TO EXPECT, EXPECT THE UNEXPECTED.
AS WE SET OFF IN PURSUIT OF A MAN ONCE DEAD, A MAN WHO WAS NOW AT BEST A TORTUOUS ABDUCTOR, AND AT WORST, A MURDEROUS FIEND...
...MY FATHER'S WORDS WERE, IN SOME FORM, ON ALL OF OUR MINDS.

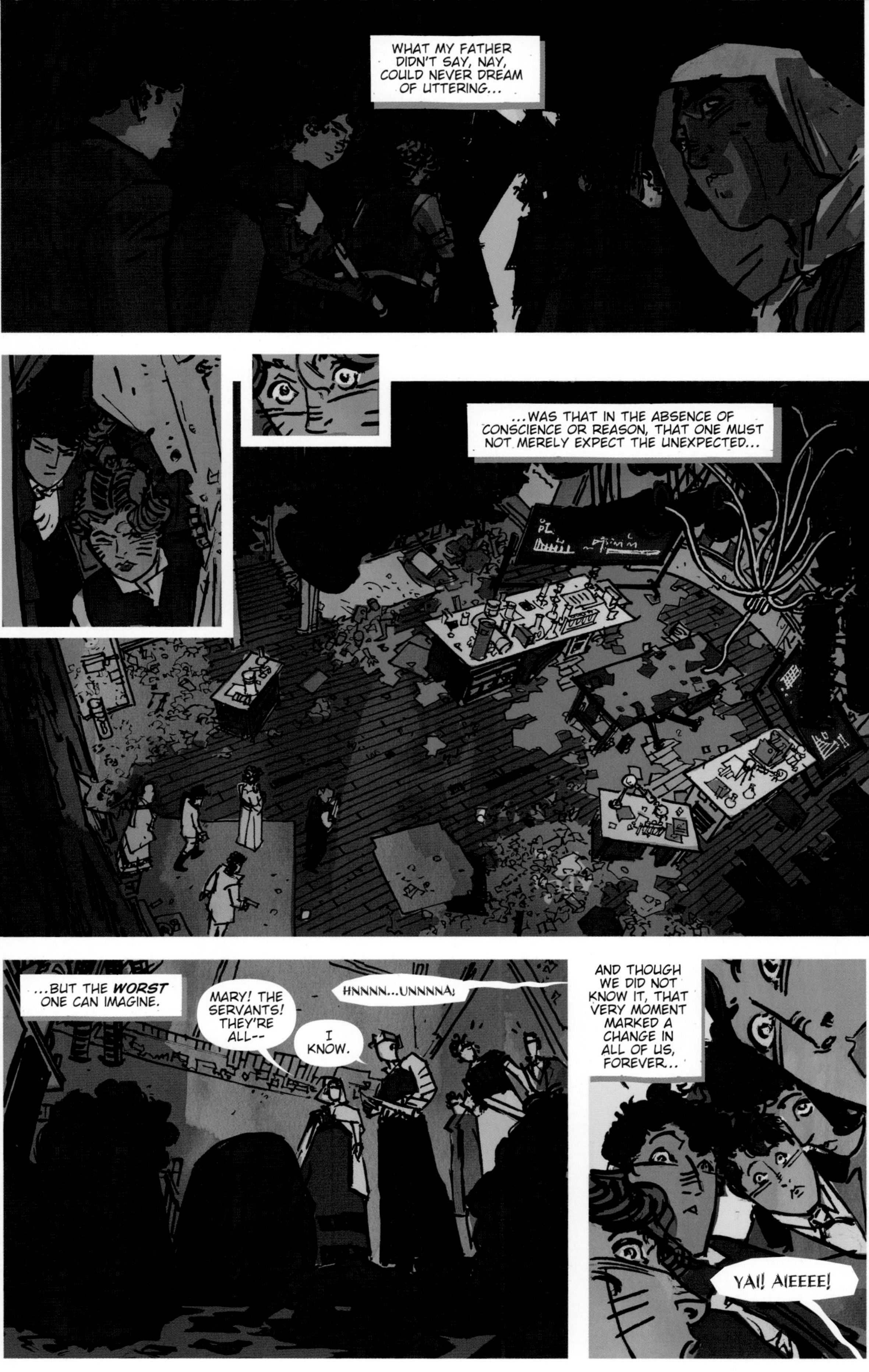
WHAT MY FATHER DIDN'T SAY, NAY, COULD NEVER DREAM OF UTTERING...
...WAS THAT IN THE ABSENCE OF CONSCIENCE OR REASON, THAT ONE MUST NOT MERELY EXPECT THE UNEXPECTED...
...BUT THE WORST ONE CAN IMAGINE.
MARY! THE SERVANTS! THEY'RE ALL--
HNNNN...UNNNNA!
I KNOW.
AND THOUGH WE DID NOT KNOW IT, THAT VERY MOMENT MARKED A CHANGE IN ALL OF US, FOREVER...
YAI! AIEEEE!

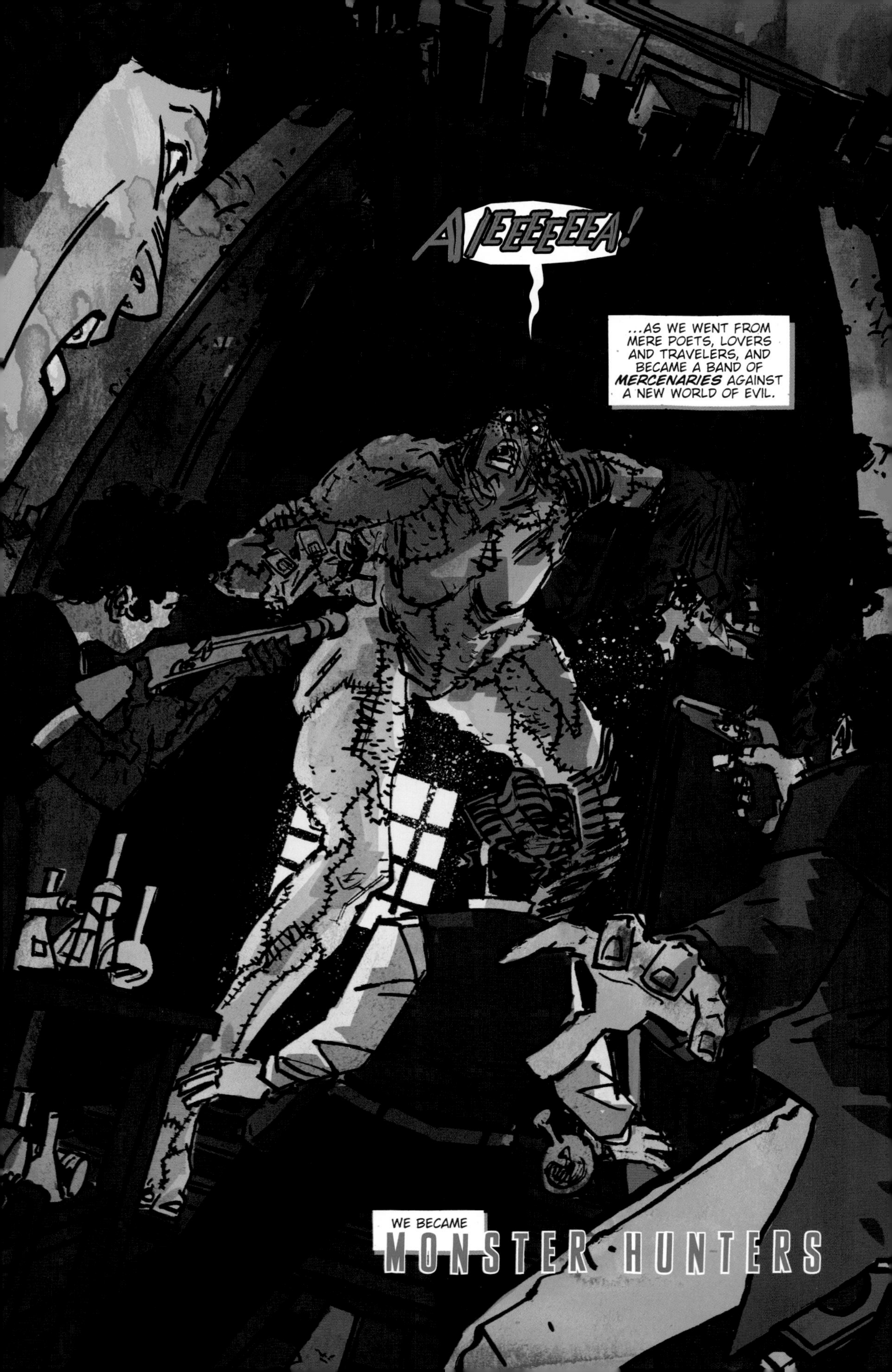
AIEEEEEEA!
...AS WE WENT FROM MERE POETS, LOVERS AND TRAVELERS, AND BECAME A BAND OF MERCENARIES AGAINST A NEW WORLD OF EVIL.
WE BECAME
MONSTER HUNTERS

5

EYE FOR AN EYE

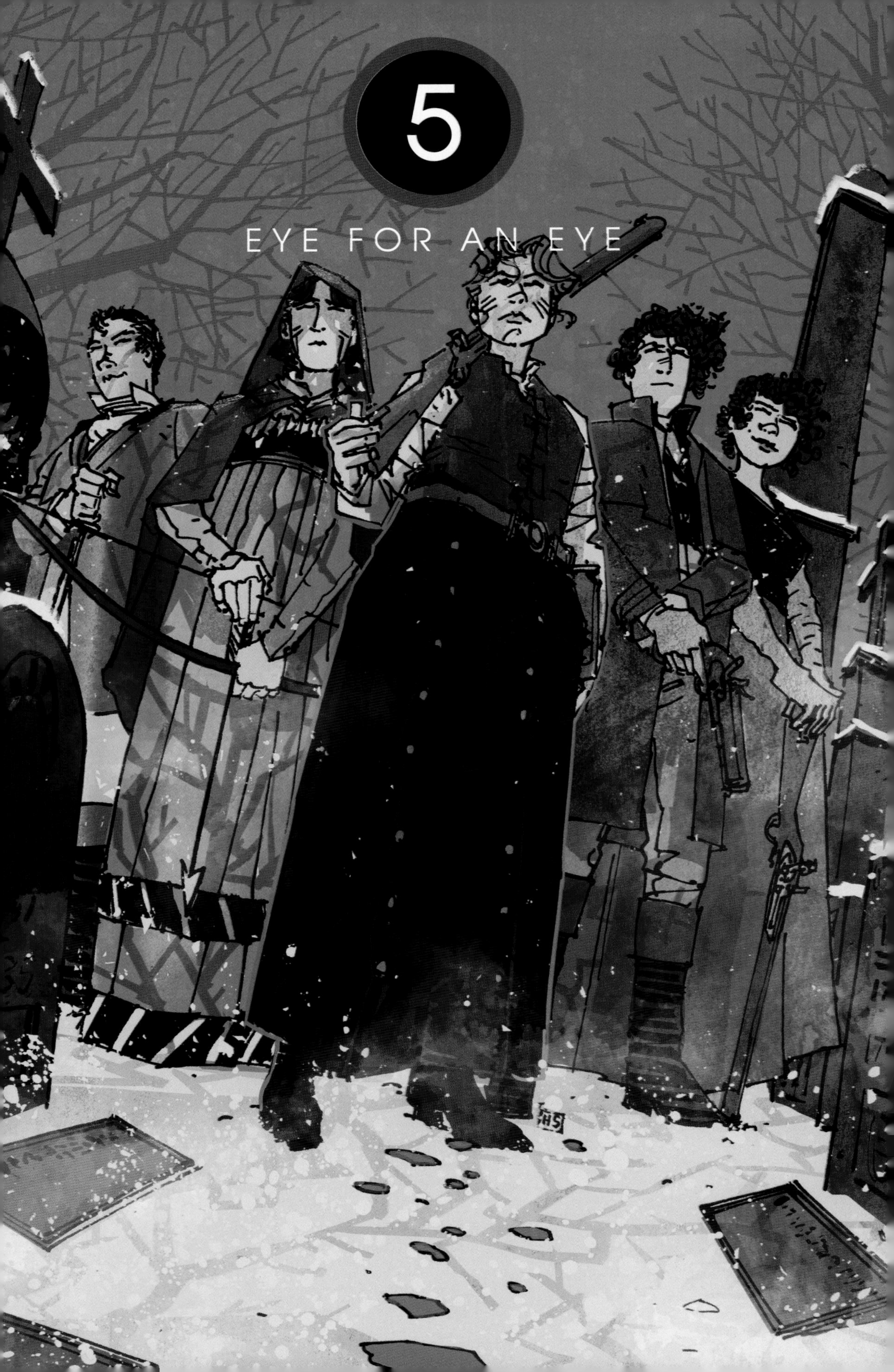

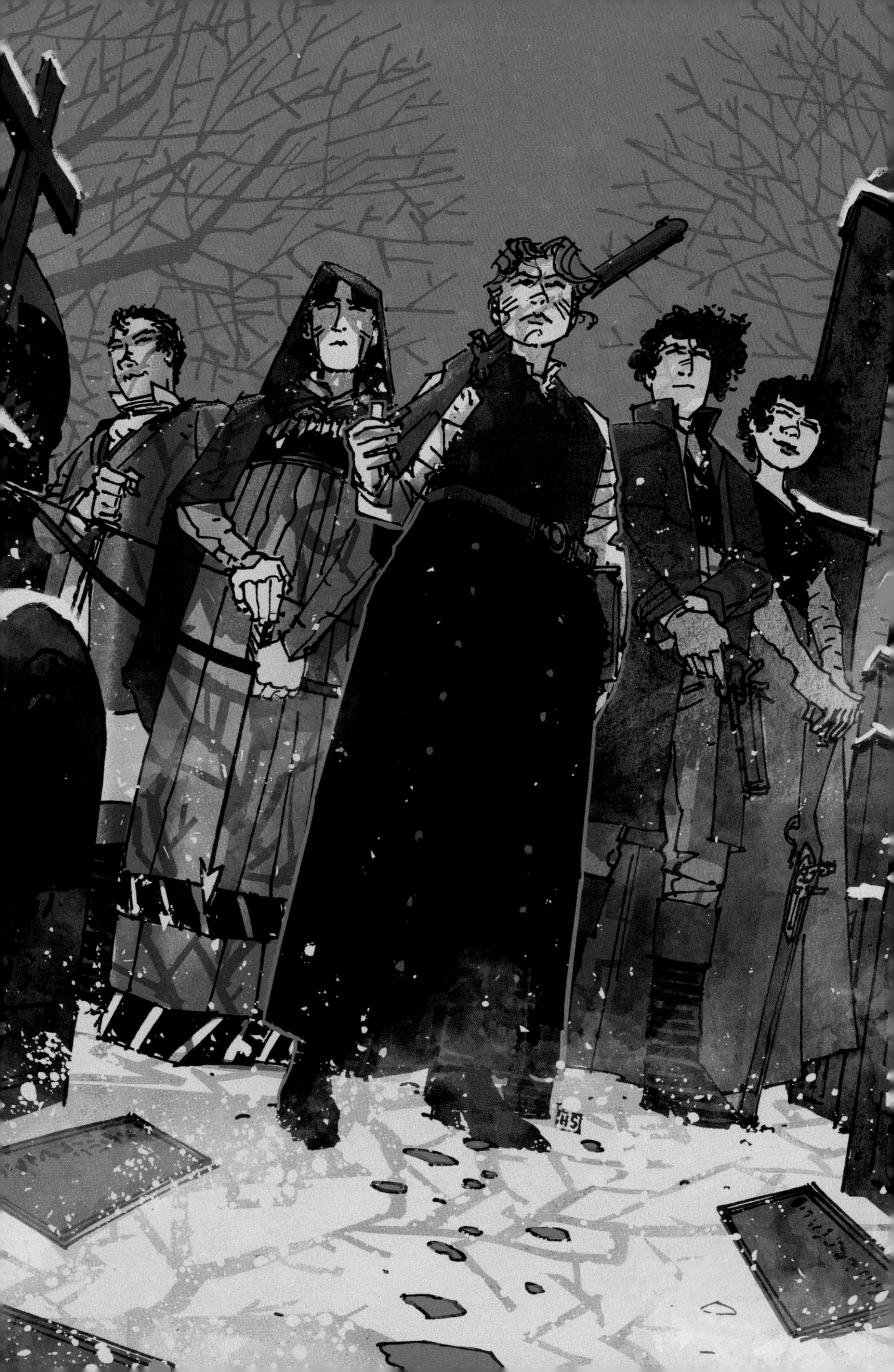

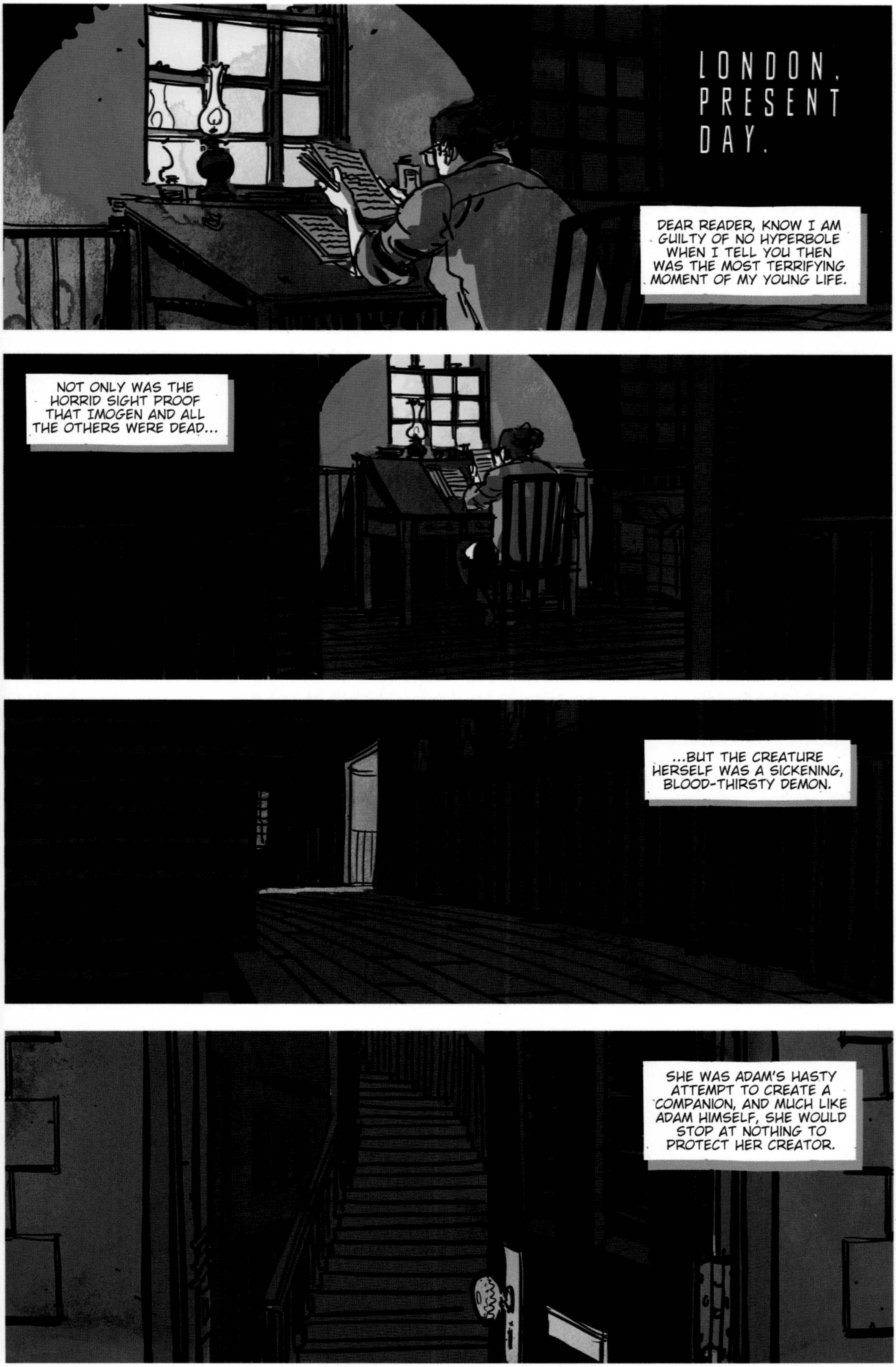
LONDON, PRESENT DAY.
DEAR READER, KNOW I AM GUILTY OF NO HYPERBOLE WHEN I TELL YOU THEN WAS THE MOST TERRIFYING MOMENT OF MY YOUNG LIFE.
NOT ONLY WAS THE HORRID SIGHT PROOF THAT IMOGEN AND ALL THE OTHERS WERE DEAD...
...BUT THE CREATURE HERSELF WAS A SICKENING, BLOOD-THIRSTY DEMON.
SHE WAS ADAM'S HASTY ATTEMPT TO CREATE A COMPANION, AND MUCH LIKE ADAM HIMSELF, SHE WOULD STOP AT NOTHING TO PROTECT HER CREATOR.

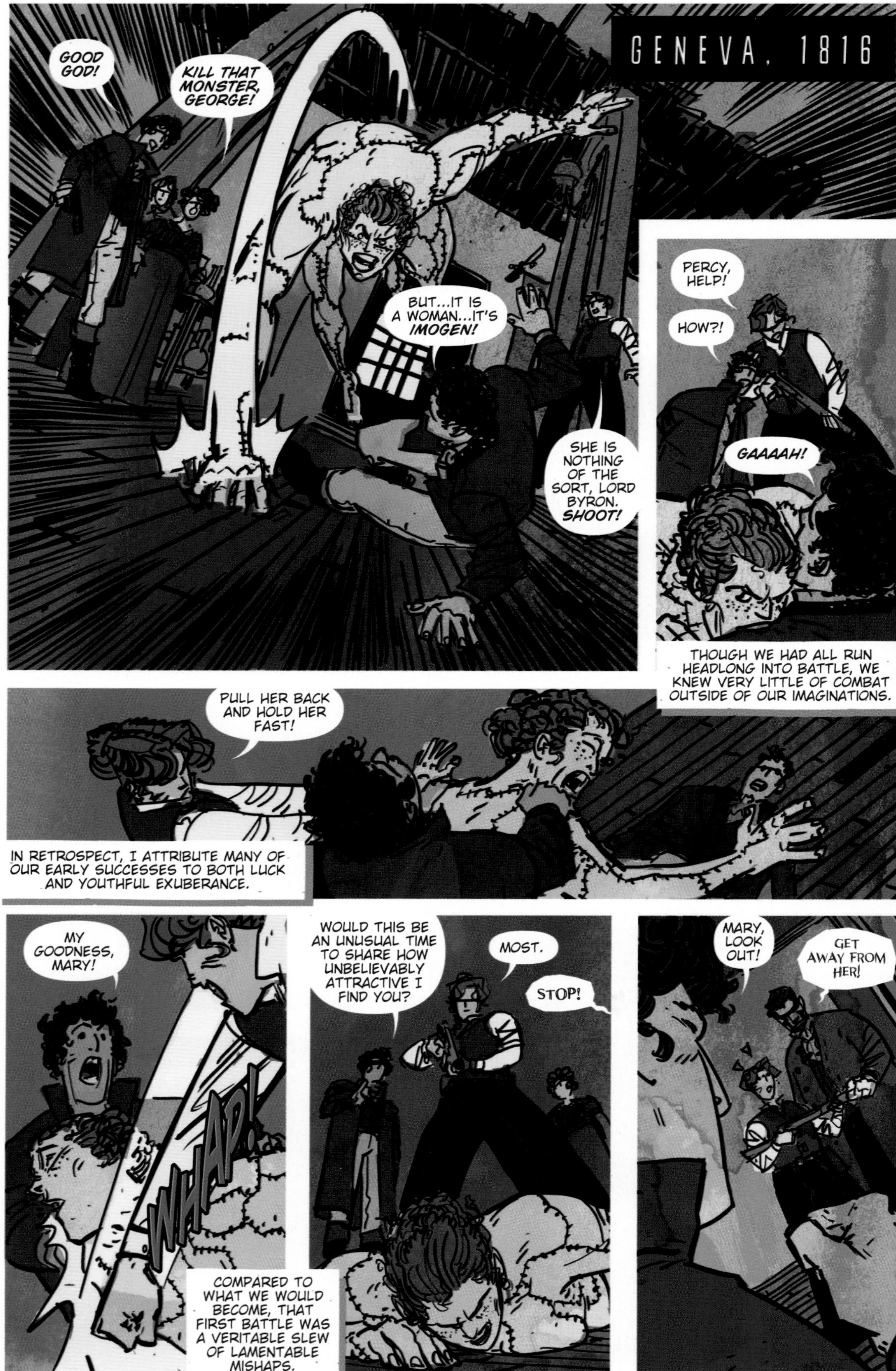
GENEVA, 1816
GOOD GOD!
KILL THAT MONSTER, GEORGE!
BUT...IT IS A WOMAN...IT'S IMOGEN!
SHE IS NOTHING OF THE SORT, LORD BYRON. SHOOT!
PERCY, HELP!
HOW?!
GAAAAH!
THOUGH WE HAD ALL RUN HEADLONG INTO BATTLE, WE KNEW VERY LITTLE OF COMBAT OUTSIDE OF OUR IMAGINATIONS.
PULL HER BACK AND HOLD HER FAST!
IN RETROSPECT, I ATTRIBUTE MANY OF OUR EARLY SUCCESSES TO BOTH LUCK AND YOUTHFUL EXUBERANCE.
MY GOODNESS, MARY!
WHAP!
COMPARED TO WHAT WE WOULD BECOME, THAT FIRST BATTLE WAS A VERITABLE SLEW OF LAMENTABLE MISHAPS.
WOULD THIS BE AN UNUSUAL TIME TO SHARE HOW UNBELIEVABLY ATTRACTIVE I FIND YOU?
MOST.
STOP!
MARY, LOOK OUT!
GET AWAY FROM HER!

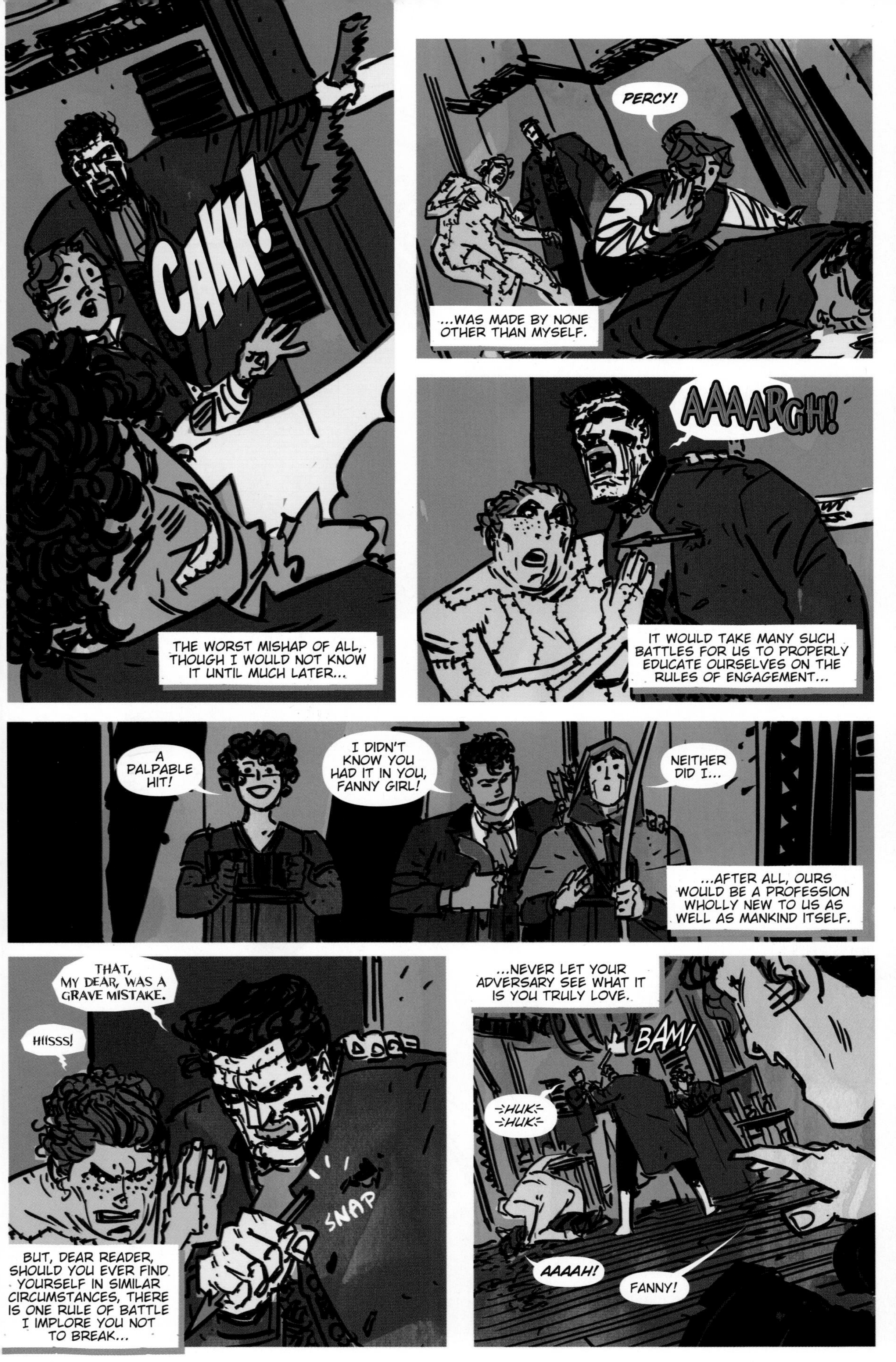
CAKK!
THE WORST MISHAP OF ALL, THOUGH I WOULD NOT KNOW IT UNTIL MUCH LATER...
PERCY!
...WAS MADE BY NONE OTHER THAN MYSELF.
AAAARGH!
IT WOULD TAKE MANY SUCH BATTLES FOR US TO PROPERLY EDUCATE OURSELVES ON THE RULES OF ENGAGEMENT...
A PALPABLE HIT!
I DIDN'T KNOW YOU HAD IT IN YOU, FANNY GIRL!
NEITHER DID I...
...AFTER ALL, OURS WOULD BE A PROFESSION WHOLLY NEW TO US AS WELL AS MANKIND ITSELF.
THAT, MY DEAR, WAS A GRAVE MISTAKE.
HIISSS!
SNAP
BUT, DEAR READER, SHOULD YOU EVER FIND YOURSELF IN SIMILAR CIRCUMSTANCES, THERE IS ONE RULE OF BATTLE I IMPLORE YOU NOT TO BREAK...
...NEVER LET YOUR ADVERSARY SEE WHAT IT IS YOU TRULY LOVE.
BAM!
HUK HUK
AAAAH!
FANNY!

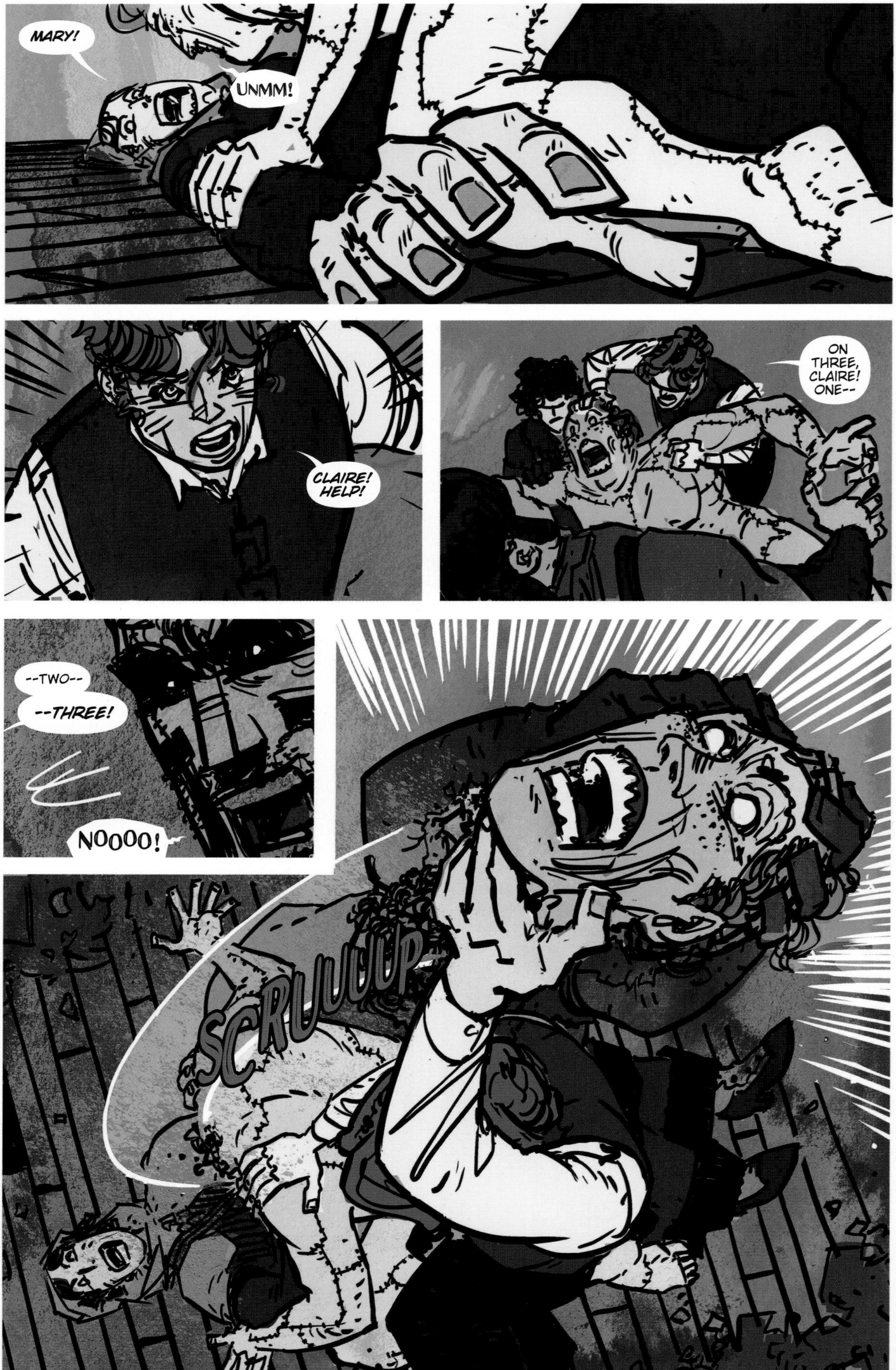
MARY!
UNMM!
CLAIRE! HELP!
ON THREE, CLAIRE! ONE--
--TWO--
--THREE!
NOOOO!
SCRUUUUP

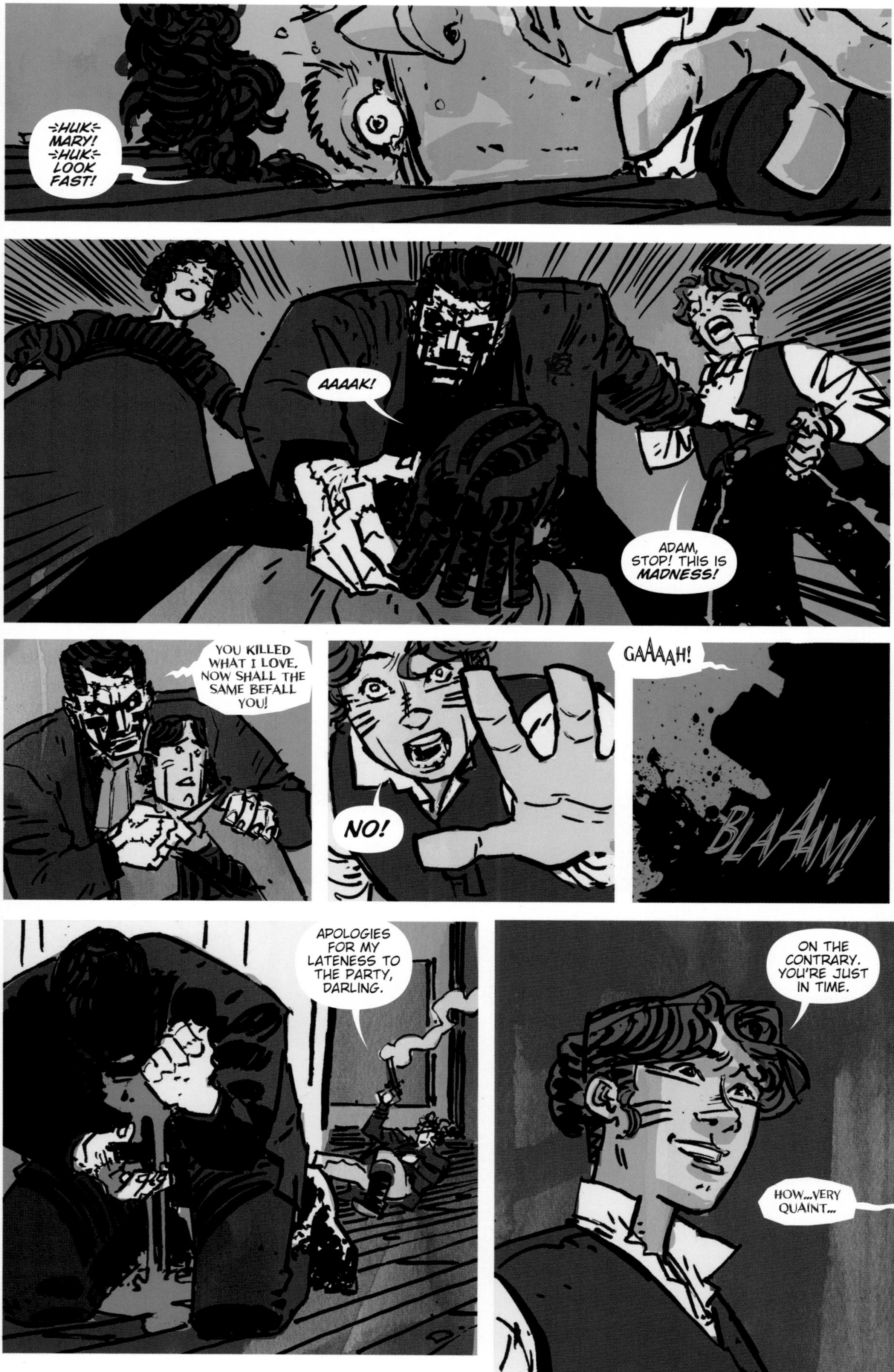

HUK MARY! HUK LOOK FAST!
AAAAK!
ADAM, STOP! THIS IS MADNESS!
YOU KILLED WHAT I LOVE. NOW SHALL THE SAME BEFALL YOU!
NO!
GAAAAH!
BLAAAM!
APOLOGIES FOR MY LATENESS TO THE PARTY, DARLING.
ON THE CONTRARY. YOU'RE JUST IN TIME.
HOW...VERY QUAINT...

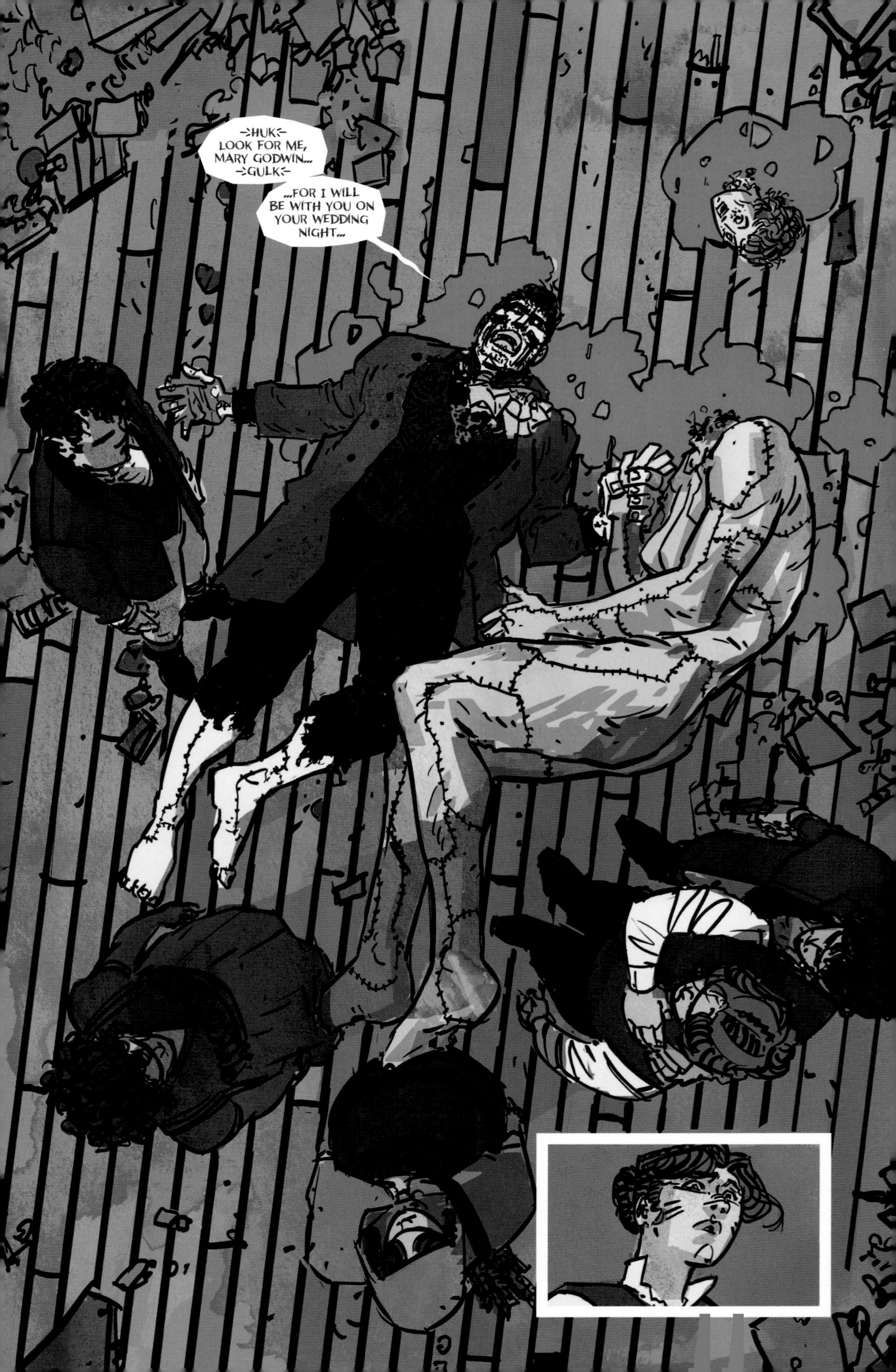
-HUK- LOOK FOR ME, MARY GODWIN... -GULK-
...FOR I WILL BE WITH YOU ON YOUR WEDDING NIGHT...

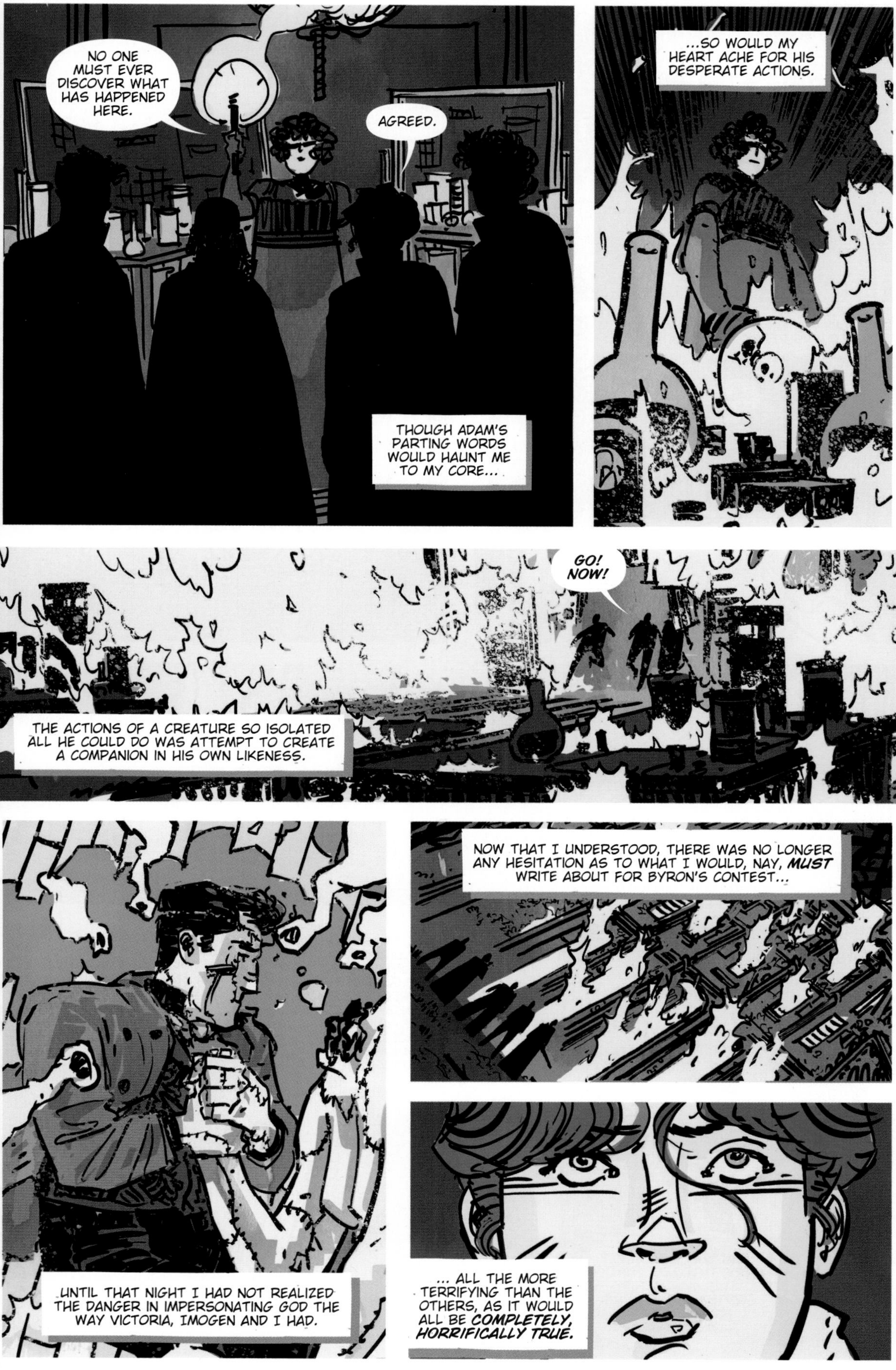
NO ONE MUST EVER DISCOVER WHAT HAS HAPPENED HERE.
AGREED.
THOUGH ADAM'S PARTING WORDS WOULD HAUNT ME TO MY CORE...
...SO WOULD MY HEART ACHE FOR HIS DESPERATE ACTIONS.
GO! NOW!
THE ACTIONS OF A CREATURE SO ISOLATED ALL HE COULD DO WAS ATTEMPT TO CREATE A COMPANION IN HIS OWN LIKENESS.
UNTIL THAT NIGHT I HAD NOT REALIZED THE DANGER IN IMPERSONATING GOD THE WAY VICTORIA, IMOGEN AND I HAD.
NOW THAT I UNDERSTOOD, THERE WAS NO LONGER ANY HESITATION AS TO WHAT I WOULD, NAY, ***MUST*** WRITE ABOUT FOR BYRON'S CONTEST...
... ALL THE MORE TERRIFYING THAN THE OTHERS, AS IT WOULD ALL BE ***COMPLETELY, HORRIFICALLY TRUE.***

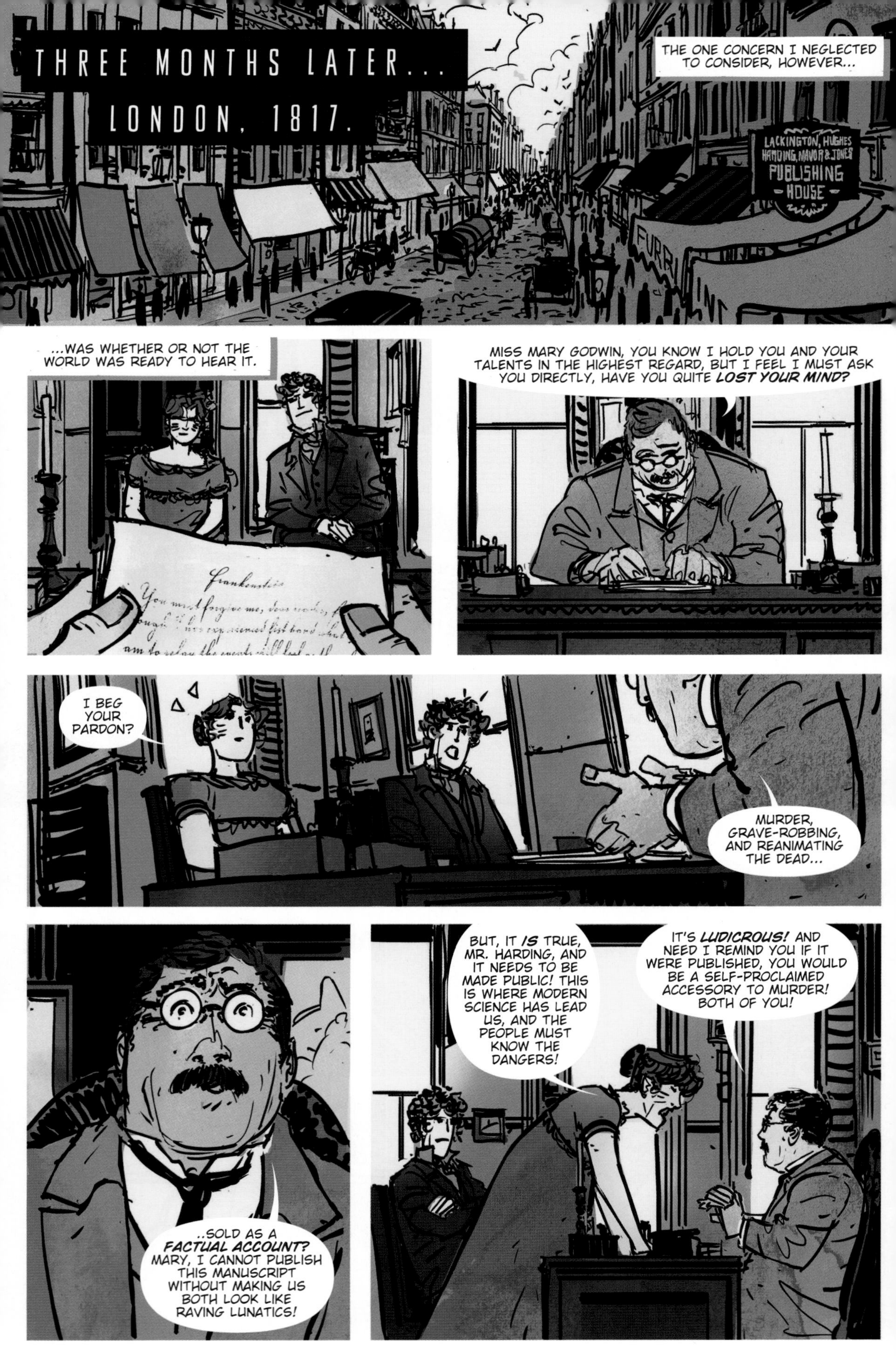
THREE MONTHS LATER...
LONDON, 1817.
THE ONE CONCERN I NEGLECTED TO CONSIDER, HOWEVER...
LACKINGTON, HUGHES HARDING, MAVOR & JONES PUBLISHING HOUSE
...WAS WHETHER OR NOT THE WORLD WAS READY TO HEAR IT.
Frankenstein
MISS MARY GODWIN, YOU KNOW I HOLD YOU AND YOUR TALENTS IN THE HIGHEST REGARD, BUT I FEEL I MUST ASK YOU DIRECTLY, HAVE YOU QUITE LOST YOUR MIND?
I BEG YOUR PARDON?
MURDER, GRAVE-ROBBING, AND REANIMATING THE DEAD...
..SOLD AS A FACTUAL ACCOUNT? MARY, I CANNOT PUBLISH THIS MANUSCRIPT WITHOUT MAKING US BOTH LOOK LIKE RAVING LUNATICS!
BUT, IT IS TRUE, MR. HARDING, AND IT NEEDS TO BE MADE PUBLIC! THIS IS WHERE MODERN SCIENCE HAS LEAD US, AND THE PEOPLE MUST KNOW THE DANGERS!
IT'S LUDICROUS! AND NEED I REMIND YOU IF IT WERE PUBLISHED, YOU WOULD BE A SELF-PROCLAIMED ACCESSORY TO MURDER! BOTH OF YOU!

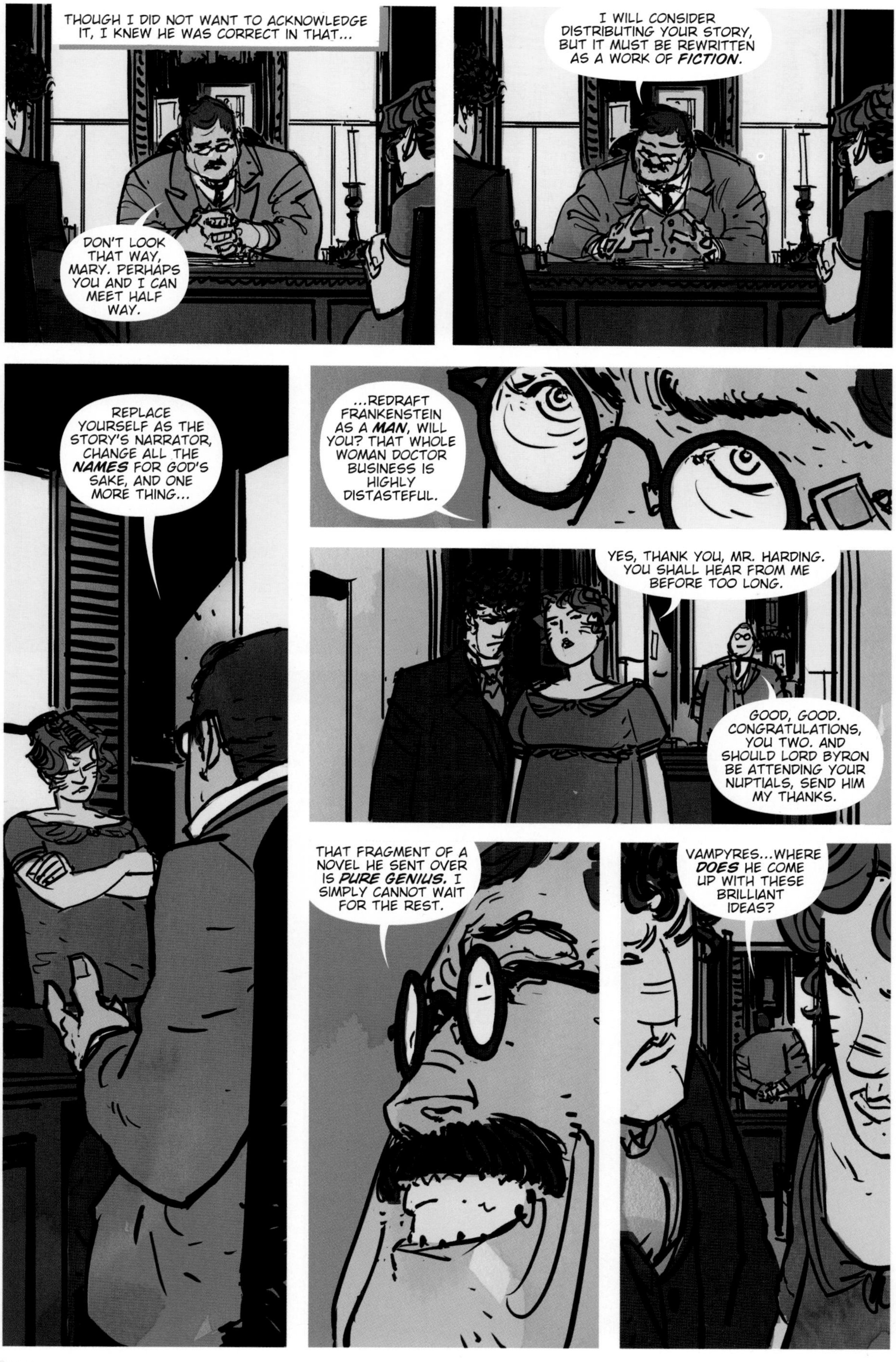
THOUGH I DID NOT WANT TO ACKNOWLEDGE IT, I KNEW HE WAS CORRECT IN THAT...
DON'T LOOK THAT WAY, MARY. PERHAPS YOU AND I CAN MEET HALF WAY.
I WILL CONSIDER DISTRIBUTING YOUR STORY, BUT IT MUST BE REWRITTEN AS A WORK OF *FICTION*.
REPLACE YOURSELF AS THE STORY'S NARRATOR, CHANGE ALL THE *NAMES* FOR GOD'S SAKE, AND ONE MORE THING...
...REDRAFT FRANKENSTEIN AS A *MAN*, WILL YOU? THAT WHOLE WOMAN DOCTOR BUSINESS IS HIGHLY DISTASTEFUL.
YES, THANK YOU, MR. HARDING. YOU SHALL HEAR FROM ME BEFORE TOO LONG.
GOOD, GOOD. CONGRATULATIONS, YOU TWO. AND SHOULD LORD BYRON BE ATTENDING YOUR NUPTIALS, SEND HIM MY THANKS.
THAT FRAGMENT OF A NOVEL HE SENT OVER IS *PURE GENIUS*. I SIMPLY CANNOT WAIT FOR THE REST.
VAMPYRES...WHERE *DOES* HE COME UP WITH THESE BRILLIANT IDEAS?

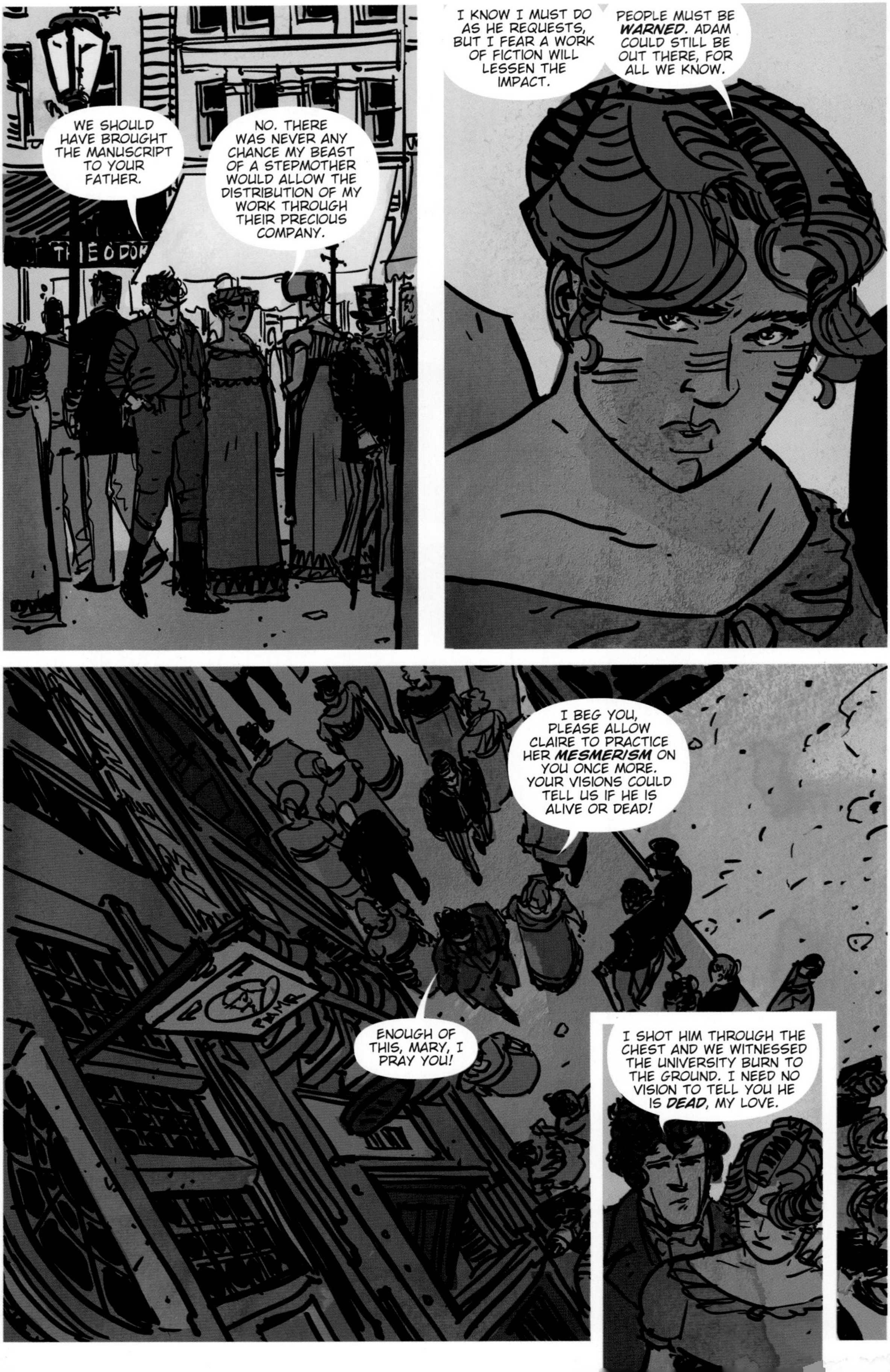
WE SHOULD HAVE BROUGHT THE MANUSCRIPT TO YOUR FATHER.
NO. THERE WAS NEVER ANY CHANCE MY BEAST OF A STEPMOTHER WOULD ALLOW THE DISTRIBUTION OF MY WORK THROUGH THEIR PRECIOUS COMPANY.
I KNOW I MUST DO AS HE REQUESTS, BUT I FEAR A WORK OF FICTION WILL LESSEN THE IMPACT.
PEOPLE MUST BE ***WARNED***. ADAM COULD STILL BE OUT THERE, FOR ALL WE KNOW.
I BEG YOU, PLEASE ALLOW CLAIRE TO PRACTICE HER ***MESMERISM*** ON YOU ONCE MORE. YOUR VISIONS COULD TELL US IF HE IS ALIVE OR DEAD!
ENOUGH OF THIS, MARY, I PRAY YOU!
I SHOT HIM THROUGH THE CHEST AND WE WITNESSED THE UNIVERSITY BURN TO THE GROUND. I NEED NO VISION TO TELL YOU HE IS ***DEAD***, MY LOVE.

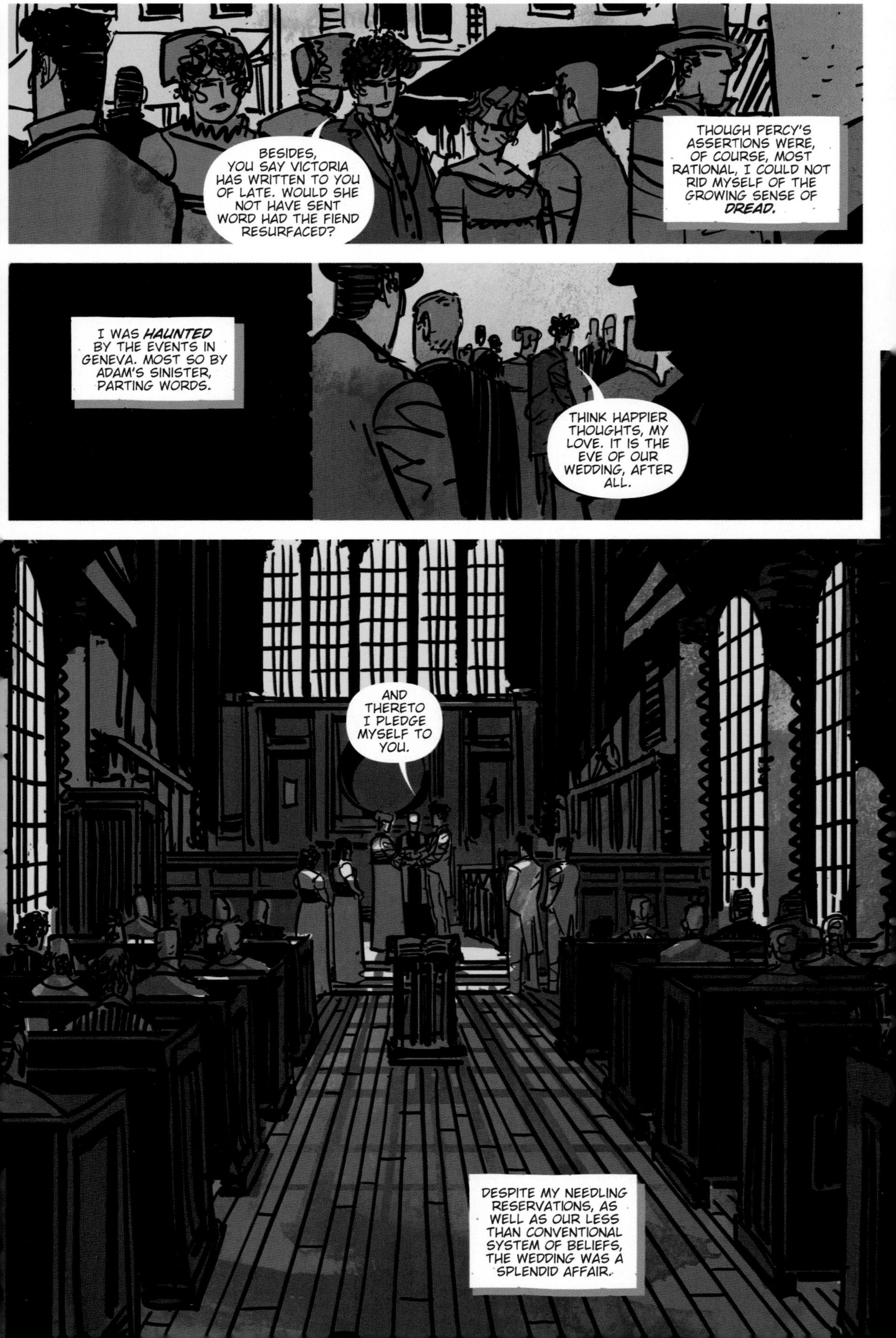
BESIDES, YOU SAY VICTORIA HAS WRITTEN TO YOU OF LATE. WOULD SHE NOT HAVE SENT WORD HAD THE FIEND RESURFACED?
THOUGH PERCY'S ASSERTIONS WERE, OF COURSE, MOST RATIONAL, I COULD NOT RID MYSELF OF THE GROWING SENSE OF *DREAD.*
I WAS *HAUNTED* BY THE EVENTS IN GENEVA. MOST SO BY ADAM'S SINISTER, PARTING WORDS.
THINK HAPPIER THOUGHTS, MY LOVE. IT IS THE EVE OF OUR WEDDING, AFTER ALL.
AND THERETO I PLEDGE MYSELF TO YOU.
DESPITE MY NEEDLING RESERVATIONS, AS WELL AS OUR LESS THAN CONVENTIONAL SYSTEM OF BELIEFS, THE WEDDING WAS A SPLENDID AFFAIR.

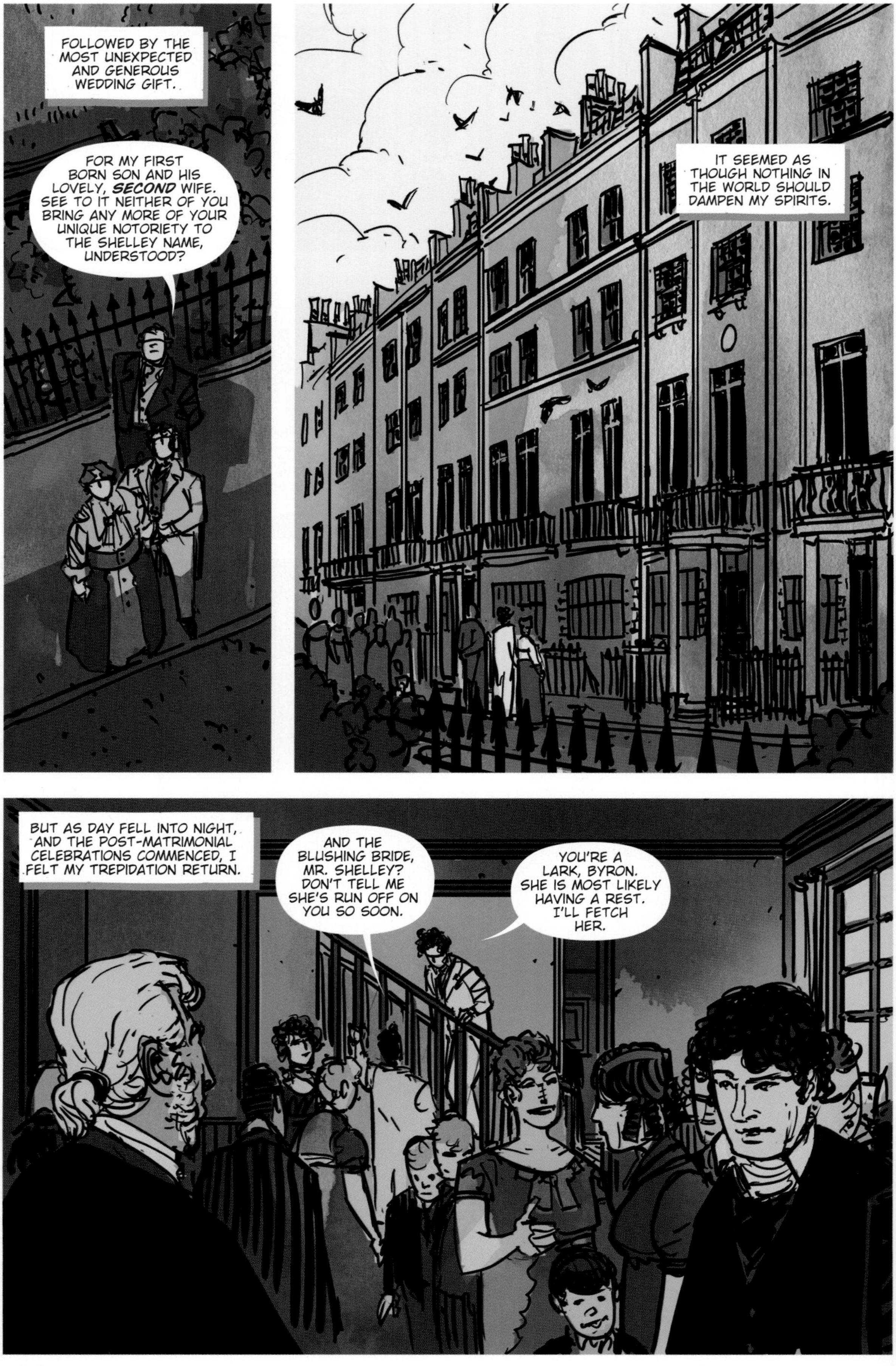
FOLLOWED BY THE MOST UNEXPECTED AND GENEROUS WEDDING GIFT.
FOR MY FIRST BORN SON AND HIS LOVELY, **SECOND** WIFE. SEE TO IT NEITHER OF YOU BRING ANY MORE OF YOUR UNIQUE NOTORIETY TO THE SHELLEY NAME, UNDERSTOOD?
IT SEEMED AS THOUGH NOTHING IN THE WORLD SHOULD DAMPEN MY SPIRITS.
BUT AS DAY FELL INTO NIGHT, AND THE POST-MATRIMONIAL CELEBRATIONS COMMENCED, I FELT MY TREPIDATION RETURN.
AND THE BLUSHING BRIDE, MR. SHELLEY? DON'T TELL ME SHE'S RUN OFF ON YOU SO SOON.
YOU'RE A LARK, BYRON. SHE IS MOST LIKELY HAVING A REST. I'LL FETCH HER.

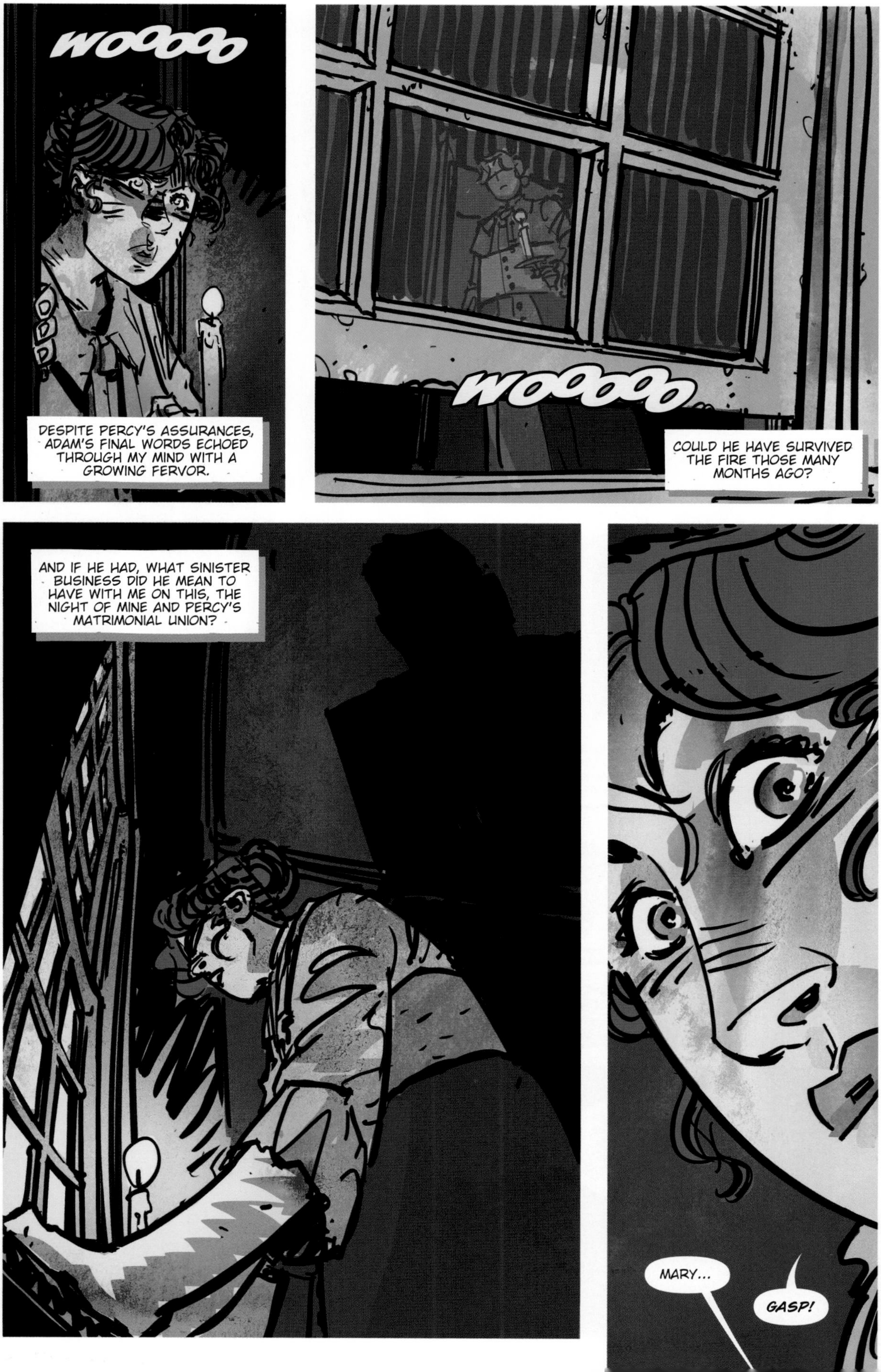
WOOOOO
DESPITE PERCY'S ASSURANCES, ADAM'S FINAL WORDS ECHOED THROUGH MY MIND WITH A GROWING FERVOR.
WOOOOO
COULD HE HAVE SURVIVED THE FIRE THOSE MANY MONTHS AGO?
AND IF HE HAD, WHAT SINISTER BUSINESS DID HE MEAN TO HAVE WITH ME ON THIS, THE NIGHT OF MINE AND PERCY'S MATRIMONIAL UNION?
MARY...
GASP!

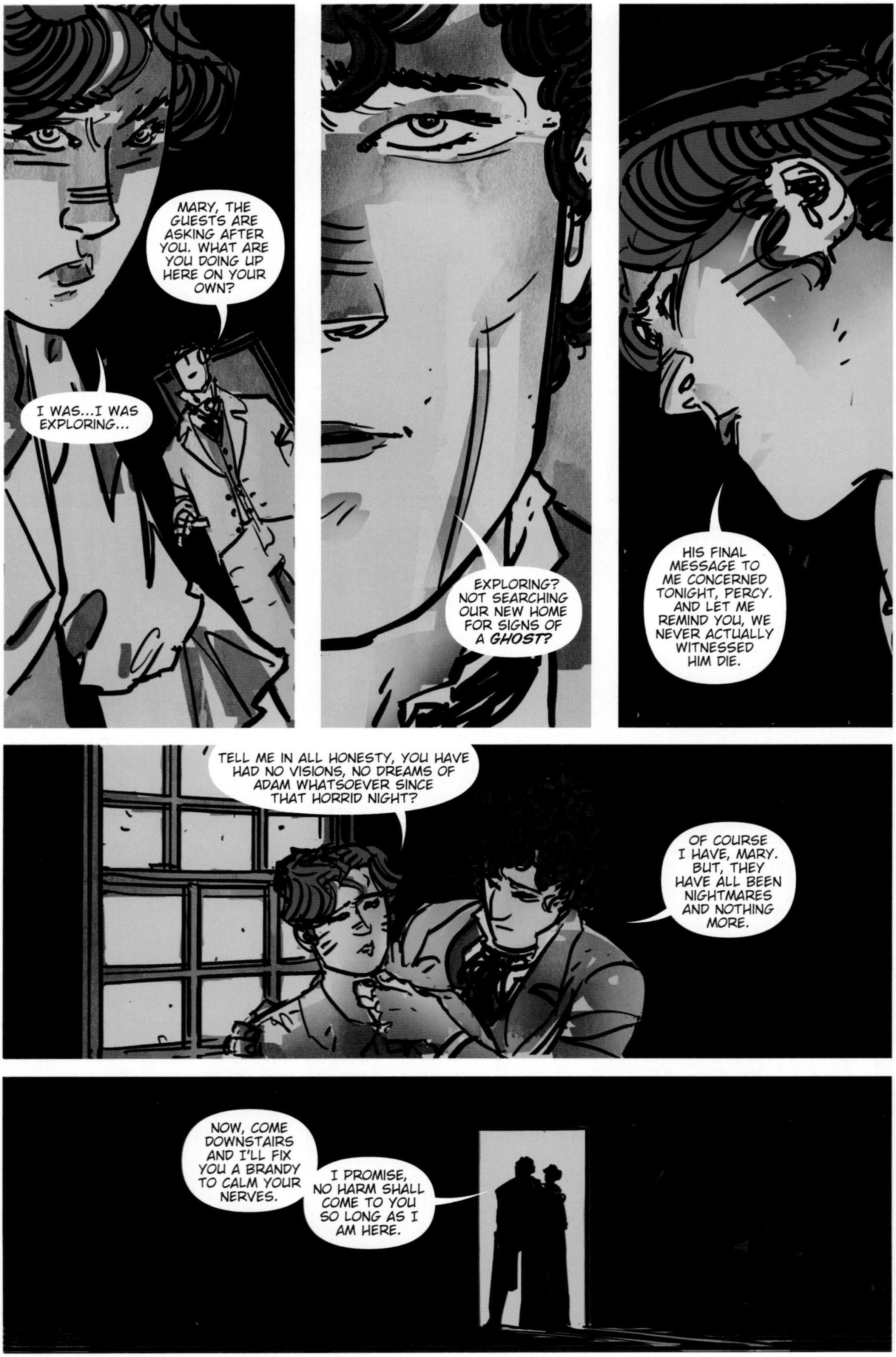
MARY, THE GUESTS ARE ASKING AFTER YOU. WHAT ARE YOU DOING UP HERE ON YOUR OWN?
I WAS...I WAS EXPLORING...
EXPLORING? NOT SEARCHING OUR NEW HOME FOR SIGNS OF A GHOST?
HIS FINAL MESSAGE TO ME CONCERNED TONIGHT, PERCY. AND LET ME REMIND YOU, WE NEVER ACTUALLY WITNESSED HIM DIE.
TELL ME IN ALL HONESTY, YOU HAVE HAD NO VISIONS, NO DREAMS OF ADAM WHATSOEVER SINCE THAT HORRID NIGHT?
OF COURSE I HAVE, MARY. BUT, THEY HAVE ALL BEEN NIGHTMARES AND NOTHING MORE.
NOW, COME DOWNSTAIRS AND I'LL FIX YOU A BRANDY TO CALM YOUR NERVES.
I PROMISE, NO HARM SHALL COME TO YOU SO LONG AS I AM HERE.

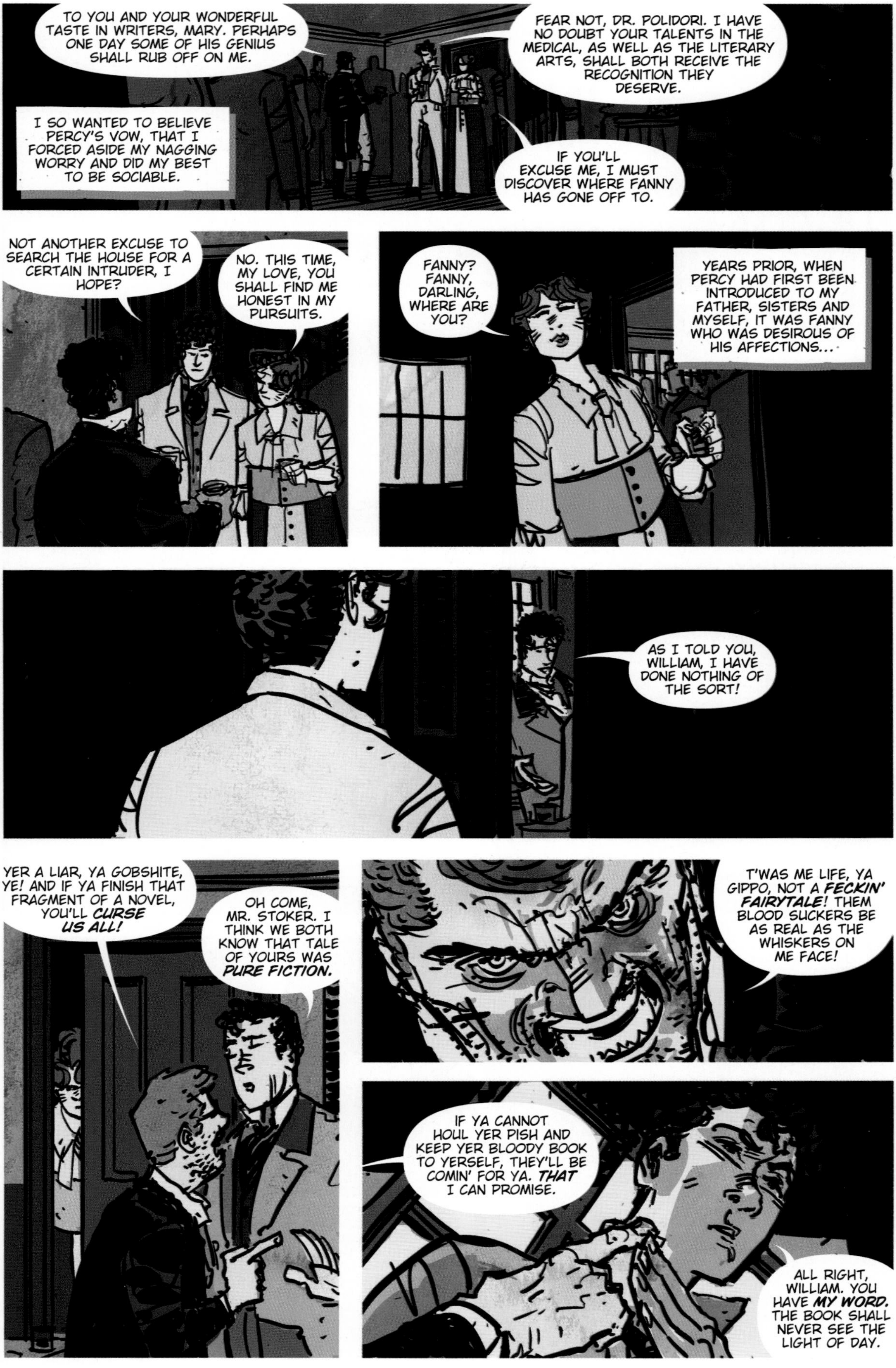
TO YOU AND YOUR WONDERFUL TASTE IN WRITERS, MARY. PERHAPS ONE DAY SOME OF HIS GENIUS SHALL RUB OFF ON ME.
FEAR NOT, DR. POLIDORI. I HAVE NO DOUBT YOUR TALENTS IN THE MEDICAL, AS WELL AS THE LITERARY ARTS, SHALL BOTH RECEIVE THE RECOGNITION THEY DESERVE.
I SO WANTED TO BELIEVE PERCY'S VOW, THAT I FORCED ASIDE MY NAGGING WORRY AND DID MY BEST TO BE SOCIABLE.
IF YOU'LL EXCUSE ME, I MUST DISCOVER WHERE FANNY HAS GONE OFF TO.
NOT ANOTHER EXCUSE TO SEARCH THE HOUSE FOR A CERTAIN INTRUDER, I HOPE?
NO. THIS TIME, MY LOVE, YOU SHALL FIND ME HONEST IN MY PURSUITS.
FANNY? FANNY, DARLING, WHERE ARE YOU?
YEARS PRIOR, WHEN PERCY HAD FIRST BEEN INTRODUCED TO MY FATHER, SISTERS AND MYSELF, IT WAS FANNY WHO WAS DESIROUS OF HIS AFFECTIONS...
AS I TOLD YOU, WILLIAM, I HAVE DONE NOTHING OF THE SORT!
YER A LIAR, YA GOBSHITE, YE! AND IF YA FINISH THAT FRAGMENT OF A NOVEL, YOU'LL ***CURSE US ALL!***
OH COME, MR. STOKER. I THINK WE BOTH KNOW THAT TALE OF YOURS WAS ***PURE FICTION.***
T'WAS ME LIFE, YA GIPPO, NOT A ***FECKIN' FAIRYTALE!*** THEM BLOOD SUCKERS BE AS REAL AS THE WHISKERS ON ME FACE!
IF YA CANNOT HOUL YER PISH AND KEEP YER BLOODY BOOK TO YERSELF, THEY'LL BE COMIN' FOR YA. ***THAT*** I CAN PROMISE.
ALL RIGHT, WILLIAM. YOU HAVE ***MY WORD.*** THE BOOK SHALL NEVER SEE THE LIGHT OF DAY.

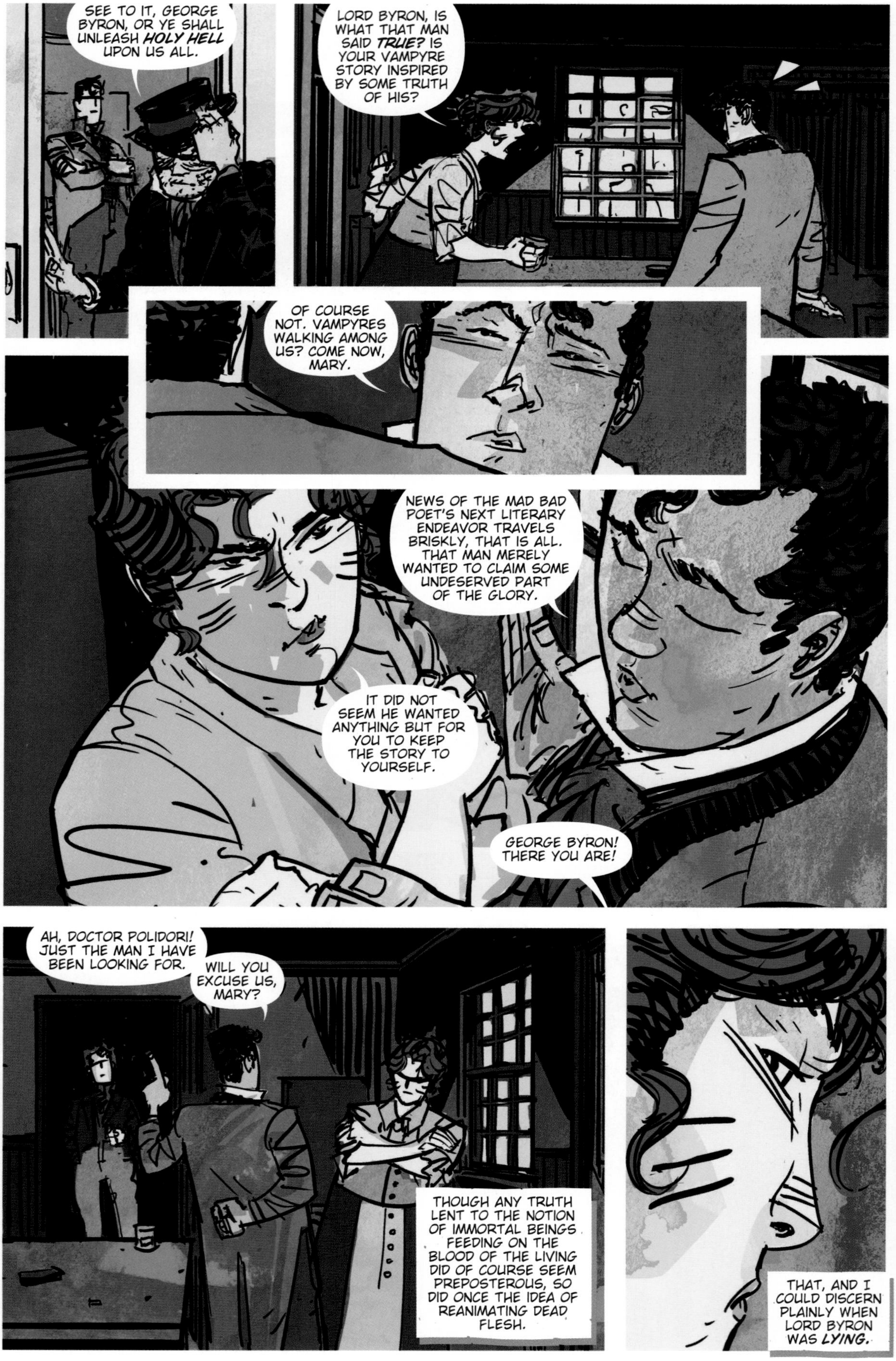
SEE TO IT, GEORGE BYRON, OR YE SHALL UNLEASH HOLY HELL UPON US ALL.
LORD BYRON, IS WHAT THAT MAN SAID TRUE? IS YOUR VAMPYRE STORY INSPIRED BY SOME TRUTH OF HIS?
OF COURSE NOT. VAMPYRES WALKING AMONG US? COME NOW, MARY.
NEWS OF THE MAD BAD POET'S NEXT LITERARY ENDEAVOR TRAVELS BRISKLY, THAT IS ALL. THAT MAN MERELY WANTED TO CLAIM SOME UNDESERVED PART OF THE GLORY.
IT DID NOT SEEM HE WANTED ANYTHING BUT FOR YOU TO KEEP THE STORY TO YOURSELF.
GEORGE BYRON! THERE YOU ARE!
AH, DOCTOR POLIDORI! JUST THE MAN I HAVE BEEN LOOKING FOR.
WILL YOU EXCUSE US, MARY?
THOUGH ANY TRUTH LENT TO THE NOTION OF IMMORTAL BEINGS FEEDING ON THE BLOOD OF THE LIVING DID OF COURSE SEEM PREPOSTEROUS, SO DID ONCE THE IDEA OF REANIMATING DEAD FLESH.
THAT, AND I COULD DISCERN PLAINLY WHEN LORD BYRON WAS LYING.

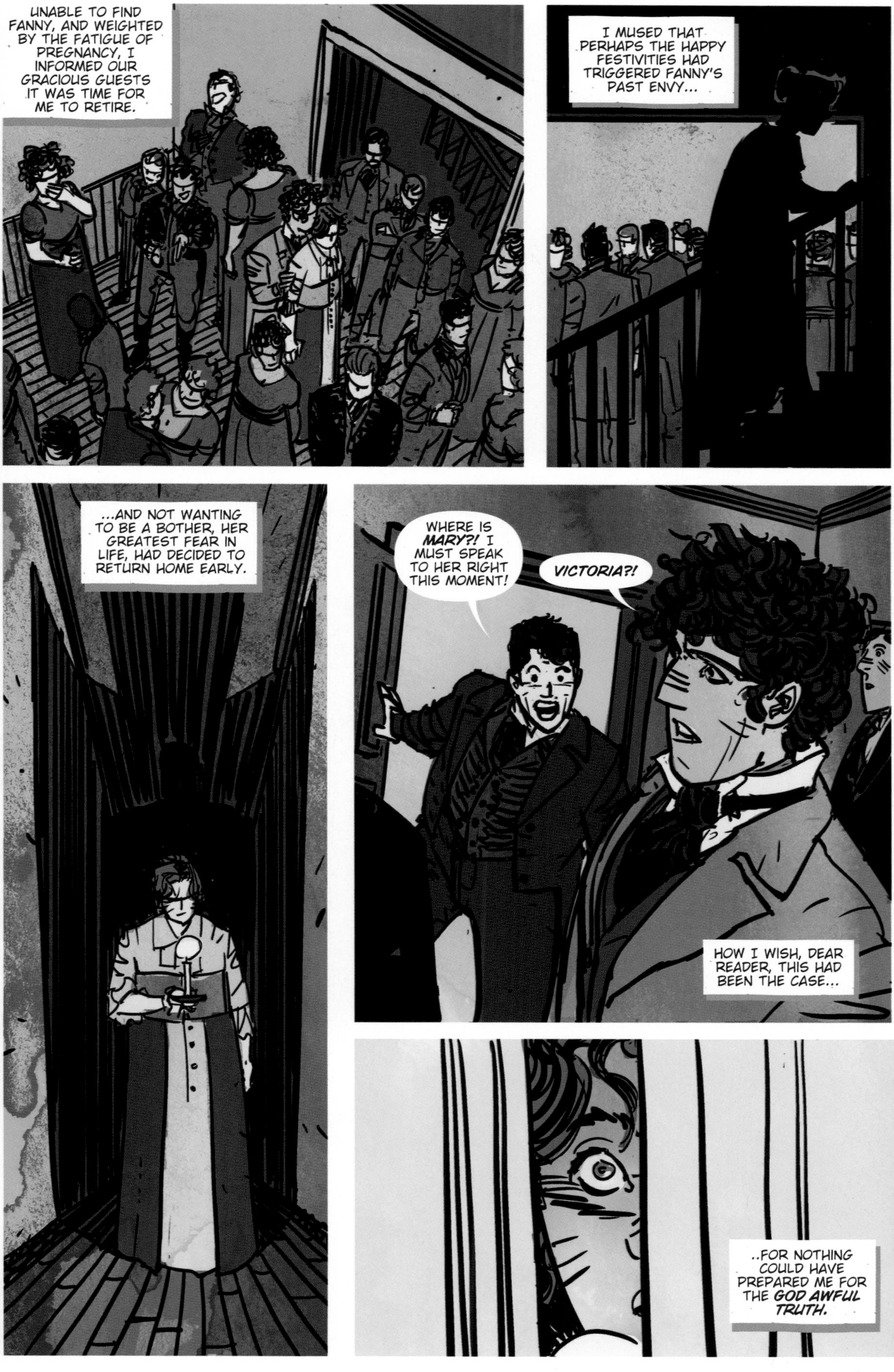
UNABLE TO FIND FANNY, AND WEIGHTED BY THE FATIGUE OF PREGNANCY, I INFORMED OUR GRACIOUS GUESTS IT WAS TIME FOR ME TO RETIRE.
I MUSED THAT PERHAPS THE HAPPY FESTIVITIES HAD TRIGGERED FANNY'S PAST ENVY...
...AND NOT WANTING TO BE A BOTHER, HER GREATEST FEAR IN LIFE, HAD DECIDED TO RETURN HOME EARLY.
WHERE IS MARY?! I MUST SPEAK TO HER RIGHT THIS MOMENT!
VICTORIA?!
HOW I WISH, DEAR READER, THIS HAD BEEN THE CASE...
..FOR NOTHING COULD HAVE PREPARED ME FOR THE GOD AWFUL TRUTH.

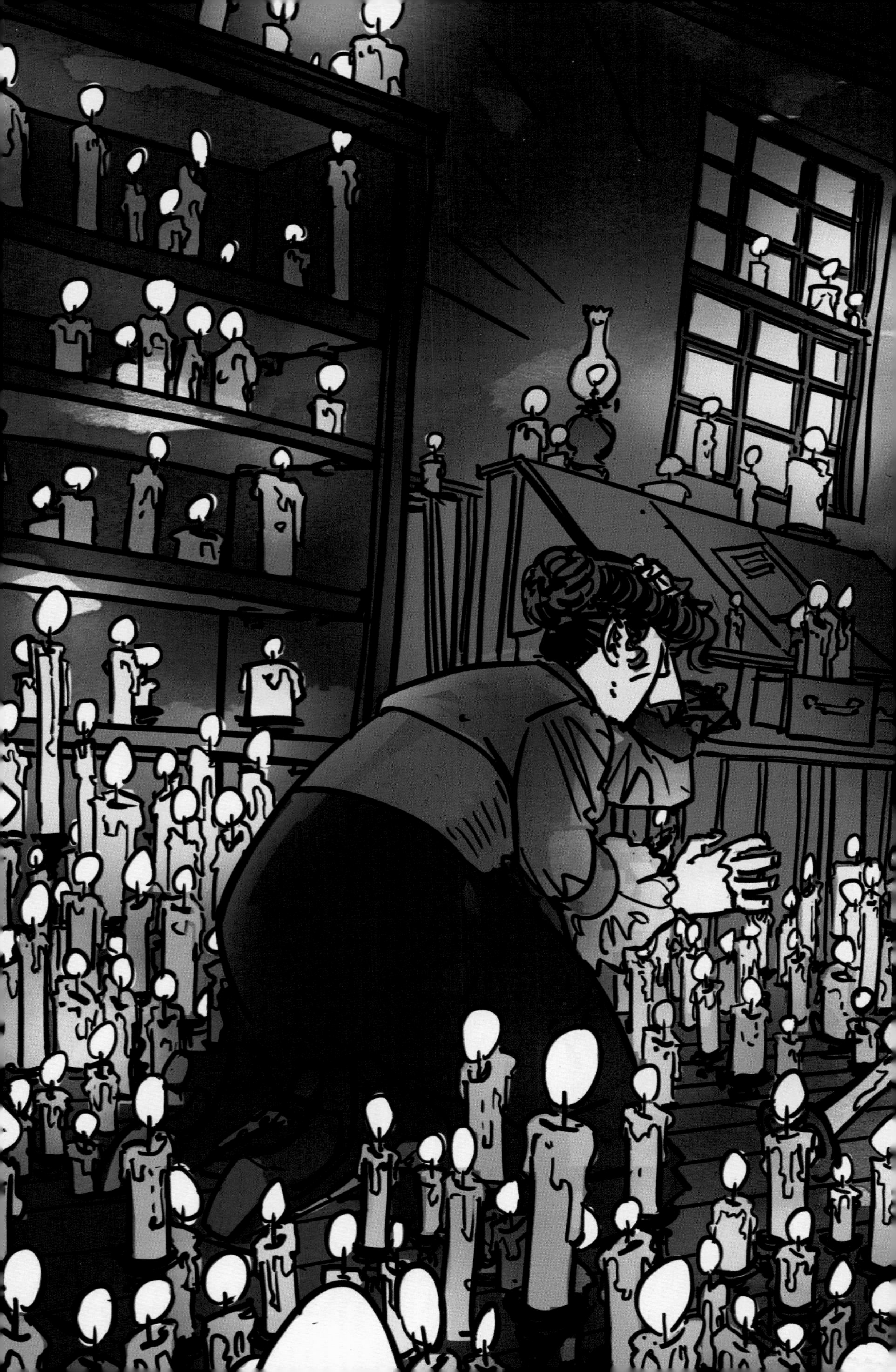

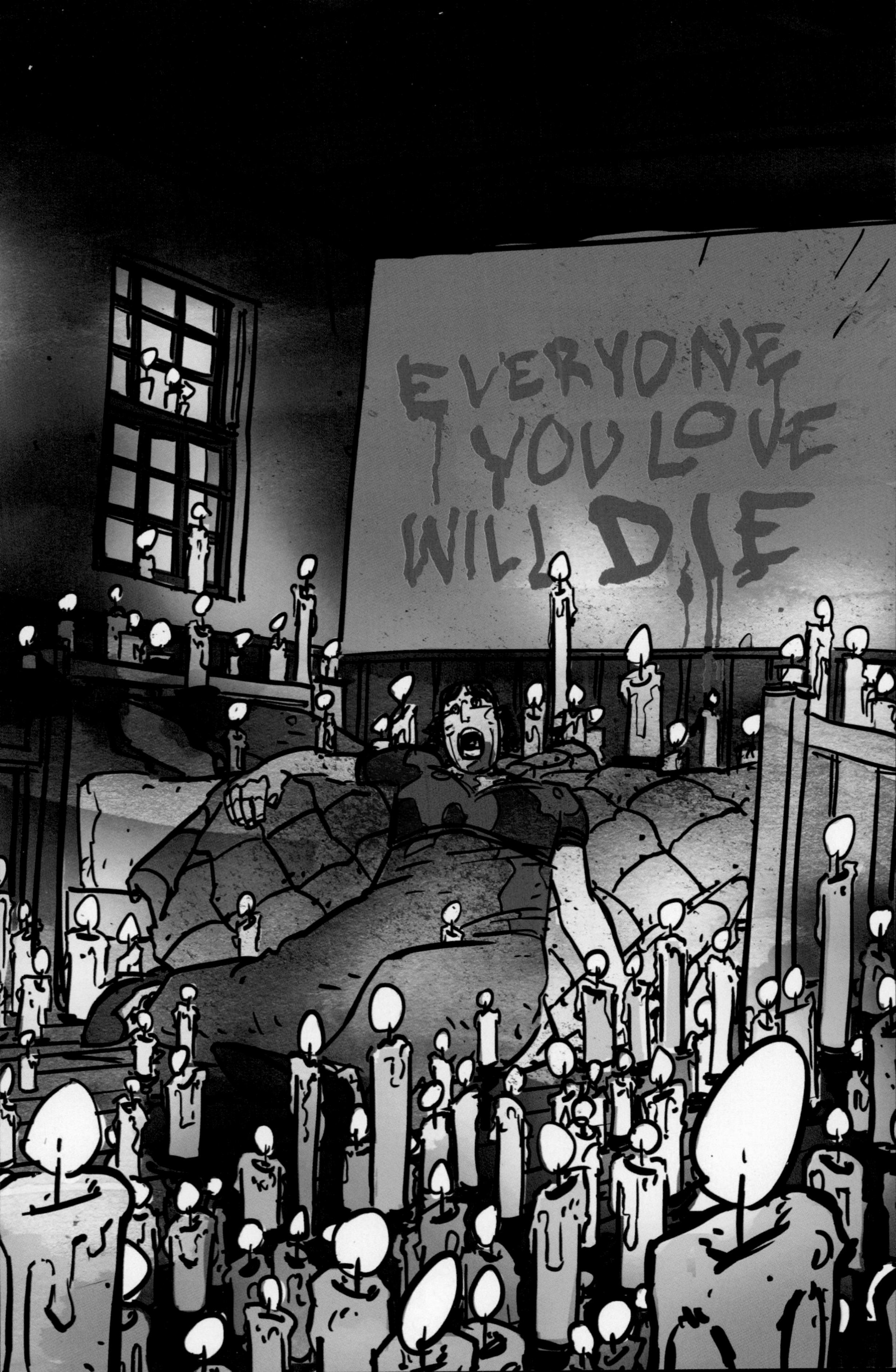
EVERYONE YOU LOVE WILL DIE

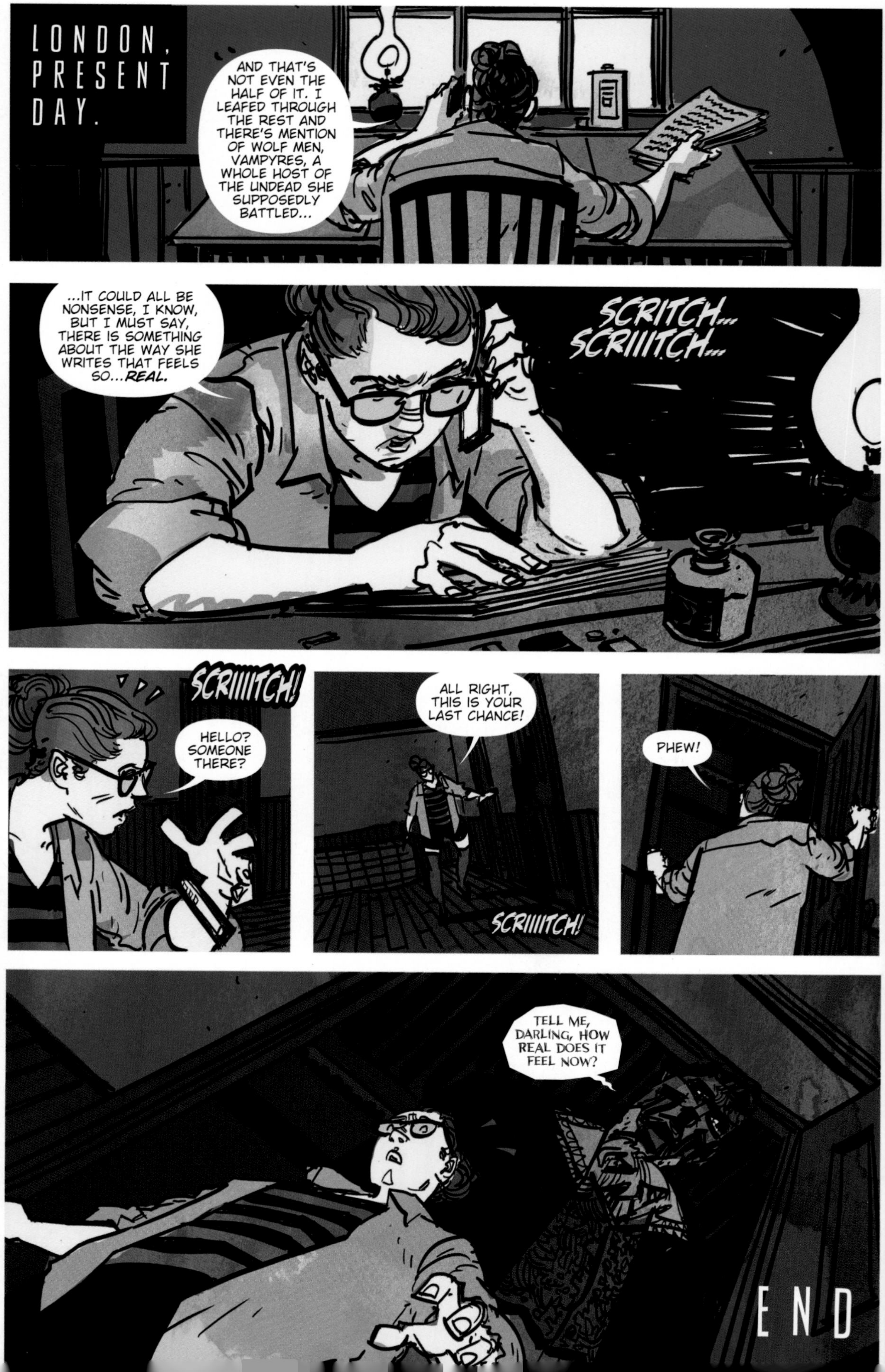
LONDON, PRESENT DAY.
AND THAT'S NOT EVEN THE HALF OF IT. I LEAFED THROUGH THE REST AND THERE'S MENTION OF WOLF MEN, VAMPYRES, A WHOLE HOST OF THE UNDEAD SHE SUPPOSEDLY BATTLED...
...IT COULD ALL BE NONSENSE, I KNOW, BUT I MUST SAY, THERE IS SOMETHING ABOUT THE WAY SHE WRITES THAT FEELS SO...REAL.
SCRITCH... SCRIIITCH...
SCRIIIITCH!
HELLO? SOMEONE THERE?
ALL RIGHT, THIS IS YOUR LAST CHANCE!
SCRIIIITCH!
PHEW!
TELL ME, DARLING, HOW REAL DOES IT FEEL NOW?
END

Mary Shelley MONSTERHUNTER ™

BEHIND THE SCENES

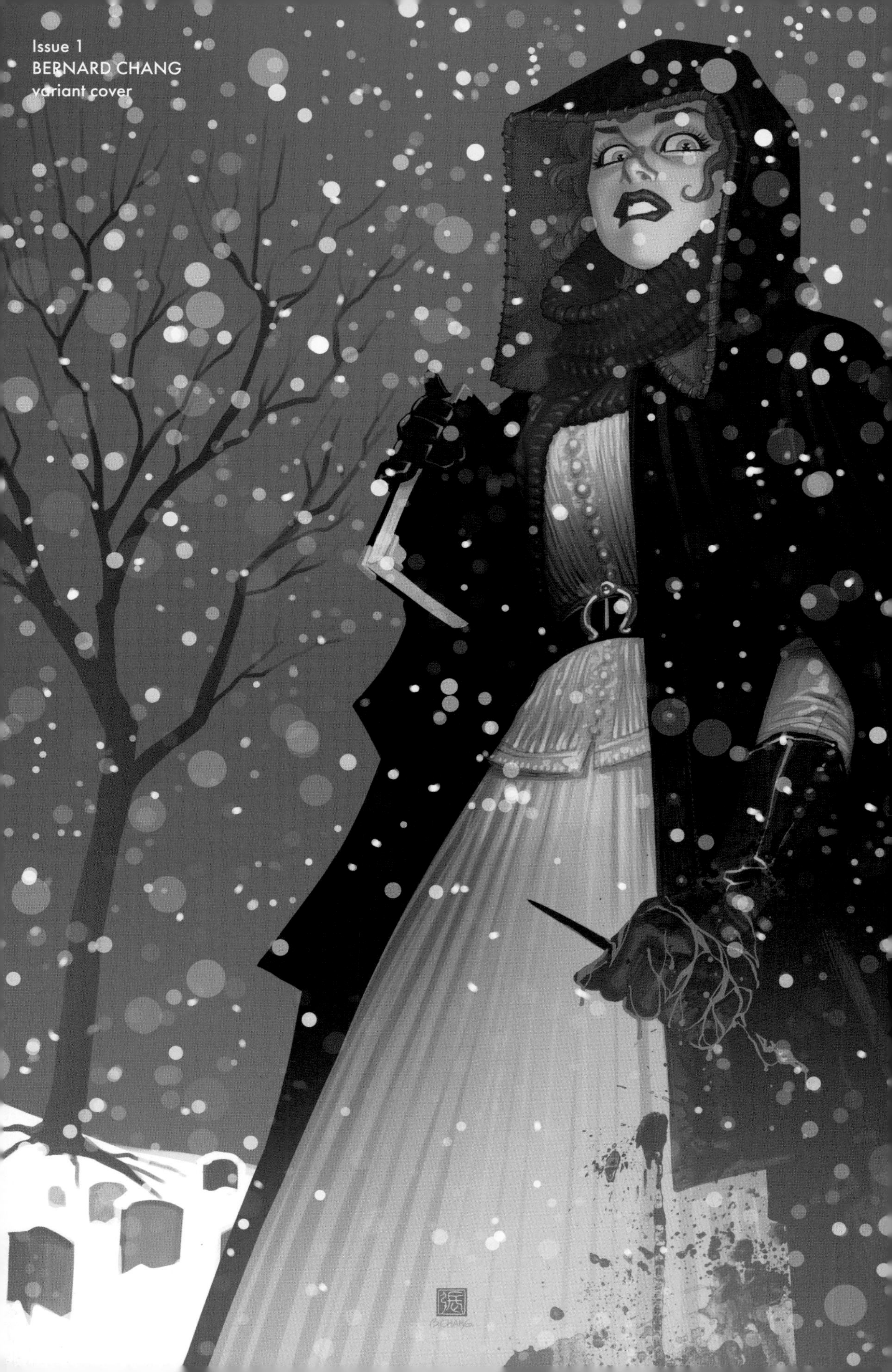
B.CHANG

Issue 1
BERNARD CHANG
variant cover

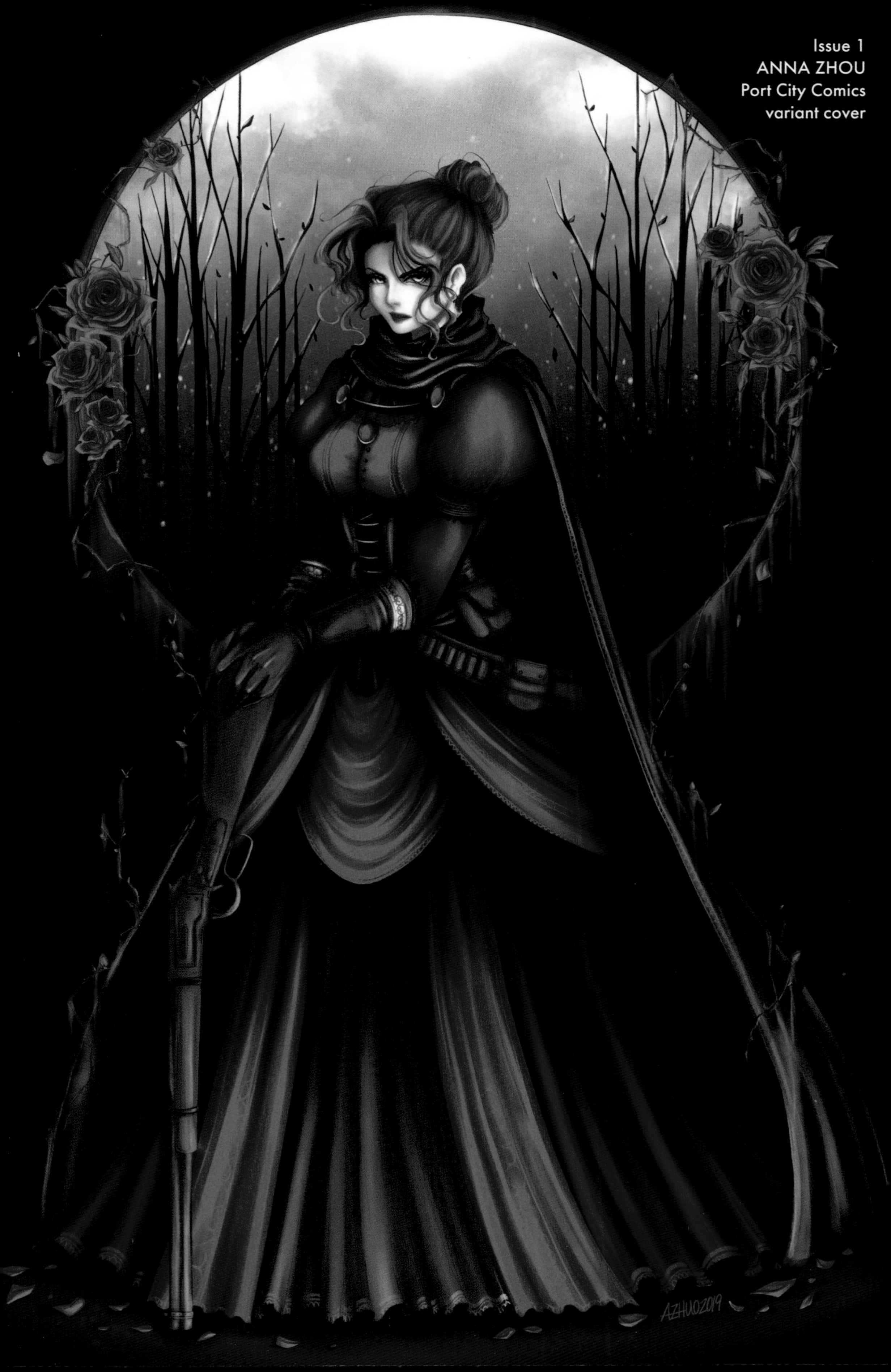
AZHU 2019

Issue 1
ANNA ZHOU
Port City Comics
variant cover

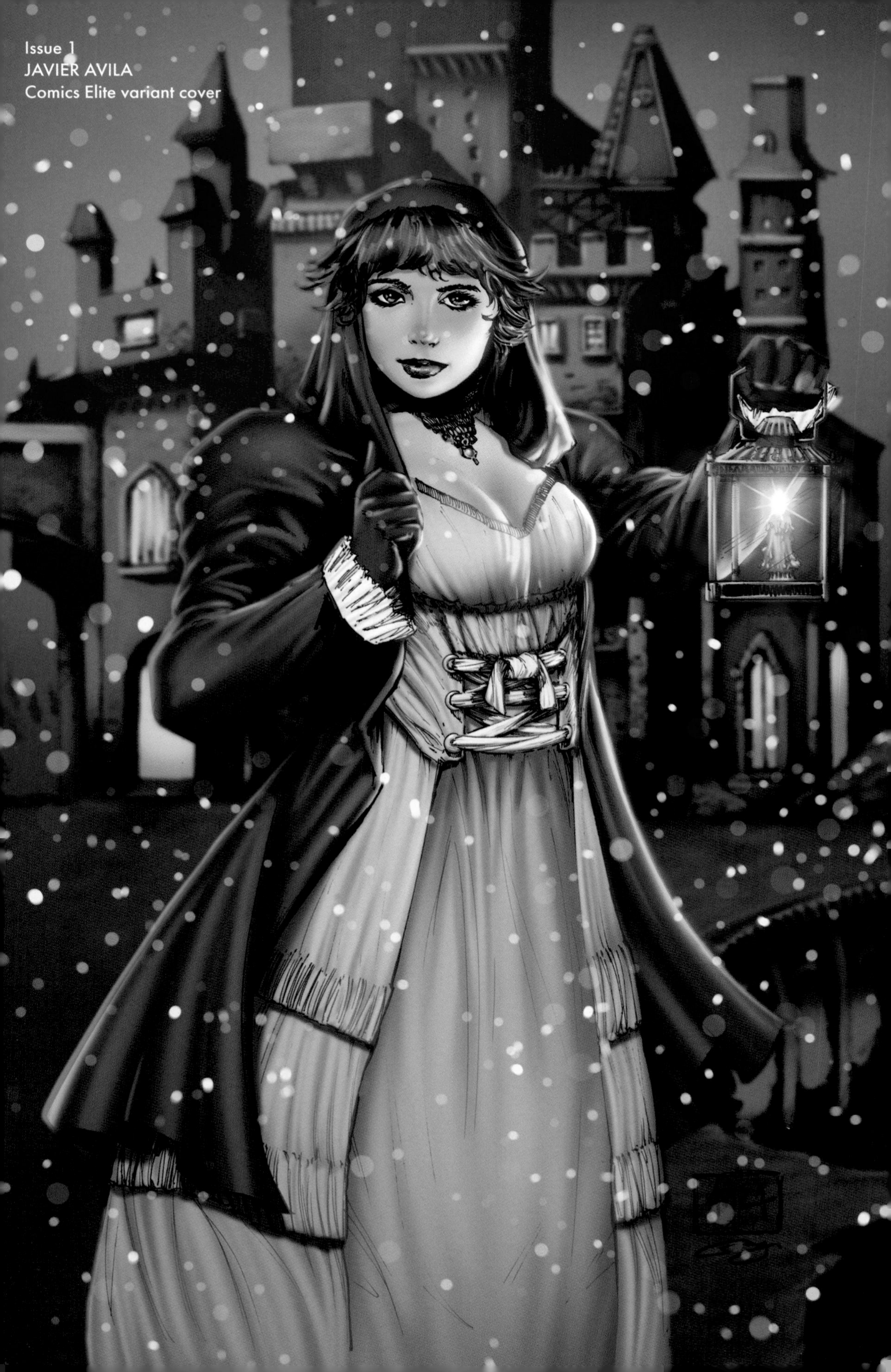

Issue 1
JAVIER AVILA
Comics Elite variant cover

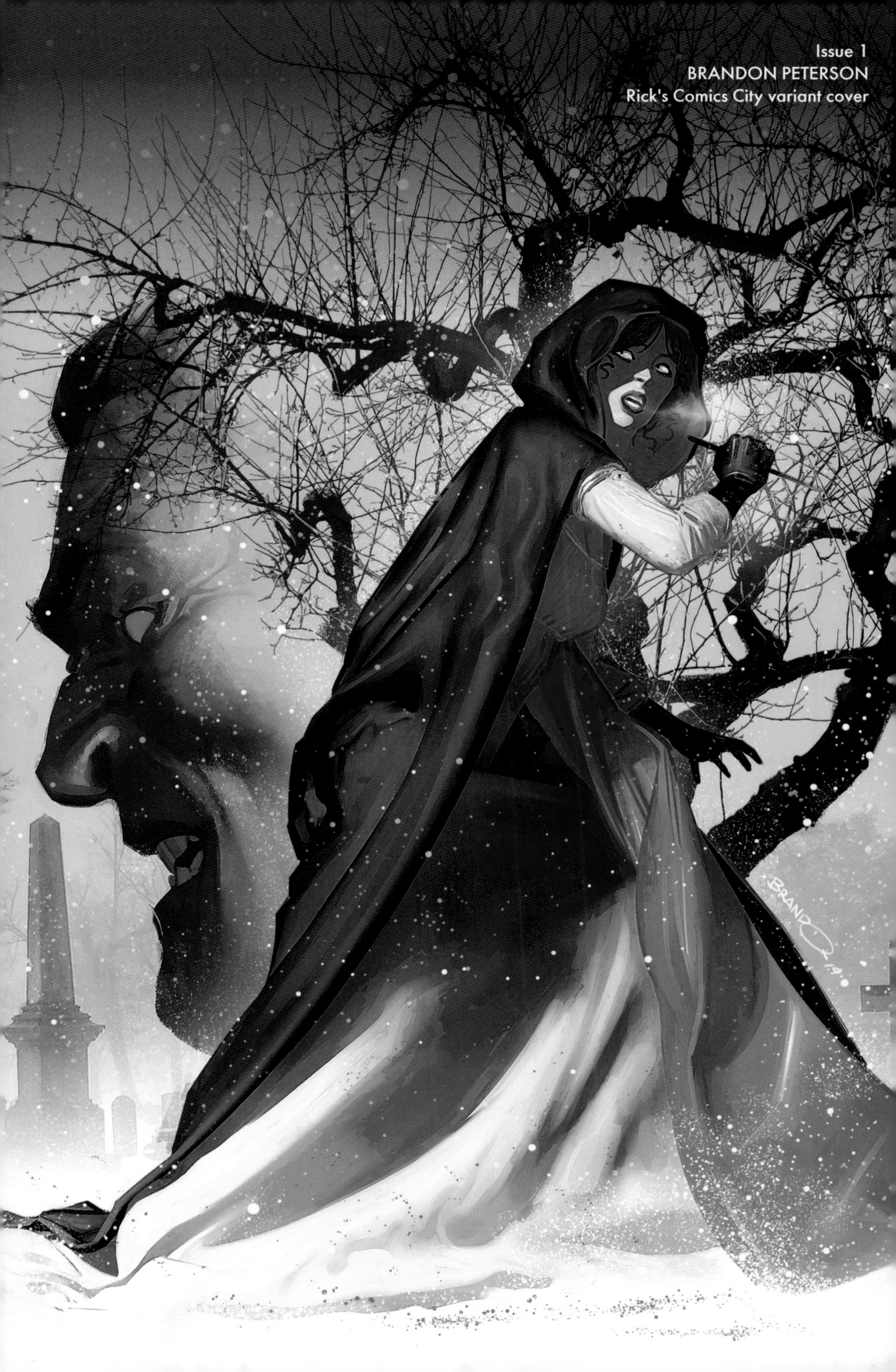

Issue 1
BRANDON PETERSON
Rick's Comics City variant cover

Issue 1
GREG KIRKPATRICK
Legends Comics & Games variant cover

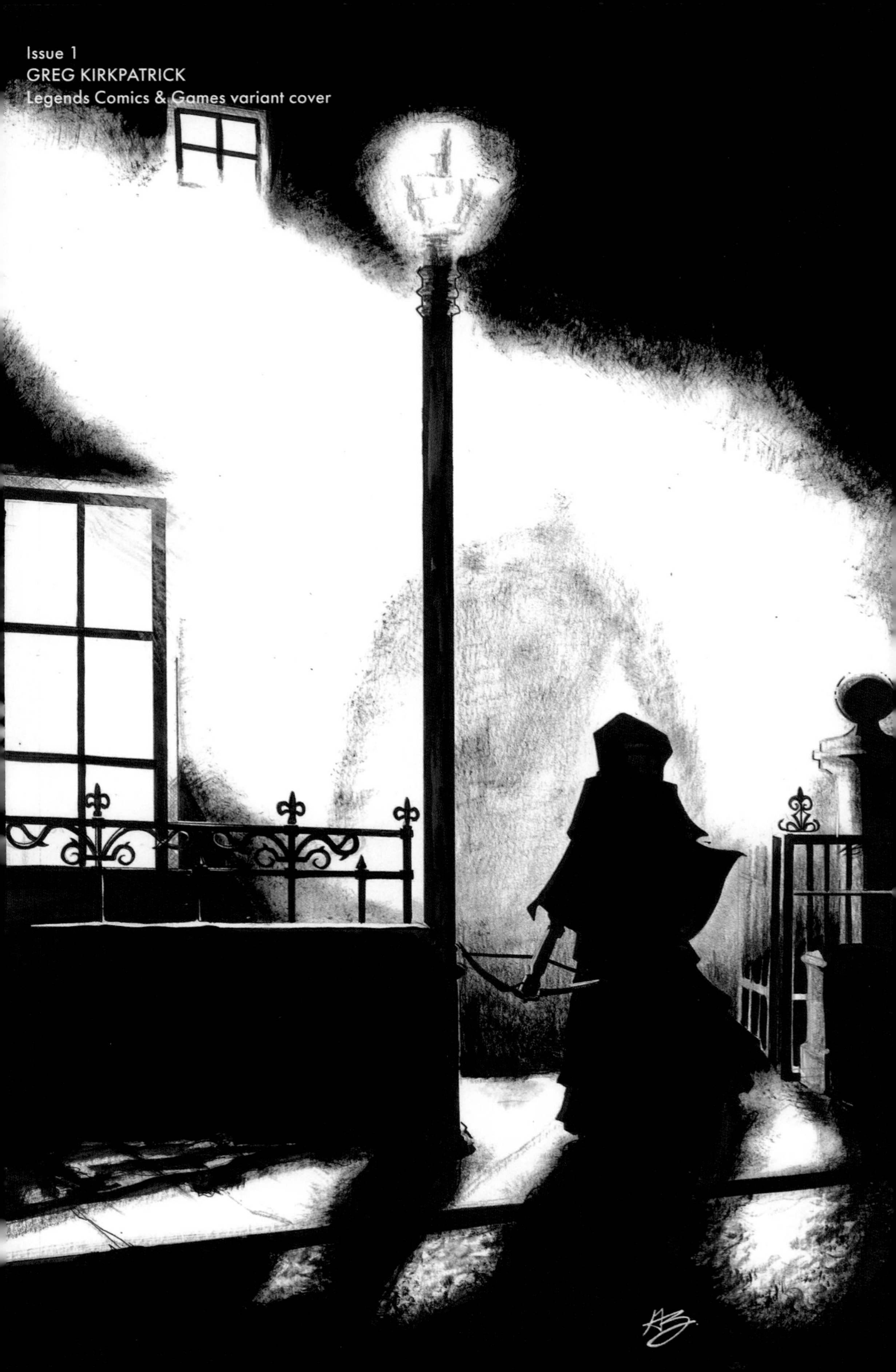

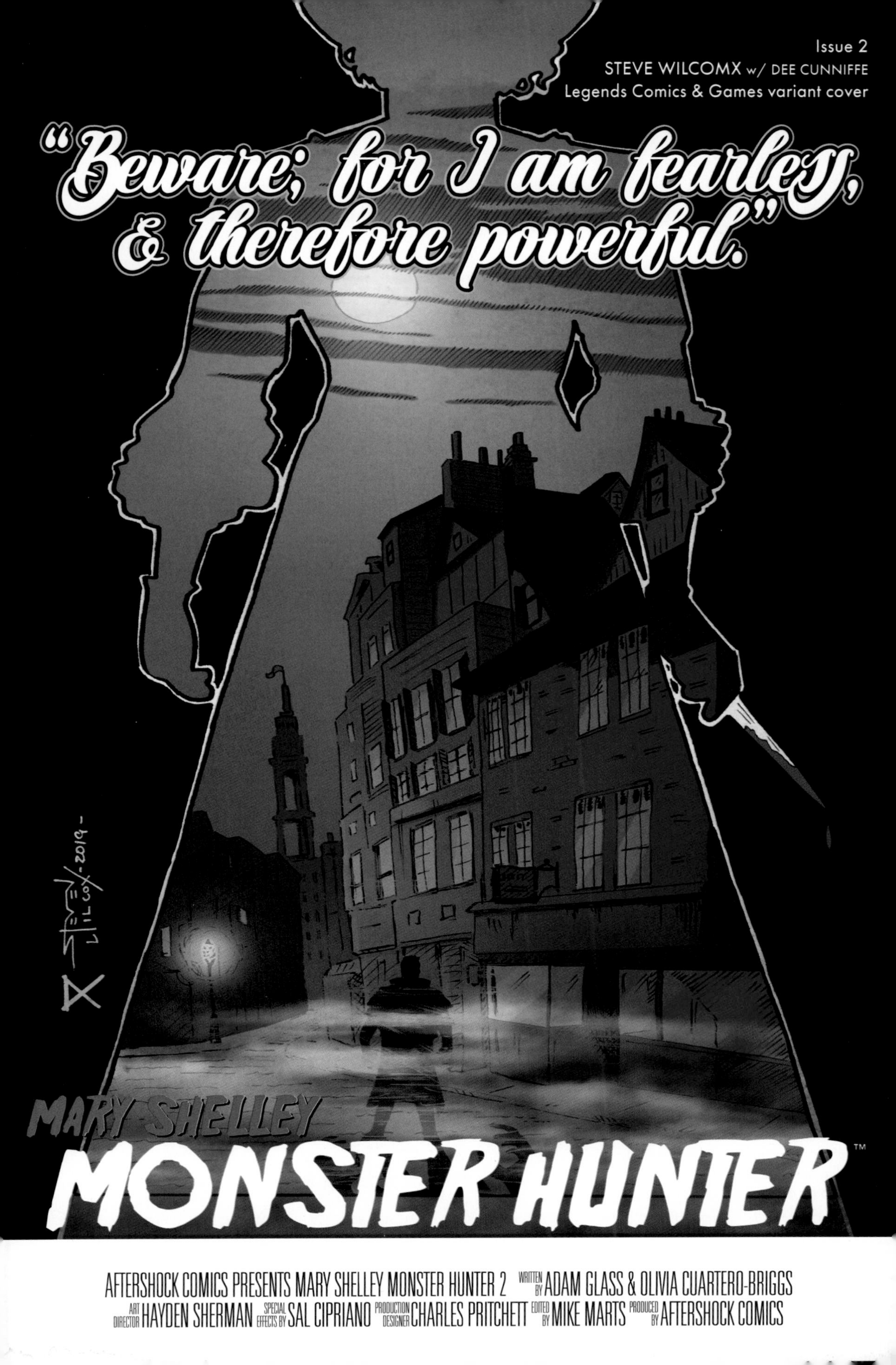
Issue 2
STEVE WILCOMX w/ DEE CUNNIFFE
Legends Comics & Games variant cover
"Beware; for I am fearless, & therefore powerful."
MARY SHELLEY
MONSTER HUNTER™
AFTERSHOCK COMICS PRESENTS MARY SHELLEY MONSTER HUNTER 2 WRITTEN BY ADAM GLASS & OLIVIA CUARTERO-BRIGGS
ART DIRECTOR HAYDEN SHERMAN SPECIAL EFFECTS BY SAL CIPRIANO PRODUCTION DESIGNER CHARLES PRITCHETT EDITED BY MIKE MARTS PRODUCED BY AFTERSHOCK COMICS

Mary Shelley MONSTERHUNTER™

Making the Monster:

An interview with artist HAYDEN SHERMAN

AFTERSHOCK: What was your favorite part of the castle to design?

HAYDEN SHERMAN: Definitely the long bridge leading up to it. It's not very present in the sketches, but when I got to drawing the final pages featuring the castle, I felt it'd be great to have the whole complex on its own mountaintop as if the rest of the surroundings had eroded away, and now there's only one long, lonely path of entry.

The first sketch for the castle was based as faithfully as I could on the actual Castle Frankenstein that you can go and visit. But after a bit, we decided to pump it up and play at the classic Frankenstein manor, But after a bit, we decided to pump it up and play at the classic Frankenstein Manor, complete with all of the massive towers and long windows.

AS: Who was your favorite character to design?

HS: Frankenstein's monster (Adam, in our story) was a lot of fun. The idea, as the story dictated, was to keep him relatively attractive. So, he's not terribly ghoulish on the surface. In response to that narrative need, I then got to play a lot more with his body. Adding different skin tones, skin qualities, age differences, or hair levels to the various patches of people that he was made with. It ultimately gets hidden by clothing, but I think it's an interesting reminder of what Adam is.

AS: How do you usually approach character design—what element do you try to pin down first? Was there a different approach in this series, as many of the main character were real-life historical figures?

HS: It's very different designing characters off of historical figures, rather than just making them up. On one hand, I want them to be distinct from one another and recognizable. On the other hand, I have a lot of respect for these characters as actual people—Mary Shelley especially. I don't want at any point to depict her as some sort of caricature. Ultimately, it meant finding the distance I could get away from their

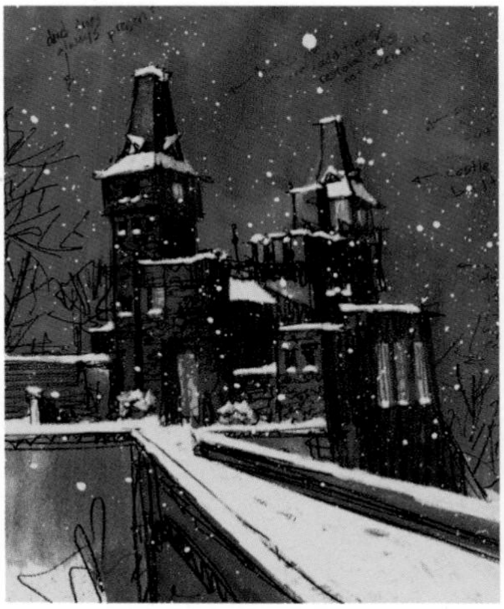

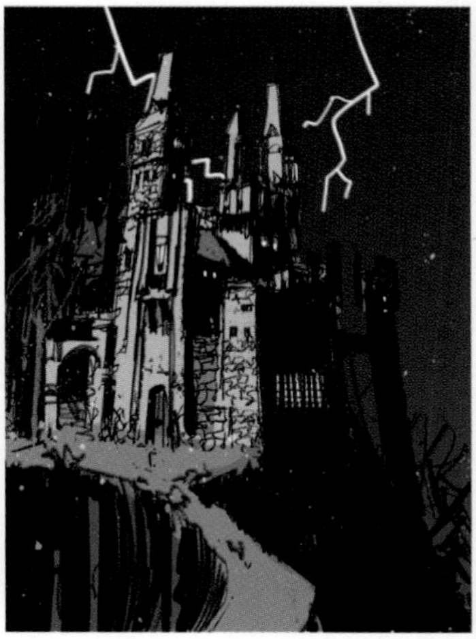

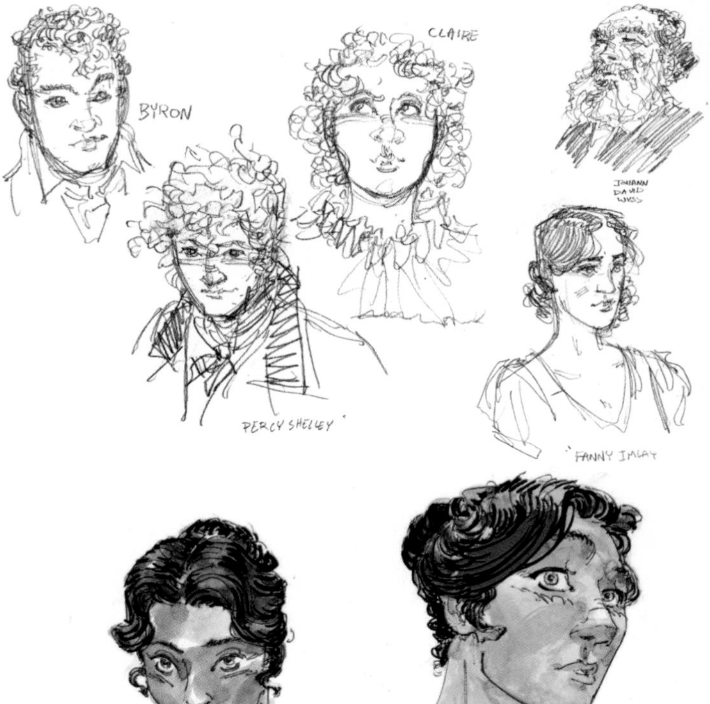
BYRON
CLAIRE
JOHANN DAVID WYSS
PERCY SHELLEY
FANNY IMLAY

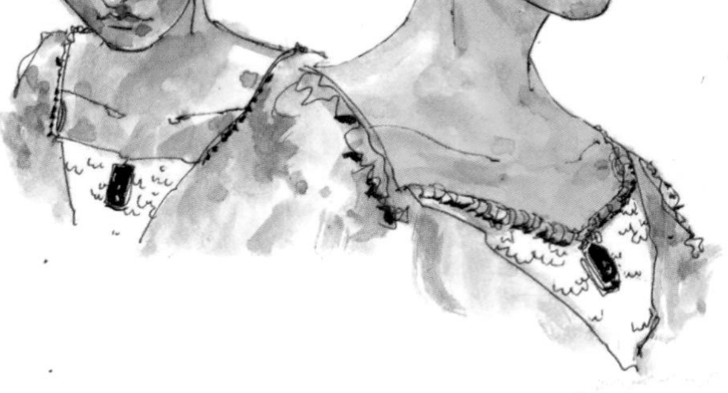

traditional portrait representations to make sure they're distinct, while making sure their acting felt deserving of their history.

It was also the first time for me doing a book with actual historical figures in it! It feels odd using real people to tell a fantastical story, so I tried to strike a balance between being true to what we know of how they looked, while at the same time keeping things a bit cartoony.

AS: What were some of the unique challenges you found in this story—it's a historical drama on one hand, a re-telling of a massively popular story on the other, and a contemporary horror comic, too. How did you reconcile all of these aspects into one cohesive unit?

HS: In the end, I took this book as its own independent thing. This story is trying to communicate things that are very different from the original Frankenstein novel. So, while being respectful to the history and people involved in making it, I tried to see MARY SHELLEY MONSTER HUNTER as something separate. The hope being that by not thinking about how strange it all might be, we could make a book that feels distinct, while still being linked with the many years of *Frankenstein*-related media.

MARY SHELLEY MONSTER HUNTER was also the first book that I didn't find myself doing as much in-depth concept work for, since the story takes place in the past. The majority of all reference material I needed was already available in books and articles that I would amass and use throughout the series. With that in mind, I just tried to familiarize myself with how the clothing worked and how places felt. It was a fun challenge.

The original style test for this book was for something much more clean and graphic. It didn't end up going this way into the final but was well worth doing all the same.

AS: You color your own work—how big of a role does color play as you design a character or location? As you layout a page?

HS: Not much, honestly. I do most of my character designing in black and white. Then I lay out pages in black and white. I don't really think about color until I've finished the inks. It keeps me guessing and lets the whole experience of making a page feel more like an experiment. Who knows how it'll end up? I don't! I like to keep an open plan so that I can change things on the day, and I'm not committed to a specific color-scheme or concept. The result feels more genuine to me.

MARY SHELLEY MONSTER HUNTER
Book Five

PANEL ONE - We are in the present day again with the Tour Guide, who reads Mary Shelley's lost manuscript while seated at Mary's old desk in her bedroom. The Tour Guide munches on a bag of chips, snack wrappers surrounding her, as well as a steaming cup of tea. Clearly she's been at this all night.

Through the windows we can see the storm still raging outside. Bright flashes of lightning streak the sky.

1. CAPTION: London, Present Day

2. MARY CAPTION: "Dear reader, know I am guilty of no hyperbole when I tell you then was the most terrifying moment of my young life."

PANEL TWO - We have moved backwards from the Tour Guide, out into the hallway now. The Tour Guide can still be seen through the open door of the bedroom, reading in the lamplight.

3. MARY CAPTION: "Not only was the horrid sight proof that Imogen and all the others were dead..."

PANEL THREE - We continue moving backwards, going down the stairs now, but still looking up toward the darkened second floor. The Tour Guide can no longer be seen, but Mary's tale continues.

4. MARY CAPTION: "... the creature herself was a sickening, blood-thirsty demon."

PANEL FOUR - We have backed ourselves to just outside the house now, where we see the front door sits slightly ajar. Crow bar marks and splintered wood tell us someone or something has broken in...

5. MARY CAPTION: "She was Adam's hasty attempt to create a companion, and much like Adam himself, she would stop at nothing to protect her creator."

script by
ADAM GLASS & OLIVIA CUARTERO-BRIGGS

PAGE
1
PROCESS

inks and colors by
HAYDEN SHERMAN

LONDON. PRESENT DAY.

DEAR READER, KNOW I AM GUILTY OF NO HYPERBOLE WHEN I TELL YOU THEN WAS THE MOST TERRIFYING MOMENT OF MY YOUNG LIFE.

NOT ONLY WAS THE HORRID SIGHT PROOF THAT IMOGEN AND ALL THE OTHERS WERE DEAD...

...BUT THE CREATURE HERSELF WAS A SICKENING, BLOOD-THIRSTY DEMON.

SHE WAS ADAM'S HASTY ATTEMPT TO CREATE A COMPANION, AND MUCH LIKE ADAM HIMSELF, SHE WOULD STOP AT NOTHING TO PROTECT HER CREATOR.

letters by
SAL CIPRIANO

MARY SHELLEY MONSTERHUNTER

#5

MARY SHELLEY MONSTER HUNTER
Book Five

Page eighteen and nineteen:
Double splash page!

PANEL ONE - Mary gapes in horror as she surveys the scene. The room is a veritable sea of lit candles, wax pooling beneath them, the light casting frightening shadows and filling the room with an eerie, orange glow. In the center of the completely blood-soaked four-poster bed lies Fanny, her wrists and throat slit, eyes still open in a frozen expression of terror. Scrawled in blood across the wall above the bed are the words, "EVERYONE YOU LOVE WILL DIE".

script by
ADAM GLASS & OLIVIA CUARTERO-BRIGGS

PAGES
18&19
PROCESS

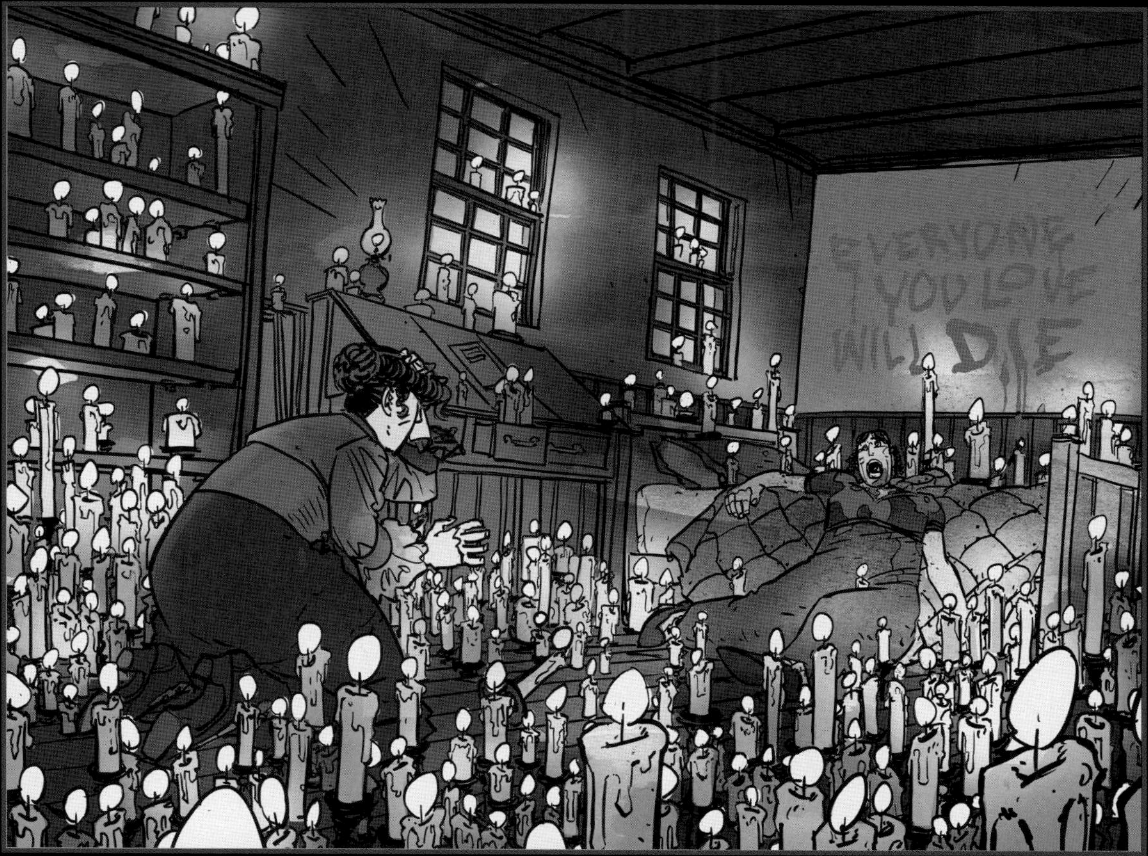
EVERYONE YOU LOVE WILL DIE

inks and colors by
HAYDEN SHERMAN

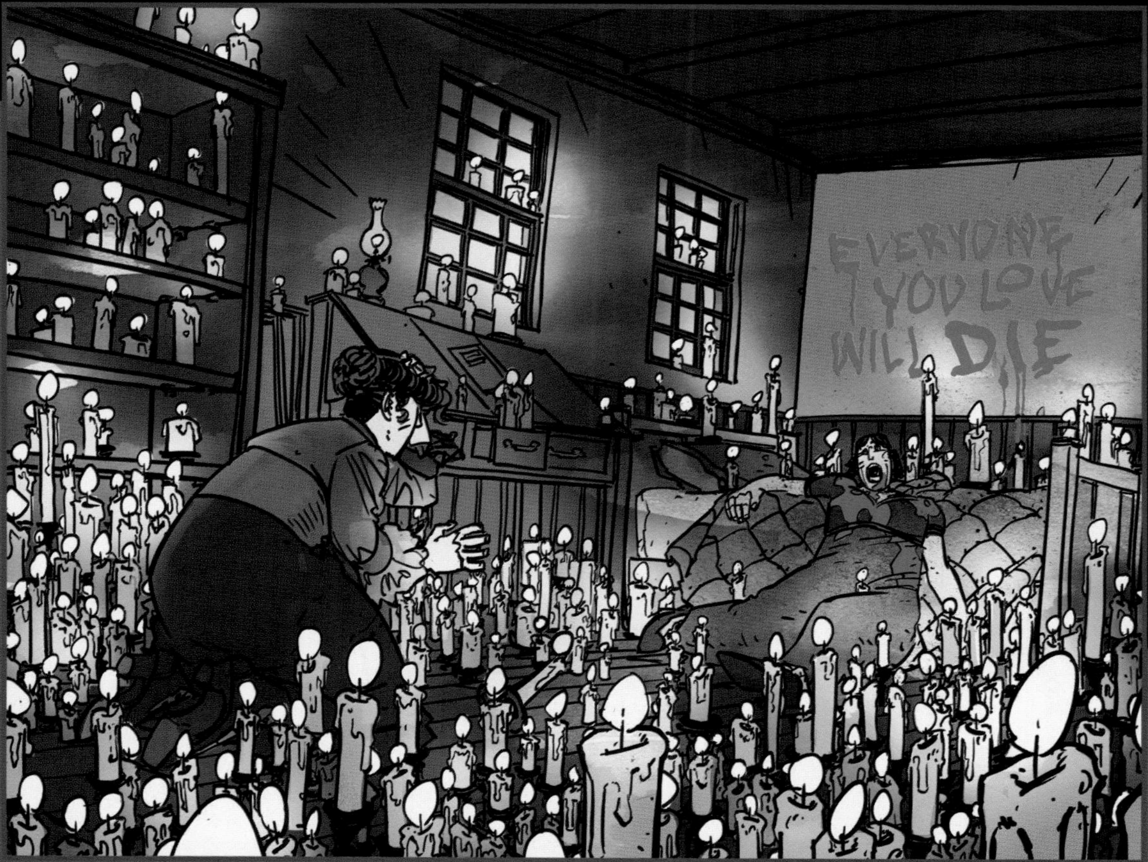
EVERYONE YOU LOVE WILL DIE

ABOUT THE CREATORS OF

Mary Shelley
MONSTERHUNTER ™

ADAM GLASS writer
🐦 @AdamGlass44

Though NYC will always be home, Adam resides in Los Angeles and is a TV Writer/Executive Producer of such shows as *SUPERNATURAL, COLD CASE* and currently *CRIMINAL MINDS: BEYOND BORDERS* on CBS. When Adam is not writing for TV or films, he's writing graphic novels. Some of these titles include: Marvel Comics' *Deadpool: Suicide Kings* and DC Comics' *Suicide Squad* — all of which were NY Times bestsellers. Other books Adam has written or co-written for Marvel are *Deadpool: Pulp, Luke Cage: Noir, Deadpool Team-Up* and *Luke Cage: Origins*. And for DC, *JLA Annual* and the *Flashpoint* series *Legion of Doom*. Most recently, Adam finished an original graphic novel for Oni Press called *Brick*. Adam's AfterShock work includes MARY SHELLEY MONSTER HUNTER, THE NORMALS, ROUGH RIDERS, and THE LOLLIPOP KIDS.

OLIVIA CUARTERO-BRIGGS writer
🐦 @oliviacbriggs

Olivia Cuartero-Briggs is a native New Yorker currently enjoying a career writing for television and comics in sunny Los Angeles. When she isn't scribbling away on her next creation, she's hanging out with her awesome daughter, Quinn, and her husband, Scott, who encourages her every day.

HAYDEN SHERMAN artist
🐦 @Cleanlined

Hayden Sherman is a recent addition to the comic industry. So far he's co-created and illustrated *The Few* along with Sean Lewis for Image Comics, as well as illustrating *John Carter: The End* for Dynamite Entertainment and *Civil War II: Kingpin* for Marvel. Hayden is also the co-creator of COLD WAR, alongside Christopher Sebela, for AfterShock. He currently lives with a couple of oddballs somewhere along the East Coast.

SAL CIPRIANO letterer
🐦 @SalCipriano

Brooklyn-born/coffee-addicted Sal Cipriano is a freelance letterer and the former Lettering Supervisor for DC Comics. His previous position at DC coupled with experience in writing, drawing, coloring, editing, designing, and publishing comics gives him unique vision as a freelancer. Sal is currently working with — amongst others — DC, Skybound, Lion Forge, Stela, and now AfterShock! Better fire up another fresh pot!